THE TEEN-CENTERED
BOOK CLUB

Recent Titles in
Libraries Unlimited Professional Guides for Young Adult Librarians
C. Allen Nichols and Mary Anne Nichols, Series Editors

THE TEEN-CENTERED BOOK CLUB

◆■◇　◆■◇　◆■◇

Readers into Leaders

Bonnie Kunzel and Constance Hardesty

Libraries Unlimited Professional Guides for Young Adult Librarians Series
C. Allen Nichols and Mary Anne Nichols, Series Editors

A Member of the Greenwood Publishing Group

Westport, Connecticut • London

Library of Congress Cataloging-in-Publication Data

Kunzel, Bonnie, 1944–

The teen-centered book club : readers into leaders / by Bonnie Kunzel and Constance Hardesty.

p. cm.—(Libraries Unlimited professional guides for young adult librarians)
Includes bibliographical references and index.
ISBN 1–59158–193–1

1. Young adults libraries—Activity programs—United States. 2. Book clubs (Discussion groups)—United States. 3. Teenagers—Books and reading—United States. 4. Reading promotion—United States. 5. Young adult literature—Study and teaching (Secondary)—United States. I. Hardesty, Constance. II. Title. III. Series.
Z718.5K86   2006
027.62′6—dc22   2005036167

British Library Cataloguing in Publication Data is available.

Library of Congress Catalog Card Number: 2005036167
ISBN: 1–59158–193–1
ISSN: 1532–5571

First published in 2006

Libraries Unlimited, 88 Post Road West, Westport, CT 06881
A Member of the Greenwood Publishing Group, Inc.
www.lu.com

Printed in the United States of America

The paper used in this book complies with the Permanent Paper Standard issued by the National Information Standards Organization (Z39.48–1984).

10 9 8 7 6 5 4 3 2 1

For my mother, who let me go to the library as often as I liked (and read my books), and for my father, who let me read the part of the Wall in family renditions of A Midsummer Night's Dream. —CH

CONTENTS

ILLUSTRATIONS

FIGURES

TABLES

SERIES FOREWORD

We firmly believe in young adult library services and advocate for teens whenever we can. We are proud of our association with Libraries Unlimited and Greenwood Publishing Group and grateful for their acknowledgment of the need for additional resources for teen-serving librarians. We intend for this series to fill those needs, providing useful and practical handbooks for library staff. Readers will find some theory and philosophical musings, but for the most part, this series will focus on real-life library issues with answers and suggestions for front-line librarians.

Our passion for young adult librarian services continues to reach new peaks. As we travel to present workshops on the various facets of working with teens in public libraries, we are encouraged by the desire of librarians everywhere to learn what they can do in their libraries to make teens welcome. This is a positive sign since too often libraries choose to ignore this underserved group of patrons. We hope you find this series to be a useful tool in fostering your own enthusiasm for teens.

Mary Anne Nichols
C. Allen Nichols
Series Editors

PREFACE

Teen-centered book clubs are grounded in the admittedly radical idea that the clubs are not primarily about library programming or even about books (!) but are all about teens. Books are the medium, the club is the method, and the goal is aiding teens in their quest for identity, meaning, and connection.

Two things set this book apart from the typical book club guide. First, it's written for librarians present and future, in public libraries and schools. It specifically addresses libraries' unique requirements: budgeting, impact on the facility and collection, censorship, and public support, to name just a few.

More important, it's the only guide that puts front and center the idea that book clubs for teens are *not* scaled-back versions of adult clubs.

What's the difference? Book clubs for adults are social clubs that connect readers with literature. Teen book clubs are social clubs that connect teens with other people—directly in club meetings or vicariously through books.

READERS INTO LEADERS . . . TOMORROW AND TODAY

We absolutely believe that teen-centered book clubs speak directly to teens' nearly existential craving for identity, meaning, and connection. We just as passionately believe that the benefits swing back around, that teens' kaleidoscopic perspectives and skewery thought-paths enrich the library in ways that go to the heart of libraries' reason for being.

It's all too easy to see teens as future parents, taxpayers, business leaders, or politicians. But our services to them are more than investments against the future. They're investments in teens' present tense. Reading books together helps us understand ourselves and connect to others. Through literature, we experience life more richly. As we explore many different answers to "Why are we here?" we think more broadly about our own lives and purpose. Teens deserve all that, for their here and now as well as for their sometime-future.

Add to that a focus on coming together to create new understanding and to get work done, and we get to the heart of teens' craving for meaning, for bringing their visions and dreams to life. That's the leadership dimension of book club. That's what transforms readers into leaders.

And if by doing all that we create raving fans, that's OK, too.

We wrote this book out of our affection for this persnickety, creative, spontaneous, exasperating, self-absorbed, and fickle Generation Whatever. We wrote it to make a real difference for them and for you—and for parents and teachers and authors and publishers and booksellers and future generations and, well, everyone, everywhere, everywhen.

That's no overstatement. When teens connect to literature, they connect to humanity. That connection sets the bells in their hearts to ringing. When you're in book club with teens, the sounds you hear are our best, brightest hopes ringing in their own futures. Your teen book club can be the place where that happens. This book can help.

The Lab Coat in the Library

The past 20 years have seen a surge of interest in young adults, particularly middle schoolers aged 11–13 years. We know more about their brain chemistry, physical mutations, social proclivities, and developmental needs than ever before. Much of what we know relates to their academic development. And that's a bad thing, because academic development is not the purpose for a teen book club (except when it is: see chapters 4 and 5).

Still, all that research helps us understand teens, and understanding points us in a direction. We can take the general truths of research, immerse them in the crucible of our firsthand experience, and develop useful ideas about what really works.

And that's what you'll find in this practical guide. In every chapter you'll find guidelines, practical tips, and suggestions for building and sustaining a teen-centered book club in your school or public library.

WHAT THIS BOOK IS—AND IS NOT

This book is a guide for adults who work with teens in library settings and want to promote, facilitate, and help maintain a book group in whatever form it takes. Though we do suggest great reads, intriguing discussion questions, and engaging activities, this is not a one-size-fits-all "cookbook" with predefined expectations and outcomes.

How to Use This Book

Take it straight from front to back or dip into whatever speaks to your heart or your immediate crisis. Every chapter is packed with ideas and tips you can use to build a club from the ground up or to make a good club even better. With detailed contents and index, it's a useful reference for troubleshooting and problem solving.

WHERE TO GO FROM HERE

Running a book club well doesn't mean you never have problems; it means that when you do have problems, you recognize and fix them. Your fixes may not look exactly like ours. You can certainly try what we suggest; the ideas are tried and true. But if they don't work, bend them, shape them, cut and paste them together. Then let us know what works for you, and we'll include it in our next edition!

It's all about process. Book club never is; it's always becoming.

HOW TO CONTACT US

Please, tell us about your book clubs! What works? What doesn't? What's fun? How did you solve a problem? What is your greatest success? Your greatest fiasco? Send us your stories, questions, ideas, observations, projects, and—yes—photos! You can email Constance at an address created for this purpose, chardesty2@yahoo.com.

ACKNOWLEDGMENTS

Thanks to all of the authors, from Bram Stoker to Julie Ann Peters, who create worlds so enticing we can't help but step in.

Thanks to all of the teens, from New Jersey to California and all points between, who stepped into those worlds with us. Our lives are richer for having known you.

Thanks to the Too Many to Name, who helped us assemble the material for this book, including especially those self-same teens; Andrew Medlar of the Chicago Public Library; the many voices of yalsa-bk and pubyac; and the incredible clerks at the Tattered Cover Bookstore in Denver.

Thanks to editor Barbara Ittner and Ron Maas of Libraries Unlimited, for believing in this book and helping us bring it to fruition. Thanks also to Apex Publishing for making us look good in print!

Thanks to all of the librarians who lead book clubs around the country, some of whom shared your experiences with us and some of whom we haven't met (yet!).

Many, many thanks to the American Library Association, for safeguarding and strengthening a most valuable national treasure.

PART ONE

◆✖◇   ◆✖◇   ◆✖◇

Before Book Club Begins:
Laying the Foundation for Success

Before you can begin to organize a teen-centered book club, it's important to understand what you're getting into. What does teen-centered mean, exactly? What does it look like? And what does it mean for your role and teens' responsibilities as the club unfolds? Chapter 1 answers these questions and more.

With those big-picture understandings in place, the first step in planning is self-evident: Get to know the teens you serve. As soon as you get approval for the club—before you even begin to think about planning, before you tentatively identify teens most likely to join—get to know all of the teens your library serves. Give yourself a few weeks to do this. As you follow the guidelines in chapter 2, you'll learn very specifically what teens want and expect, and how book club can deliver it.

Now the nuts-and-bolts preparation begins. Chapter 3 details how to plan a club and how to structure it behind the scenes so it serves teens well. Chapters 4 and 5 detail several types of book clubs from which to choose. And chapter 6 helps you create buzz with a variety of marketing strategies.

1

◇■◇　◇■◇　◇■◇

WHAT'S A
TEEN-CENTERED
BOOK CLUB?

What's the difference between a teen book club and an adult one? Too often the answer is "not much." Traditional teen book clubs tend to be scaled-down versions of adult ones. Book selection, taboo topics, what's to eat: If those are the most important things setting your teen book club apart from adult ones, you could be missing a huge opportunity.

Megamonstrous is more like it. According to the U.S. Census Bureau (2004), more than 40 million people between the ages of 10 and 19 years live in the United States. (More than 19 million are between the ages of 15 and 19 years.) And according to the most recent (though deplorably ancient) national survey of library use, nearly 25 percent of library users are young adults. In a survey by the National Center for Education Statistics (1995), almost every library reported that young adults are heavy users of library services. Granted, many are working on school projects, and we can expect Internet fun time to whittle away at the rest. But the fact is there are lots and lots and *lots* of teens out there—and a book club is a great way to lure them in, serve them, and (yes!) have a whole lot of fun.

OPPORTUNITY LOST . . . AND REGAINED

Book clubs are common, common, common library services. And no wonder. Teen book clubs have huge potential to further a whole range of library goals, from bringing more patrons in the door to building communitywide awareness and support to promoting lifelong learning. Teen book clubs promote developmental assets (Benson 1997), benefiting the library and community well into the future. And on a purely practical note, clubs help YA librarians fulfill their obligations to provide a given number of programming hours per month.

So why do so many teen book clubs fail? Few kids come, they don't come regularly, they don't read the book, they talk about everything but the book, they walk as soon as the snacks are gone, or they spend the whole time taunting one another and grabbing body parts. And that's *not* the worst-case scenario. In some of the best cases, attendance is loyal and teens connect with books and one another—all three of them.

In the words of Adrian Mole, "Why? Why? Why?"

True to the age, teens turn every assumption on its head. Adults join book clubs because of the books; teens join book clubs because they are clubs. The traditional book club is a place to connect to literature; the teen-centered book club is a place to connect. For teens, in fact, the club may be about everything *but* books.

Vibrant, dynamic teen book clubs, the kind teens eagerly anticipate and attend session after session, are teen-centered. They're not merely "by, for, and about" teens. They're places where teens take the lead in shaping, planning, and implementing the club.

Borrow from Business to Build a Better Book Club

If you think of teens as the customers of your book club, you can find analogies in business, where the term is *customer-centered.* Here's how it works:

Until recently, most American companies manufactured products and then beat us over the head until we bought them. All that's been turned on its head. During the past 20 years, leading firms have learned to ask consumers what we want and need *before* creating products. Based on our feedback, companies modify existing products or create something entirely new. Along the way our role as consumers has changed: We're no longer passive purchasers; we're practically design consultants. Businesses discovered that they could be more successful and their products more popular when they took a customer-centered approach.

You can do the same thing with your teen book club.

WHAT A TEEN-CENTERED BOOK CLUB LOOKS LIKE

When we began research on this book, Constance asked Sydney, aged 15, and Nicole, aged 13, to describe the ideal teen book club.

"My friends would be there," Sydney said.
"Would you be talking about the book?" Constance asked.
"If it was interesting."
"And if it wasn't?"
"Then we wouldn't talk about it!"
Nicole said, "There's food and music. There's an adult in the corner. He's old, and he's sitting at a computer. He has his back to us. He's ignoring us."
"What about the adult in your club?" Constance asked Sydney.
The Blank Look. "What adult?"

It's easy enough to say that a teen-centered book club begins with teens' wants and needs, progresses according to their interests and abilities, and ends with their triumphant emergence as thoughtful readers and leaders. But when it comes to the doing, what does it really look like?

Teen-Centered Means . . .

- Teens' preferences drive decision making—even if their preference is to leave it all up to you.
- Even when teens choose not to become involved in planning, you are mindful of their preferences in every decision you make.
- You avoid unexamined assumptions based on vague notions of the teen age or personal memories. (Chapter 2 helps you get real.)
- The club takes shape and evolves with teens as they learn and grow, cycle in and out, or simply change their minds.

It's All about Teens

Teen-centered means that the first point of reference for every decision and plan and action is teens' longings and desires and interests, stated and unstated. Teen-centered means going to the source—asking teens questions and *listening*—and then putting the answers to work. Even when teens' answers clash. Even when teens don't say what they mean or mean what they say. Even when their ideas don't mesh with yours. Especially when their ideas don't mesh with yours.

Nicole, a middle schooler, likes the security of an adult in the background. Sydney, after some thought, found a role for the adult in her book club: bringing the food! The good and bad news are the same: No blueprints here. What teen-centered book clubs look like, what they do, how they function, who holds the power and how they wield it—all depend on what we know directly and indirectly about what's important to the teens we serve.

Wants and Needs: Not!

To say that teen-centered book clubs put teens' wants and needs front and center barely begins to scratch the surface of what it means to be teen-centered. It's not as if you can simply refer to the Master List of Wants and Needs (and there *are* some out there!), pick and choose a few likely ones, and cobble them together into some kind of program.

Instead, a teen-centered book club creates a safe space where teens do what teens do: explore, question, and work things out for themselves. The club doesn't "address" or "answer" teens' wants and needs; it creates a neutral zone where teens can create their own answers.

WIN* with *What's Important Now

To get at the heart of what's important to teens, you need to drill down through their interests, needs, and desires. Sports *interest* them; they *need* a prom date; they *desire* status. You'll never build a successful book club around those issues.

Teens care, and care deeply, about identity, connection, and meaning. These are the major concerns of literature as well; it's easy to see that almost any book club can speak to teens' hearts.

YOUR ROLE IN A TEEN-CENTERED BOOK CLUB

In every conversation about teen book clubs, sooner or later, a few good questions arise.

1. If teens take the lead, where does that leave me?

Leading right alongside them. Someone must set the stage, coach the players, and support them as they grow into new patterns of thinking and acting. Teen-centered book club challenges you to do that without taking control of the club. How?

- Sustain a safe atmosphere and consistent structure.
- Model, facilitate, coach, support, remind, nudge, and occasionally instruct or intervene to foster leadership/book club values and behaviors.
- Provide all the behind-the-scenes support the club needs to succeed.
- Get out of the way!

A safe space is consistent and predictable, nurturing and encouraging, respectful and confidential, noncompetitive and nonthreatening, congenial rather than critical. Needless to say, it takes just one breach to lose a teen or to set a precedent. Chapter 3 describes simple things you can do to foster a safe atmosphere for book club.

Officially your role is to offer support from the sidelines. Realistically, teens will need a balance of direct help and sideline support. You'll find suggestions for fostering leadership and book club values and behaviors in chapters 6, 9, and 10 of this book.

Teen-centered book clubs will test your tolerance for ambiguity and chaos, ideas that never fully develop, conversations that never reach resolution. Sometimes you'll need to quash your urge to rescue teens as they struggle to speak their truths; other times you'll need to step in to prevent key ideas from being lost or ridiculed. Knowing when to get out of the way and when to jump in is as much a matter of empathy as experience.

Is a Teen-Centered Book Club Right for You? And Vice Versa?

Doing all of this takes personality and skill. Liking teens is a good start. You'll need the usual laundry list of characteristics for YA librarians: patience, creativity, friendliness, helpfulness, and the ability to carry on a conversation with teens. Teen-centered book clubs are a good fit if you are ready to do the following:

- Examine yourself, your attitudes, and assumptions
- Let teens examine and challenge your thoughts and opinions
- Give up control over things small and large
- Wallow in the messiness as teens explore, discover, and wrestle with new ideas and new ways of perceiving and thinking
- Commit the time and energy book club demands

---

2. Does this mean I have no agenda of my own? My library director/board is not going to support a free-for-all.

Of course not. Book club is teen-centered, not librarian-annihilating. Being teen-centered doesn't mean teens get to do whatever they want however they want on your time and dime. Everyone lives with constraints, and teens are very much aware that they're no exception. The two most obvious constraints are as follows:

- It's library-sponsored
- It's a *book* club

To trot out the business model again, businesses don't sacrifice their ultimate goal (profit) to become consumer-centered. Nor do they turn over the keys to the factory. They simply become sensitive to consumer preferences to further their goals. That said, you're in a tight spot. As a librarian you have certain responsibilities to the library, the community, and yourself; as a *teen-centered* librarian you hold teens as the central point of reference for every decision. And where they don't meet? How do you work out the kinks? Through consensus. In the best of all possible worlds, you and the teens will explore ways to mesh your agenda with their preferences, and you'll all come out stronger and smarter. More likely you'll stumble along—and it's in the stumbling that the real growth happens. Working out the messy details of compromise, you face the ultimate test of your commitment to teen-centeredness.

Clearly, although we talk a great deal about teen leadership, you serve as the anchor, the touchpoint that ensures that the club remains teen-centered. This should be invisible to teens. They don't need to hear you harping on "teen-centered this or that" if they can see the result, that is, their collective idea of a great book club coming to fruition.

As with most leadership endeavors, you and teens cocreate the club. However, because of the power inherent in your position, you always have the potential to exert a direct influence over the club. Be careful in how you go about "leading from within" to ensure that the focus remains on teens. This is their club, all the way.

3. What if teens don't want to take the lead? Where does that leave the leadership piece? Front and center still. Think of leadership as having two dimensions. On the one hand is the nuts-and-bolts, get-it-done skill set. On the other are the staunch interpersonal qualities that inspire others to action. If teens don't leap at the chance to "get their hands dirty" managing the club's operations, they can still engage in conversations and encounters with peers and book characters that build the disciplined awareness and empathy from which leadership qualities grow.

When teens' passivity is about to drive you to distraction, take heart: As teens become more engaged in the club, they become more invested in how it unfolds. And as they become more invested, they become more eager to take the reins. Meanwhile, book club, with its focus on understanding human behavior and communicating with peers, can't help but stretch teens' leadership abilities.

READERS INTO LEADERS: HOW TEEN-CENTERED BOOK CLUBS FOSTER LEADERSHIP

Leadership Defined

Over the past decades, building on Peter Drucker's earlier work, there's been a sea change in accepted notions of what leadership means and what makes a great leader. Where it was once considered mostly a matter of outward-directed authority and control, all about amassing accomplishments, today leadership is considered a much more inward thing: Leadership is all about building relationships, and the authority a leader wields emerges not from power but from inner resources and interpersonal skills. This has been encapsulated in the cliché: Leadership isn't about doing things right but doing the right things.

Frances Hesselbein (2002), former chief executive officer of the Girl Scouts of the USA and chairman of the board of governors of the Leader to Leader Institute (formerly the Peter F. Drucker Foundation for Nonprofit Management), sums up the most current thinking about leadership in a way that applies perfectly to teens: "Leadership is a matter of how to be, not how to do it." Anyone can learn to perform the common tasks of leadership, like running a meeting or negotiating a compromise. But, as Hesselbein (2002, p. 3) explains, "All the how-to's in the world won't work until the 'how-to-be's' are defined."

Hesselbein—and most American MBA programs—are not alone in defining leadership in this way. The U.S. Army, considered one of the world's most expert team-building and leadership development organizations, also takes this approach (Shinseki and Cavanagh 2004). We are delighted that they do. Contemporary "how-to-be" definitions of leadership are music to our ears because they align exactly with teens' overriding interests in who they are (identity), what they envision (meaning), and how they relate (connection).

To say that leadership is all about the inner self does *not* imply that leaders are born. Indeed, the U.S. Army is renowned for turning "plain Janes and Joes" into extraordinary leaders far away from battlefields. So what does it take to become a leader? It takes rigorous, disciplined effort to understand ourselves, examine our assumptions, and build relationships. To do those things we perform certain tasks (like self-assessment), develop certain skills (like self-control), and practice certain habits (like empathy). Those tasks, skills, and practices are the how-tos that give rise to the how-to-bes. They are the quintessential leadership behaviors.

We've identified several leadership practices and skills book clubs are uniquely suited to foster in teens. Focusing on the how-to-bes, we chose four practices: emotional self-control, self-awareness, empathy, and thinking. To that we added three skills essential to both book clubs and leadership: literacy, communication, and action.

Some feel that this approach to leadership is too soft, that it doesn't get to the nitty-gritty of making things happen. Our response is twofold. We agree with Drucker, Hesselbein, and others that leadership is not about making things happen; it's about relating to self, others, and the world so deeply and authentically that one can create and communicate a compelling vision. It's about connecting so deeply and authentically with others that they are inspired to set aside existing priorities to flock to the new vision. Second, because these personal aspects (which are plenty tough, after all) form the foundation of leadership, because they align almost perfectly with teens' consuming interests, and because literature is obsessed with those same consuming interests—for all of these reasons, a teen-centered book club is the perfect place to foster solid, foundational leadership skills and traits, including the following:

Self-awareness: Discovering and defining your character, values, beliefs, standards. Knowing which values and standards are subject to change and which are bedrock. Sticking to values and standards in the face of choice and pressure. The self is the "home base" from which leaders step into action; there can be no strong action without a strong base.

Emotional self-control: Knowing what sets you off, recognizing signals from your body that you are being hijacked by emotions or impulses, interrupting your emotions, detaching from them, and calming down. Self-control is the starting block of leadership; you can't perceive, think, relate to others, or act reliably until you learn to separate heat from light.

Empathy: Thinking and feeling with others; temporarily setting aside your own assumptions and truths to enter into another's viewpoint without abandoning your own. Tuning in (being sensitive) to what, how and why people feel and think the way they do (Stein and Book 2001).

Thought: Critical and creative thinking, verifying facts and substantiating opinions, persevering, detaching, researching, appreciating the value of multiple viewpoints, making connections, coming to conclusions and explaining them. Just as carpenters use the right tool for the job, so leaders employ thinking skills that suit the situation at hand.

Literacy: When we talk about literacy, we're talking about more than reading comprehension. We're also talking about information literacy, including media literacy, and the higher-level comprehension that comes from empathetic, thoughtful reading. Literacy begins in rote skills and ascends to a level where reason and empathy meet.

Communication: Speaking, writing, and using body language to convey attitude and information, to persuade or negotiate, and to connect.

Action: Taking responsibility (volunteering), working alone and together to set and achieve goals, learning how to do new things, remembering to do them, recognizing the value of teamwork.

Can a book club really foster all this? Yes! It may not transform teens overnight, but it will help them make a start from wherever they are. Reading for insight and understanding rather than sheer entertainment . . . moderated, thoughtful discussion rather than opinionated outbursts . . . relationships built on common ground rather than pecking order: By its very nature, book club guides teens to insight and reflection.

And that's what it does on autopilot. Imagine what book club can do when you deliberately sustain an atmosphere that encourages exploration and self-disclosure . . . when you stand back as teens wrestle with questions about identity, meaning, and connection . . . when you plan activities that challenge teens to dig for surprising truths . . . when teens take charge of their own growth, with focus on what Hesselbein reminds is the core of leadership: who we are, not what we do.

TEENS TAKE CHARGE

In traditional teen book clubs, the adult organizer comes up with the plan, sets a schedule, gets the word out, chooses the first book, does some research, photocopies a prefab discussion guide, buys snacks, arranges chairs, and at the appointed hour asks the question that has launched a thousand book clubs: So, what did we think of the book?" The discussion is scintillating, of course. And there's a nice bit of chat afterward.

Right. A nice bit of chat. Nicole thinks *dancing* would be cool.

Teen-centered book clubs start not with a plan but with *intent*—to build the club around teens. Some clubs will be teen led as well as teen centered. In others, teens will rely on you to provide a bridge between what they envision and what they can realize. While teens determine their level of involvement, our highest hope is that they will take the lead in creating thought-provoking questions, facilitating discussions, selecting books, marketing and promoting the club, and so on.

Note the word *take.* When you *give* leadership to teens, you're still holding one end of the leash. When teens *take* charge, the club is all theirs. It's a subtle but important distinction that goes to the heart of this question: Are you holding back control of the club?

Teens may start merely as active participants, but the ultimate goal is larger than that: We want them to become leaders as well as readers. One of the fundamental uses of book club is to help teens grow, and teen-centered book clubs help them grow into leaders.

References

Benson, Peter L. 1997. *All Kids Are Our Kids: What Communities Must Do to Raise Caring and Responsible Children and Adolescents.* San Francisco: Jossey-Bass.

Hesselbein, Frances. 2002. *Hesselbein on Leadership.* San Francisco: Jossey-Bass. National Center for Education Statistics.

Services and Resources for Children and Young Adults in Public Libraries. Report 95–357. Washington, DC: U.S. Department of Education Office of Educational Research and Improvement. Available at; http://nces.ed.gov/surveys/frss/publications/95357/.

Shinseki, Eric K. and Richard Cavanagh. 2004. *Be Know Do: Leadership the Army Way.* San Francisco: Jossey-Bass.

U.S. Census Bureau. 2004. "General Demographic Characteristics: 2003 American Community Survey Summary Tables." Available at: http://factfinder.census.gov/servlet/STTable?_bm=y&-geo_id=01000US&-qr_name=ACS_2004_EST_G00_S0101&-ds_name=ACS_2004_EST_G00_.

2

◇■◇　　◇■◇　　◇■◇

LISTENING TO LEARN: STRAIGHTFORWARD TIPS AND SNEAKY TRICKS FOR GETTING TO KNOW THE TEENS YOU SERVE

It's tempting to think we can imagine our way into teens' heads by remembering what we were like as adolescents. Nothing doing, as a group of college students in a YA lit class quickly discovered. Trying to figure out how teens would react to novels like *Staying Fat for Sarah Byrnes* (Crutcher 2003) and *Rule of the Bone* (Banks 1996),

> We came to realize that we were relying all too often on our hazy memories of adolescence . . . to construct a "virtual adolescent reader." . . . Who knew what "real kids" would think? (O'Donnell-Allen and Hunt 2001)

That's a common mistake—and it's not the only one that even experienced researchers make. According to Harris Interactive, Inc.,

> There is a presumption that because "we were all young once" or "we have teenage children at home or "all kids in this age group are pretty much the same," that we somehow now understand the entire youth market. . . . We fail to appreciate generational differences or differences across regions and countries. (Geraci et al. 2000, p. 4)

Clearly, to build a teen-centered book club we must get out of our heads and into teens'. That means learning about teens in general as well as the teens our libraries serve. Adapting the tools and strategies of market research, we can get to know our "customers" and use what we know to develop a product, brand it, and create a marketing and promotion campaign that speaks directly to teens.

Through it all, we focus primarily on these questions: What type of club should we build? What will we read? What will we do? What atmosphere (e.g., caring, challenging, entertaining, educational) will we create together?

That's a lot to pack into a few weeks of research, but it's entirely doable. All it takes is a plan.

GET TO KNOW TEENS IN FOUR EASY STEPS

You can read dozens of research reports and enjoy lengthy, enlightening conversations with teens—but what you learn won't necessarily help you build a better book club. To do that you need to focus on relevant, *actionable* information. Getting to know teens is a research problem; it's all about putting information literacy skills to work. Here's the plan:

1. Define what you need to know.
2. Listen to learn.
3. Round it out with research.
4. Put it to work.

Step 1. Define What You Need to Know

It's easy to amass so much information you become lost in it. Avoid the confusion by beginning with the end in mind: What do you need to know to create a successful book club?

You'll need to start by defining *successful.* You're free to do that any way you like (e.g., boosting circulation or attendance, gaining publicity for the library, fulfilling developmental needs). After you've defined success, simply

- decide what you need to *do* to make book club succeed,
- decide what you need to *know* to get the job done, and
- write questions that elicit the information you need.

All market research begins with questions, and they all boil down to the following: Who are your prospects? What can you do to serve them? Teens wax loquacious when they find an adult who cares. All you have to do is ask—and listen.

Step 2. Listen to Learn

Easy and popular ways to "listen to learn" are written surveys, interviews, and focus groups. We'll look at a few general principles first, then take a closer

---

The Book Club Generation Gap

Adults say they join book clubs to give great literature a second read, out of a nostalgia for college literature courses, or to exercise their intellect. There is no equivalent to that in teen thinking. Teens haven't given literature a first read yet; they certainly don't need an alternative to school; and after a full day of exercising their brains they'd rather exercise their right to free speech and the pursuit of happiness—socializing and eating and, by the way, books.

look at the old standbys, and finally toss out some sneaky tricks that go beyond simple question and answer (Q&A).

None of this is rocket science, and no single approach is essential. To start, pick one or two tactics, like a survey and a focus group. When you have a block of useful information, move forward. You can always go back to the well as the need arises.

The Key to Q&A Research: Ask Questions that Get Answers

According to Harris Interactive, Inc., teens "seriously contemplate questions and answer choices . . . and are frustrated when questions are not clear" (Geraci et al. 2000, p. 4). Whether you pose questions through written surveys, interviews, or focus groups, the way you frame your questions determines whether you get an answer—or an answer you can *use*. To ask useful questions, keep in mind the following:

- **Focus.** Stick to questions that truly help you build a better book club. Ask yourself, "Will knowing this *really* help me build a better book club?" Expect library staff to ask if they can piggyback a few questions of their own onto your Q&A. Just say no!
- **Be clear and direct.** Have a colleague or teen review your questions to be sure they ask what you mean them to ask and they don't hint at a preferred answer.
- **Be actionable.** "What is your schedule like?" is a good conversational question, but a more actionable one is "What is the best day for you to attend book club?"
- **Ask only one question per question.** Unbundle combo questions like "What do you like best and least about book clubs?"
- **Don't let one question influence another.** If you first ask a teen, "Do you like science fiction?" and later ask, "What kind of club would you join?" you are skewing the results toward science fiction.

No one writes perfect questions the first time out. Give yourself a chance to revise them. Set the questions aside for a few days and then review them to be sure they work.

Building the Foundation: Trust and Respect

Wouldn't it be great if trust could be built in a day? By the early teens you've got a tough sell on your hands. Teens in general live in a perpetual show-me state—and rightly so. Since being discovered by corporations and funding agencies (about nine months before birth) young people are bombarded by marketers and do-gooders eager to pander to their wants and needs or to "help" (i.e., reshape) them.

Librarians have a special obstacle to overcome. Many teens have expected library staff to be "unhelpful and controlling," according to Mary K. Chelton, one of the leading researchers and writers on library service to teens. Judging from messages on Listservs, many librarians oblige. Too often when library staffers look at teens, they don't see people but "problems that walk on two legs" (Mary K. Chelton, quoted in Jones and Shoemaker 2001).

Six Great Reasons to Listen to Teens

1. Listening to teens reveals valuable information about their styles, attitudes, habits, interests, needs, and desires. And that's the least of it.
2. Initiating conversations, taking time to chat and to *listen,* demonstrates that you respect teens and care about what they think. That builds trust, which provides fertile ground for relationships to blossom.
3. Consulting teens during planning builds support for the club; it's another key recruiting tool.
4. Consulting teens after the club is up and running promotes retention.
5. Equally important, consulting teens ensures that you build the club they want.
6. Getting to know teens demolishes assumptions and stereotypes. It opens your eyes to whole new worlds—theirs. That in itself is a fine reward: Though most adults say they'd never want to live there again, the adolescent world is a fascinating place to visit.

On top of all that, teens are hypersensitive to real or imagined hurts. You admire one boy's nose ring and the other feels slighted. You ask a swimmer how the meet went and she's convinced you *know* she blew it. Teens aren't paranoid; they *have* been slighted and hurt; they *have* been ambushed by friends and adults alike.

What to do? Take your time and cast your net wide. Talk to teens every day, not just when you want to pump them for information. Talk about their lives, hobbies, families, pets. Tell them about yours. Share jokes. Commiserate. Keep your judgments and advice to yourself. Solicit teens' opinions on what to read, where to hang up the new poster. Take their advice. Pay attention, maintain eye contact, nod often, make interested noises. Slow down. Give them time to get their thoughts out and let them revise. Never stop; teens are always evolving, and the only way to stay abreast is to keep talking. Allow your genuine interest to shine through, showing each teen you get it: You know they are their own one and only.

Then you can pump them for info.

The Big Three of Q&A: Surveys, Interviews, and Focus Groups

Written Surveys

Written surveys in print and online are without a doubt the most popular way to reach out to teens. They're easy, simple, fast, versatile, and affordable. And, because teens haven't yet been inundated with them, teens have fun completing them. You can easily create a written survey that will tell you exactly what you need to build a better book club. After you write a half dozen good

Don't Delay; Start Today!

Talk to teens every day, not just when you want to pick their brains. Top salespeople fulfill a quota of so many calls per day. Set yourself a goal—speak to five teens per day—and do it consistently. Starting now. Put this book down and don't come back until you've hit your quota.

questions (see previous tips), consider adding the following finishing touches to make your survey even more effective:

- **Keep it short.** Ask a half dozen questions with brief, specific answers. Multiple choice is good. Remember, you'll compile the results later, so frame questions in a way that will make your job easy!
- **Leave the door open.** Written surveys offer no opportunity to probe for meaning. Create follow-up opportunities by appending an invitation to "Tell Me More!" If library policy allows, collect teens' contact information so you can schedule a meeting.
- **Announce your audience.** Be sure your survey gets into the right hands. Give it a headline that screams audience and purpose. For example, "13+ Book Club Survey" works.
- **Offer the online option.** Be sure your printed questionnaire includes the address of its online counterpart. That way, teens can go online to complete the survey without returning the hard copy to you.

How to Choose Which Teens to Talk To

Of course you'll chat with every teen who crosses your path. But for book club, narrow your focus to the teens you want to attract. For example, if scheduling constraints require you to hold the book club on Wednesday, focus on teens who are in the library on Wednesday. Do your interviews every Wednesday for a month, interviewing different teens each time, and you'll cover a good sample of teens available to join book club.

Figure 2.1 is a sample survey that can be printed on a 4 × 6 card.

Written surveys can be distributed in dozens of ways, in print and online. For maximum return, match distribution to audience:

- Leave questionnaires in the stacks, inside popular books, at computers, on work tables, near circulation centers, and at the exits.
- Link from the library teen page to your survey.
- To reach teens outside the library, distribute surveys at malls, outdoor basketball courts, coffee shops—anywhere teens hang out.
- To reach teens at school, buy a classified ad in the school newspaper. Include a teaser and a link to the online survey.

FIGURE 2.1
A Small Survey that Can Be Printed on an Index Card

13+ Book Club Survey!

1. Are you at least 13 years old? _____

2. How many books have you read just for fun since school started? _____

3. Check off the kind of book club you would join:

   ☐ read a book, then watch the movie
   ☐ read a book about a social problem, then do a service project to fix it (and earn service learning credits!)
   ☐ everybody reads the same book, then talks about it together
   ☐ everybody reads whatever they like, then tells each other what they read
   ☐ read one kind of book (mystery, romance, etc.) What kind?
   ☐ my idea of a great book club:

4. How often should book club meet? _____

5. What day and time is best for you to come to book club? _____

6. What days and times can you *not* come to book club?

   _____

Signoff!

What's your name? _____

What's your email? _____

Fill out this survey online: www.mylibrary.gov

To improve response rates, generate excitement in advance. A few weeks before you distribute the survey, post teasers around the library, on the Web and in the stacks, promising a worthwhile incentive to the first 25 teens joining in. Change the teasers each week, each time revealing another clue to what's coming. When you make the survey available, post "calls to action" on the Web, in the stacks, and everywhere teens roam.

Reward teens for taking the survey. Concrete incentives include forgive-all-your-fines, an invitation to a by-invitation-only event, free books, trinkets, brand merchandise, or entering teens' names in a drawing for movie tickets or gift certificates. Or, make it affordable: On the Web, post a banner-ad look-alike (teaser) at the top of the survey page and end with a link to a site offering cool videos or free downloads.

Individual Interviews and Chats

Individual interviews or chats in person or online yield detailed information. You can verify or clarify questions and answers, expand a train of thought, use props (like book covers or sample room arrangements), and probe for hows and whys. In addition to all that, personal interviews build rapport, a key motivator for teens to become involved in library activities.

But interviews and chats have their downsides as well. They're time-consuming and they tend to be biased. Teens will tell you what they think will impress you most or what you most want to hear. They will respond to subtle cues as well as the question. And they will respond to you personally. So, how can you communicate well with teens?

- **Watch your tone.** Be conversational. If abrupt or brusque is your natural style, force yourself to slow down and speak in a neutral tone.
- **Use a script.** Scripts help you gain confidence and remind you of the points you need to cover. Obviously, you can't read a script verbatim, but you can glance at it often as you work through your questions.
- **Follow up on the fly.** Depart from the script to ask for clarification or detail.
- **Give teens the lead.** Even as you ask prepared questions, give teens plenty of latitude to cover the ground they want to cover. Don't cut them off too soon.

As with written surveys, it's a good idea to reward teens for sharing their insights. Offer them a choice from a grab bag of prizes. And give them the big prize: Remember their names.

Focus Groups

Marketers use focus groups to test new ideas before taking them live. In a typical group a facilitator leads 6–12 participants through a series of carefully planned questions to learn what people think, why they think it, and how they came to their decision.

Focus groups foster relationships among participants and with the facilitator. If teens in focus groups hit it off with one another and/or with you, recruiting will be that much easier.

You can plan an effective focus group in about 30 minutes. Don't plan on learning universal truths about adolescence, but do try to get a feel for your little corner of the world. To create an insightful discussion, consider the following:

- **Focus on your goals.** Know what you need to know and don't ask about anything else.
- **Invite teens who share characteristics you seek in book clubbers.** Do you want to attract poor readers? Girls? Teens who rarely visit the library? Invite them to your focus group.
- **Write a logical series of questions.** Keep them short, and build from the simple to the complex.

Conducting a focus group is just as easy. Gather teens, introduce one another and jump right in:

- **Use prepared questions as your agenda.** Read the questions from a cheat sheet to be sure you get the language and the order of questions right.
- **Facilitate, facilitate.** Keep the conversation focused on actionable information and short-circuit groupthink (the tendency for everyone to play follow-the-leader in answering questions). See chapter 10 for tips on facilitation.
- **Give equal attention to everyone.** Avoid the temptation to focus on discussion dominators or trendsetters.
- **Take notes.** Make very brief notes during the focus group and flesh them out immediately after adjourning.
- **Play host.** Serve light snacks and beverages. Thank everyone for coming and sharing their thoughts.

Many libraries use teen advisory boards (TABs) as sounding boards for new ideas. That's fine if your goal is to attract TAB members to book club. But if you want to involve other teens, you'll need to extend your reach.

Sneaky Tricks: Getting to Know Teens on the Sly

Observe

Observation is cheap and easy! As you go about your business, keep an eye out for the following: Where teens congregate. When they arrive and leave. How much time they spend doing homework, chatting, reading, playing games, and so on. Which staff has best rapport with teens. Who the natural teen leaders are. What items teens check out. What they leave on the tables. Whether they talk about books.

Visit other libraries' teen book clubs. Notice when teens become lively and engaged and when they are barely there. After the meeting, talk to clubbers about why they joined book club. Later, check with the facilitator for additional insights.

Observe patterns in circulation to get a feel for reading preferences. If you want to form a theme or genre book club, recruit teens based on what they check out (you can do it without violating library policy).

Host Special Events

Take observation to the next level. Invite teens to a special book-centered event (e.g., author reading, conference, winter-break reading program). Design activities, book displays, and so forth to glean information you need from teens. For example, if you want to know whether teens would rather talk about fiction or nonfiction, schedule a miniconference with tracks for each. Count attendance and monitor the excitement in each track. Fewer teens with greater excitement equal better book club possibilities than a large group of lukewarm teens.

Seek Professional Help

Draw on colleagues' expertise in person or online. What matters to their teens? What works and what doesn't? When do they meet? What lessons have your colleagues learned? What new things have they tried? Have they encountered any surprises? How do they recruit?

Trust Your Intuition

Throughout the research process you'll pick up subtle signals. Pay attention to them. Back up your hunches with solid research to separate intuition from stereotypes and assumptions; then heed what your gut is telling you.

Step 3. Round It out with Research

From Harris Interactive to SmartGirl.org, from *Not Much Just Chillin'* to U.S. Department of Education reports, you'll find an avalanche of research on teens. Use these resources to gain big-picture overviews (formal research on large samples), anthropological views (narrative studies by authors who immerse themselves in teen life), and psychological insights (based on professionals' work with teens).

Space constraints prevent us from detailing research findings, but the resources listed at the end of this chapter are a treasure trove. If this kind of information appeals to you, you'll find plenty more by following footnotes, links, and references within the published reports.

Skim the reports that seem most likely to give you information you can use. Flag the interesting but less relevant information to peruse at your leisure.

Step 4. Pull It Together and Put It to Work

The purpose of all this research is to put you inside the heads of your most likely book club prospects so you can appeal to them and serve them *as they are,* not as conventional wisdom assumes them to be (or dictates they *should* be).

As you gather information, note the big ideas and things that grab your attention. Jot them in a notebook. These are your first impressions. To dig deeper, organize your notes. This doesn't need to be a fancy affair. Start a notebook or word processing file with sections for each of the actions you intend to take (referring back to your goal-to-action plan). Then take an hour or two to group

---

Repeat. Repeat. Repeat.

Never stop getting to know the teens you serve. Talk to them informally, ask them purposeful questions, and once every year or two do a survey to get back inside their heads. Teens will think you are magic when you "out of the blue" suggest a book or activity (or a whole new approach to book club) that suits them *exactly*. That's the magic you can work when you listen to teens.

---

like ideas and place them in the appropriate sections. Look for information that will tell you the following:

- What type of club to create in terms of reading material, activities, and atmosphere. This is the number one thing you need to learn.
- Why current clubbers come to book club.
- What drives teens' decision to join book club (e.g., friends, time of day or time of year, parental encouragement or restrictions, rapport with you, boredom, books).
- How teens feel about book club (e.g., Is it passé? What would give it cachet?).
- What social, emotional, intellectual, and developmental needs teens themselves feel.
- What types of rewards or recognition motivate prospective clubbers.
- Where they stand in terms of maturity, discussion styles, reading ability, and so forth.

Now step back for a few days. Then take an hour to brainstorm things you can to do create excitement for book club. Now you're getting to the point: using what you've learned to design a book club that speaks so directly to teens it's as if they created it themselves! The first thing you'll need to consider is: What type of book club? If you think read-and-discuss is your only option, keep reading! Chapters 4 and 5 highlight 12 very different kinds of book clubs.

References

Banks, Russell. 1996. *Rule of the Bone.* New York: HarperCollins/Perennial.

Crutcher, Chris. 2003. *Staying Fat for Sarah Byrnes.* New York: HarperCollins/HarperTempest.

Geraci, John, et al. 2000. "Understanding Youth: What Works and Doesn't Work When Researching and Marketing to Young Audiences." White paper presented at "Reinventing Advertising—The Worldwide Advertising Conference," Harris Interactive, Inc.

Jones, Patrick, and Joel Shoemaker. 2001. *Do It Right! Best Practices for Serving Young Adults in School and Public Libraries.* New York: Neal-Schuman.

O'Donnell-Allen, Cindy, and Bud Hunt. 2001. "The Lure of Young Adult Literature—Reading Adolescents: Book Clubs for YA Readers." *English Journal* 90 (3): 82. (*English Journal* is published by the National Council of Teachers of English.)

A Sampling of Research on Teens

There are literally thousands of studies on teens available. These are some that we found interesting and useful.

Army Teen Panel. "Teens' Top Concerns." Available at: www.redstone.army.mil/armyouth/teensrva.htm.

Benson, Peter L. *All Kids Are Our Kids: What Communities Must Do to Raise Caring and Responsible Children and Adolescents.* San Francisco: Jossey-Bass, 1997.

Bostrom, Margaret. *The 21st Century Teen: Public Perception and Teen Reality: A Summary of Public Opinion Data.* Washington, DC: The Frameworks Institute, 2001.

The Frameworks Institute. For many research reports on teens, mostly focusing on communications, go to http://www.frameworksinstitute.org/products/youth.shtml.

Geraci, John, et al. "Understanding Youth: What Works and Doesn't Work When Researching and Marketing to Young Audiences." White paper presented at "Reinventing Advertising—The Worldwide Advertising Conference." Harris Interactive, Inc., 2000. Available at: http://www.harrisinteractive.com/expertise/pubs/Youth_WhitePaper.pdf.

Harris Interactive, Inc. *Trends & Tudes:* Newsletter highlighting current topics in youth and education research. Vol. 2, No. 10 (October 2003) features "A Brave New Media World," results of a research into media habits of 13- to 24-year-olds.

Horatio Alger Association. *A Portrait of Contrasts 2000–2001: A Comparison of the Horatio Alger Scholars and the State of Our Nation's Youth Survey.* Alexandria, VA: Horatio Alger Association, 2001. Available at: http://www.horatioalger.com/pdfs/portrait00.pdf.

———. *The State of Our Nation's Youth 2005.* Alexandria, VA: Horatio Alger Association, 2005. Available at: http://www.horatioalger.com/pubmat/state05.cfm.

National Mental Health Association. "What Does Gay Mean?" Teen survey conducted by ICR/International Communications Research. Available at: http://www.nmha.org/whatdoesgaymean/WhatDoesGayMeanTeenSurvey.pdf.

O'Donnell-Allen, Cindy, and Bud Hunt. "The Lure of Young Adult Literature—Reading Adolescents: Book Clubs for YA Readers." *English Journal* 90:3 (2001): 82. *English Journal* is published by the National Council of Teachers of English.

Perlstein, Linda. *Not Much Just Chillin': The Hidden Lives of Middle Schoolers.* New York: Ballantine, 2004.

Pipher, Mary. *Reviving Ophelia: Saving the Selves of Adolescent Girls.* New York: Ballantine, 1995.

Simmons, Rachel. *Odd Girl Out: The Hidden Culture of Aggression in Girls.* Harvest Books, 2003.

Young Adult Library Services Association and SmartGirl.org. "Teen Read Week 2002." Available at: www.smartgirl.org/reports/1493716.html.

Zollo, Peter. *Getting Wiser to Teens: More Insights into Marketing to Teenagers.* Ithaca, NY: New Strategist Publications, 2003.

3

◈✦◈　◈✦◈　◈✦◈

PLAN TO BUILD
A BETTER BOOK CLUB

Most of us are familiar, at least in theory, with the traditional read-and-discuss model of book clubs. To make the shift to a teen-centered book club, you'll need to change your perspective just a bit. But as anyone familiar with the Mona Lisa can tell you, change your perspective and you change the whole picture. When you build a teen-centered book club, you work *with* teens and *in view of* a host of interested parties. You also work *in relationship with* your school or library, its policies, requirements, and structure.

Careful planning helps it all come together. You'll plan in two stages: The first stage focuses on high-level issues—for example, refining the goals and scope of the book club and aligning it with library goals (e.g., serving at-risk teens, building community support). The second stage is all about logistics. Of course, it's not as linear as all that; you'll hop back and forth between the two stages, and teens will move in and out of the process as you go.

This chapter outlines what you need to think about and do to start a club and keep it going strong. If you're familiar with book clubs and teen programming, you'll easily be able to apply this to your current program. If you're a newbie, look to the rest of the book for details.

PLANNING WITH TEENS . . . OR NOT

It's ideal if teens help you plan, but it's not necessary. With the research you've amassed you have plenty of information to build your plans around teens' preferences and interests.

Perhaps you assume that without teen involvement every step of the way, the club is not really teen-centered. But remember, "teen-centered" and "teen-led" are two different things. Following teens' lead, even when it upsets your assumptions, is what being teen-centered is all about. Certainly, if you like, invite teens to help you plan and encourage them with your enthusiasm. Their involvement now will certainly build their sense that this is their club. But if teens are not willing, able, and available to help, don't become discouraged. As they become more engaged, they'll become more involved in planning.

Plan to Involve Teens

When you begin to consider logistics is the perfect time to invite teens to join in planning. But to do that, you'll need to overcome two hurdles: teens' tight schedules and the general perception of planning as time-consuming and dull.

During your initial research (chapter 2), find out what dates and times are generally best for meetings. Then schedule the meeting when the most committed teens are available. To make it clear this is not going to be a droner of a meeting, emphasize the social (connect with book lovers!) and creative (give us your ideas!) aspects. When teens show up for the planning meeting, deliver on your promises: provide plenty of opportunities for them to socialize, and make the planning active and exciting.

Planning Meetings that Sizzle

The best way to make planning sizzle is to put together a series of tightly focused, timed, decision-making activities and rotate through them quickly. For example, to set the date, post a huge, undated, 30-day calendar on the wall. Give each teen a marker and tell them they have 1 minute to converge on the calendar to mark out the days they *cannot* meet with a big, red X. Blow a whistle to start and stop the game. When time is up, see which dates are left un-Xed (or lightly Xed). This is a great icebreaker, as teens compare notes on their schedules. You may have to do some negotiating on dates, because it's highly unlikely that you'll find one that works for everyone. (See step 5 "Set the Date" later in this chapter.)

For other planning ideas, distribute fishbowls and stacks of colorful index cards on the tables, floor, and windowsills around the room. (If you want teens to be creative, you be creative, too.) Each bowl gets labeled with a decision point, such as "What's to Eat?" "Our First Meeting," "Read This First," "Let's Try This" (activities), and so on. Turn teens loose with pens, encouraging them to scribble as many ideas on as many cards as they can as fast as they can. Every minute, blow your whistle, indicating it's time to move to a different topic. When time is up, gather the fishbowls, withdraw cards one by one, read the ideas aloud, and ask teens for a thumbs-up or thumbs-down on each. Tie votes are set aside for further discussion after the thumbs have their say.

You don't need to finalize every detail at this meeting, but teens will have substantial say in the details that matter most to them, and you'll gather plenty more input to use as you fill in the rest.

Even if your planning meeting draws a good number of teens and all goes well, remember that planners are not necessarily clubbers and vice versa. If you schedule a planning meeting, you will attract the planners. Some may also be clubbers, but in general, you can expect a greater number and variety of teens to show up for the club itself than for a planning session.

A Low-Stress Alternative

Book club requires lots of detailed planning, and the sheer magnitude can put teens off. Make planning more palatable by breaking it into bits, or planning moments. Each planning moment deals with one issue, such as when to meet or what to do about food. Then take the "eyedropper" approach. Establish the general parameters based on what you know from your research, but leave several decisions open-ended. (A particularly good decision point to leave for book club meeting itself is "Name That Club!"). During the first book club meeting, alternate icebreakers, planning moments, and book discussion or activities. Continue to "eyedropper" planning moments into successive meetings as needed.

TWELVE STEPS TO BUILDING A BETTER BOOK CLUB

1. Listen to Teens

Follow the guidelines and tips in chapter 2 to learn about the teens you serve or would like to serve. The most important thing you'll need to learn is whether your idea is realistic: Is there enough strong interest to move ahead? The second thing you need to know is: What type of club would teens actually join? (Chapters 4 and 5 describe several types of clubs.) Be specific, and listen for intensity of interest. You don't need to know what type of clubs teens think would be fun; you need to know which clubs they would commit to attend month after month and would even take charge of running.

Reflect on what teens have told you. Listen between the lines. What do they find irresistible, not because of its flash and dazzle but because it strikes a deep chord within them? Most likely you'll find greatest resonance around issues of identity, meaning, and connection.

2. Begin with the End in Mind

There's an old proverb that's been credited to everyone from Chinese philosophers to Norwegian bachelor farmers: If you don't know where you're going, that's probably where you'll end up. In short: Begin by defining your book club's purpose, goals, and measures of success. Then plan to them.

There's no need to go through an elaborate process here. You have a lot on your plate, and unless teen book club is a cornerstone library initiative, why drive a Hummer when a Chevy will do?

Start with your library's mission and goals. If your library adopted the YALSA Vision Statement (1994), its mission might include this: "Young adults are actively involved in the decision-making process." If your library has recently launched a fundraising drive, the goal might be to build community support. If your performance goals for the year include serving at-risk teens, there's your purpose. When you have a handle on the larger goal or vision, simply answer the question: How will *this* teen-centered book club further it? Then translate the answer into specific, doable, measurable goals.

To help you begin thinking about mission and purpose, here is a sampling of some of the many ways book clubs serve various groups and goals.

Teens

- Connects sociable readers to other sociable readers
- Provides a safe place to explore new ideas
- Promotes empathy, reason, and judgment
- Opens the door to questions about identity, the meaning of life, and human relationships
- Exposes teens to many viewpoints, life stories, cultural norms, assumptions, and other influences, yielding fresh insights into why people think, act, and feel as they do
- Hones conversational skills, including civil disagreement
- Broadens the answer to the question "What's to read?"
- Complements formal education with a broader base of prior knowledge and more finely developed thinking skills
- Improves reading mechanics and comprehension

The Library

- Strengthens the link between reader and library
- Builds awareness of the library as a place to go for informal lifelong learning
- Proves the usefulness of library for research and recreation
- Increases circulation beyond the bestsellers
- Promotes the use of a variety of library resources
- Introduces readers to new writers
- Provides a place where people can connect: readers to readers, writers to readers, and so on

The Community

- Supports school curriculum
- Promotes civic values
- Encourages intellectual freedom and understanding of its complexity
- Boosts notion of freedom of speech and understanding of its complexity
- Develops knowledge-based decision making
- Prepares teens for roles as workers
- Provides a community-based developmental asset for teens (see Benson 1997)

The Librarian

- Fortifies ties with a core group of young, involved patrons
- Keeps job interesting and enlivened
- Fulfills job requirements
- Can provide insights/information to influence collection development
- Warms the heart, stimulates the mind, and gives hope for the future

Working from your purpose or mission (and your research into teen interests), create three to five specific, doable, measurable goals or priorities. (We prefer the

Whose Club Is This? A High-Level Planning Priority

Gaining a sense of who your "best customers" are is key to higher-level planning for teen-centered book clubs, because your planning decisions flow from what you know about your customers. Decisions about whom you include in the club, how you recruit them, and how many you sign up go a long way toward establishing the tone of book club. Is book club limited to teens at a certain school or service area, grade level, age, sex, reading ability, or curricular area? Do you want to attract teen/adult pairs, sci-fi fans, teens hanging out after school? Do you need to limit the size of the club? Or is everything up for grabs? Your library's mission may answer this question for you (e.g., the library is focusing on at-risk teens this year). Or you may find as you talk to teens that the most committed potential clubbers fall into certain groups.

Be sure to identify your target audience during the first stage of planning so you don't waste your effort planning a perfect book club—for the wrong group of teens.

term *priorities* because it denotes more flexibility than the word *goals* does.) For each priority identify a measure of success and what you will do to achieve it. Congratulations—you've just created your goal-to-action plan!

Put the plan in writing and refer to it often so that every decision and action moves you toward your goals. For example, if your action plan calls for writing in books, you'll need to consider the budget; if it calls for small group activities, room size and arrangement must accommodate that.

Figure 3.1 is sample a goal-to-action plan; chapters 4 and 5 list measures of success for several types of book clubs; and chapter 12 walks you through assessment.

3. Plan within Parameters

Using what you've learned about the teens you serve, as well as the purpose of the club, round out your vision of the book club. The club will be teen-centered, of course, but will it also be teen-led? How much real leadership can you expect of teens? How much support and backup can you expect from the library? the Friends of the Library? the community? Will you market the club to draw teens primarily from your branch, or will you extend your reach districtwide? What constraints (e.g., funding, book availability, time) affect planning, and how can you work with (or around) them?

With all of these things in mind, outline some of the club's defining parameters or boundaries, such as amount of time you'll devote to it, portion of programming budget you'll allocate to it, priority you'll assign to it, minimum number of members, and so forth. Compare these parameters to your goal-to-action plan to be sure your plan is still reasonable.

Now you're ready to fill in the details.

FIGURE 3.1
Goal-to-Action Plan

Purpose	Priorities	Measures of Success	Action
Developing Empathy: Teens think and feel with characters who are unlike the teens.	1. Teens suspend their personal judgment or emotional response to a book character. 2. Teens find common ground with difficult characters. 3. Teens are less quick to dismiss books with characters they dislike or don't understand.	1. Teens can note the moment they experience their first strong emotional response to a character by underlining (or flagging) the exact words or phrases that set off the emotional reaction. 2. Teens can identify an important emotional moment for the character by flagging the passage. 3. Teens can look past the story to name the core emotion at work in the passage. 4. Teens can link the character's emotional experience to one of their own. 5. Teens can name a dozen words or phrases that indicate the teen is judging the character based on the teen's own feelings or beliefs. 6. Teens can justify the character's motivations, emotions, thoughts and actions *and* explain how all of these differ from the teen's own. 7. Teens complete at least one book featuring a character the teens initially disliked or didn't understand.	1. Give teens colorful post-its and ask them to flag the passage with a color that suits their response (red for angry, blue for cold, yellow for happy, etc.). 2. Give teens colorful post-its and ask them to flag the passage with a color that suits their response (red for angry, blue for cold, yellow for happy, etc.). 3. Teens who have chosen the same passages get together during book club to talk about what the core emotion is, what color they assigned it and why. Small groups report back to the club. 4. Share as a club. 5. Play a game where teens write on colored cards (red for stop, green for go) words that indicate the teen is judging or empathizing. 6. Role-play with teens questioning the character about his motivations, and so forth. Teens take turns playing the character, answering the same questions. 7. Ask for a show of hands and record the number!
Thinking: Teens avoid the Big Three thinking flaws: generalizations, assumptions, and stereotypes.	1. Teens will catch the thinking flaws that other people make during book club discussion. 2. Teens will catch themselves in the act of making thinking flaws in book club discussions. 3. Teens will catch themselves in the act of making thinking flaws as they read or reflect on their reading.	1. Teens can name a dozen words or phrases that indicate assumptions, generalizations and stereotypes. 2. Teens can name which thinking flaws appear most often in book club discussions. 3. Each teen can name which thinking flaw he or she most often falls prey to. 4. Teens name the ways they catch themselves in the act of thinking or voicing a thinking flaw. 5. The number of thinking flaws voiced in book club discussions decreases over time.	1. Play a card game in which teens write on colorful cards (blue for generalization, purple for stereotypes, etc.) words or phrases and what thinking flaw they indicate. 2. During book club discussions, teens award one another the colorful cards. 3. Teens choose the card that best represents their thinking flaw. 4. Teens group themselves by thinking flaw and brainstorm ways to catch themselves in the act. 5. Track the number of thinking- flaws cards that change hands (and whether they should change hands more often than they do).

From *The Teen-Centered Book Club: Readers into Leaders* by Bonnie Kunzel and Constance Hardesty. Westport, CT: Libraries Unlimited. Copyright © 2006.

> ### Special Planning Issue: Who's on Top?
>
> What if teen interests don't align with your agenda? That's not the show-stopping obstacle it appears to be. Yes, it's all about teens... but being teen-centered is *not* librarian-annihilating (see chapter 1, "Your Role in a Teen-Centered Book Club"). You and the library may establish the arena in which the club operates. It's the equivalent of saying, "We're building a house (not a grocery store), and teens are the architects."

4. Build Your Infrastructure

You'll need three resources to make book club work: time, money, and support from your supervisor, director, and decision makers.

Depending on the type of club you have, you'll need a few hours (or more) per month to prepare, meet, recruit, gather and distribute books, promote the club, and evaluate it. Before you go any further with planning, put together a time estimate and be sure you can commit to it. Or, look for ways you to shrink the club's scope. The good news is that there's a book club for every schedule. Bookchatters takes almost no time outside of meetings. At the other end of the spectrum, service-learning and readers-into-leaders clubs require substantial preparation. (See chapters 4 and 5 for descriptions of these and other types of clubs.)

Book club must run even when you are absent. Make it easy for colleagues to fill in unexpectedly. Prepare a fact sheet with essential information: date and time, meeting room location and setup, where you keep supplies, what you do for food, a list of upcoming books with Web sites for prefab book club guides, and even brief notes on members. If you can, designate a pinch hitter whom you can invite to visit book club a few times to see how it operates.

Besides staff time, you'll need money. Direct costs include acquiring books, snacks, and supplies; printing or copying promotional materials and special costs for activities, guests, and so on. Indirect costs include staff time, interlibrary loan use, use of the room, Internet access for email, and the library's Web space for recruiting and promotion. Indirect costs are often uncounted, but when you seek funding, your proposal should state *all* costs.

Track all expenses so you can explain them and justify requests for additional funds. If you can, make book club a separate line item within the YA budget; it may help prevent funding being diverted into other programs.

After you know the costs, you can build a cost-benefit case. Articulating tangible costs and intangible benefits makes it easy for funders to say "yes" to book club. Taking the time to do this is well worth your while: It's nearly impossible to strip funding from effective, popular, *visible* programs. To build your case you'll need to document your successes. (Chapter 12 tells you how.)

Finally, you'll need support for answering challenges within and outside of the library. Challenges might include budget or staffing cuts, conflicting priorities, and attempted censorship. If you have recruited people who will champion the teen book club, and you've promoted the program in general, you'll have

---

Need Something? Go Get It!

- Not enough staff support for book club? Recruit volunteers: teens, friends of the library, senior citizens, members of service organizations, and other interested parties.
- Not enough money for book club? Look to alternative sources of funding: community foundations, corporate sponsors, publishers, granting organizations, and individual donors.

---

allies to call on when you need them. (Chapter 6 gives guidelines and tips for building support.)

5. Set the Date

Recreational book clubs in schools or public libraries generally meet once a month for 45–90 minutes. Often they're seasonal, meeting September to November and January through April or even May. Most clubs take a break as spring activities heat up and summer sets in. (Some libraries are bucking that tradition: We're hearing about more and more clubs that meet in the summer.)

Working around all school, extracurricular, and vacation schedules is impossible. Be realistic: You can't catch *all* the fish in the sea. Even if teens have told you their schedules at an initial planning meeting, double-check with local schools to establish a schedule. Beware of Mondays (too many holidays), school breaks, seasonal quirks, and big events (e.g., homecoming week). Be alert to unusual opportunities: If your library is near a school and teens hang out at the library during lunch, try a Read 'Em and Eat! book club.

Once you've established a schedule, stick with it even if some teens have to miss some meetings.

Literacy-enrichment and other curriculum-support clubs may meet more often, three to five days each week. Work with the reading specialist or classroom teachers to create a schedule that works for you, them, and the teens.

6. Pick a Place, Build a Space

Check out the room the library has been using for teen book club. Does it really work, or does it need a little help? Room size, location, arrangement, furniture, décor . . . all set the stage for book club.

Size: People don't like to fill a space to capacity, and they don't like cavernous spaces. Figure seating for 10 if you hope to draw 8 people.

Location: Here's a no-brainer: Meet in a room that's easy to find. Or, make it easy to find with tape arrows on the floor or signs along the way. Though centrally located, the room should be private and quiet, with a door you can close for privacy and noise control. Easy access to the bathrooms is good.

Hint: Barring policy restrictions or budget, there's no reason why book club has to meet in the library. Some clubs meet in coffee houses or bakeries. You can even meet outside when the weather is nice.

Arrangement: Arrange the room into areas for discussing, doing activities, and eating. Or make sure the room has enough space to push chairs out of the way when it's time to play Literary Twister.

Cookies Speak Louder than Words

Once you've established the why and how, it's time to set up the chairs and bring out the cookies. Assuming you're having cookies. Are you? That's what logistics is all about. The down-to-earth details can make or break a club, whatever your lofty goals.

Lowly logistics—whether you serve cookies or dinner, meet after school or on Saturday, sit around tables or lounge on the floor—all clearly convey messages about book club. As you plan, ask yourself how each decision will affect book club. What messages are you sending? What kind of atmosphere are you creating?

Furniture: Soft, comfy surfaces relax the body and open the mind. Pillows and fabric-covered foam mats work. So do papasan and beanbag chairs. Even hardback chairs work, as long as they surround a table so teens have a place to put their elbows to prop up their heads. The only thing that really doesn't work is hardback chairs in a big circle. No one can get comfortable.

Obviously, you can't spend the book club budget on furniture. But you can borrow and beg! Perhaps the story time room has mats and pillows you can borrow, or you can add beanbag chairs to the wish list in your annual book club report.

Décor: Decorate the room for each meeting (see chapter 6). Start with a colorful tablecloth in the center of the discussion circle; arrange The List and other book club gadgets artfully on it. Create a tabletop or book cart display. Give teens something to look at as their eyes roam.

7. Announce the First Meeting

As you talk to teens about book club, interest will build. By the time you're ready to announce the first meeting, teens should already be asking about it. The more compressed the time frame, the greater the excitement. Plan your schedule so that about six weeks elapse between your initial research and the first club meeting. Announce the club about three weeks before it actually begins, to give teens time to circulate the word and put it on their schedules. That gives you three weeks of research and initial planning, and then three more weeks (after the announcement but before the meeting) to put all the final details in place.

Chapter 6 offers many ideas for recruiting teens, but nothing works like the personal touch: The more teens you talk to, the more teens will sign up.

Recruiting gets easier as time goes on. Plan ways to make it worth their while and teens will return—and bring their friends. With a relaxed, friendly atmosphere and surprising, fun, and thought-provoking activities, you'll build a core group of loyal clubbers who will spread the word about this cool thing at the library. The

---

Atmosphere Is Everything

Creating a safe space sets your teens free. It's the foundation of everything else you do—and everything you do must reinforce it. People, processes, policies all affect book club atmosphere just as surely as room size and location do. As you plan book club, be sure every decision, plan, and action reinforces an atmosphere of caring, respect, and inclusion.

This is where your role is most important and intrusive. You may need to occasionally nudge, prod, or directly intervene to maintain civil and courteous discussion. At other times, you'll be busy creating and sustaining the atmosphere by engaging fully and positively with teens, praising every good thing they do, every rigorous thought, every insightful comment.

Simply put, a safe book club space is an atmosphere where people can speak their minds with the certainty that they will be respectfully and *care*fully heard. Manners and ground rules are the superficial means to the end, but safety is much larger than that. It's a sense of respect and value and care for one another that informs each person's language and actions. You can build that atmosphere by talking openly and frequently about book club values and by making sure of three simple things:

- Everyone always feels included,
- Everyone is always respected, and
- Everyone is always honored (wholeheartedly accepted, even when their behavior isn't).

---

momentum will carry over as members return for a second (and, if you're lucky, even a third!) season of clubbing.

8. Choose Great Reads

In traditional book clubs, the librarian selects the club's first book . . . and possibly the second book ... and often all of the books. That gives you plenty of lead time to gather and distribute books.

In teen-centered book clubs, teens pick the books at every meeting or two. Give careful thought to how you do this. Since you can't predict which book teens will choose, you are under pressure to provide speedy turnaround. The ideal, of course, is to distribute books immediately after they are selected, but few library collections support this.

A second-best solution is next-meeting delivery: Borrow books from several libraries. Distribute them at the following book club meeting, then discuss them at the following (third) meeting. Of course, you run the risk that, during the interval between book selection and discussion, interest in the book will wane. The only protection against that is to be sure that book selection is based on real interest and not on whim or a popularity contest. (Chapter 7 offers more detail on book selection, including how to handle challenges.)

> **If You Could Do Only One Thing . . .**
>
> Book handling can easily eat up great chunks of time. The best solution? Get funding so you can buy what you need when you need it. Write a grant proposal, appeal to community organizations, hold a car wash! Nothing will make your life easier than streamlining this process.

Caution: Don't use collection development funds for book club. It hides the true cost of book club and it doesn't build a balanced collection. An exception is curriculum-support book clubs in schools. In that case, the library could buy a set of books with some assurance that they would be used year after year.

9. Plan the Program

What do you do with the books you've selected? The only limits to programming are time, cost, policy, and safety. Deciding on programming ideas is a great "planning moment" activity. Do it often, even setting out a fishbowl for ideas at each meeting. Don't worry if you don't get to one-tenth of teens' ideas. Brainstorming is half the fun.

The most common book club activity is talk, and for teens that usually centers on:

- **Identity:** Who is this character and why did he behave the way he did? Was he right? What was he thinking? How am I like him and how am I different? What would I do? What does that say about me?
- **Meaning:** Why are we here? Why can't we all live in peace? What matters? Is this all there is?
- **Connection:** What do those people have to do with me? Am I one of them? Where is my place? What is my part in all this?

Plan how the club will generate discussion questions. Will teens create them, or will you? Chapter 10 offers many ideas for generating questions, along with a list of 50 open-ended questions that focus on identity, meaning, and connection. Whatever you do, avoid the dreaded plot–theme–character drill. This isn't school.

Clubbers will certainly suggest many program ideas other than discussion. Whether they decide to read to the elderly, make scrapbooks, watch a movie, role-play, keep blogs, or play strategy games, try to work in some discussion that brings clubbers together around the books they have read.

When teens choose individual activities like crafts, include time at the end of the meeting for looking at one another's creations, or create a group display for the library. The more you can do to help clubbers hang together, the more committed teens will become.

Caution: Some activities can be done on the spur of the moment. Others take some planning and prep time. When you plan programming, try to move from idea to action as quickly as possible (before interest shifts)—but be sure that you and/or teens have enough time to gather the resources (e.g., materials, guests, books) you need to make the program happen. Unless you're planning a major event, one month should be all you need to prepare.

10. Integrate Lessons in Leadership

Teen-centered book clubs focus on leadership basics: self-knowledge and self-control, empathy and reason, communication and reflection. Of course, teens still take action in planning, assuming responsibility, working together. But the primary focus is on the internal. Why? Because life gives teens plenty of opportunity to *do* but little opportunity to reflect.

By their nature book clubs encourage teens to think and feel with others, to focus on their inner selves in a meaningful way, and to build shared understanding. You can offer teen-centered programs that move clubbers toward that end. Games or activities that promote book club values, emotional intelligence, empathy, thinking, communicating, or doing will serve your purposes. Leadership manuals are full of such games and activities.

Any activity takes a leadership turn when you stop abruptly and ask teens to examine their thoughts and actions. Doing so, you're asking teens to become self-aware, a defining element of leadership. Likewise, in asking teens to role-play an unfamiliar or even distasteful point of view, you're asking them to empathize or delve into issues of identity.

11. Plan to Evaluate

Build time into the club (and into your book club planning/preparation time) to collect and record statistics and stories, observations, and thoughts. Explore your personal response to book club and reflect on its usefulness or potential. Focus especially on your purpose and goals—and the measures of success you identified in your goal-to-action plan. Be sure to revisit those plans periodically to ensure that your goals are still your goals, the measures of success are still relevant, and so on.

All of this will come in handy as you document your success (see chapter 12) and reflect on the experience.

12. Stage Your Exit

Decide in advance what criteria you will use to decide when book club has run its course. If your club is closed-ended (e.g., a three-of-a-kind club, a school-based club), you'll have no problem marking its demise. Otherwise, you'll need to plan to make the decision to end book club when you can no longer justify the resources it requires. That decision may be based on attendance, level of energy or engagement during meetings, a change in your job status, or shifting priorities for the library.

To make the end as painless as possible, plan your exit strategy before you call the first meeting. Decide what criteria you will use to make the decision to disband, when and how you will let teens know, how you will begin the transition, and how many meetings will elapse between your announcement and the final meeting. Also think about what you will do with the props and book lists clubbers have amassed.

Finally, plan to include a closing ritual in the last club meeting—but don't fill in the details. When the time comes, ask the teens to do that.

MOVING FORWARD

Don't worry about making perfect plans set in stone. In the first place, you can't make a perfect plan. In the second, teens' preferences are constantly changing. It's entirely possible that in the weeks between the planning meeting and the first book club meeting, the club's membership will change and the club will be tweaking all those well-laid plans on the fly. Focus on higher-level planning to create a strong and flexible framework, and then let teens shape it to suit them.

Over time (sometimes very little time), you can expect even the framework to change. Every club Constance has participated in has seen these shifts: the senior citizen club infiltrated by middle-aged youngsters; the literary club that became as much about leadership as literature; the save-the-discards club that became a read-and-share club; the Old Classics book/movie club that oscillated between old and modern classics.

Planning is just for starters. At some point, every good club takes on a life of its own. If you trust your instincts, watch for bias and assumptions, and keep your focus on teens, then your club will grow organically, shifting and evolving with its members. Plan on it.

Reference

Young Adult Library Services Association. 1994. *YALSA Vision Statement.* Adopted June 1994. Available at: http://www.ala.org/ala/yalsa/aboutyalsab/ yalsavisionstatement.htm.

4

❖◼❖ ❖◼❖ ❖◼❖

LET'S GO CLUBBING! SIX TRADITIONAL AND INNOVATIVE BOOK CLUBS

If ever there was a candidate poised to burst out of its box, it's teen book clubs. And they are beginning to do it: Once, all clubs were shoehorned into the read-and-discus model; now teens can choose from online, book/movie, leadership, and many other types of clubs.

Ongoing read-and-discuss clubs continue to be ubiquitous for good reason: They familiar, they're fun and easy, and they work well enough. However, their appeal is limited to people who like to talk about what they read. Worse, after a few months the read-and-discuss formula can become formulaic, even monotonous.

So why not shake it up? Rethinking book club can add spice to meetings and extend your reach to teens who don't fit the traditional book-club profile. In a few weeks of off-and-on brainstorming, Constance imagined more than 35 different ways to spin book club. By looking at what other libraries do and what we've done over the years, what works well and better, what we dreamed of doing if only the budget and schedule allowed . . . we winnowed the list to 13. This chapter and the next highlight those innovative clubs.

READ AND DISCUSS

What it is. This traditional club meets every month to discuss a book everyone has read. Members *join the club;* they come every month regardless of what's on the schedule. Group discussions take up most of each meeting, spiced up with occasional parties, author visits, or other treats.

Purpose. This is the most "clubbish" of all book clubs. It's about *belonging* as well as books. As teens connect around books, they learn more about themselves and about life. Ultimately, we hope they grow in understanding, reason and compassion—all by reading and talking about books.

How it works. Between meetings everyone reads the same book. During meetings everyone discusses it. (See chapters 9–10.)

Advantages

- What could be more heartwarming than watching teens mature and bond over time? or more exciting than those "ah-ha!" moments?
- Lively, friendly discussions encourage teens to jointly explore their thoughts and feelings.
- Even as book club encourages intellectual and emotional leaps, it holds teens responsible for what they say.

Disadvantages

- These clubs can become tired. If you've been doing a traditional club for a while and attendance or energy is waning, try another type of club for a while.
- It takes effort to organize and deliver a memorable book club.
- Polite disagreement is becoming a lost art. Expect to spend a fair amount of time training teens to keep it civil and to stand up for themselves.

Measures of Success

- Consistent attendance.
- Teens plumb questions of identity, meaning, and connection: Who am I, why am I here, and what are all you people doing on my planet?
- Teens become competent readers and discussion artists.

Tips

- Go with the flow. Great book clubs develop over time.
- Prevent or circumvent clashes that grow out of discussion styles. Help teens focus on substance, not style.
- If teens seem to be skating on the surface, ask a question with no easy answer.

Great Books for Read-and-Discuss Clubs

Airborne. Kenneth Oppel. New York: HarperCollins/Eos, 2003.

A captivating caper featuring Victorian-era fantasy with a luxury airship, cabin boy, wealthy girl passenger, pirates, shipwreck, and an undiscovered species of flying cats. 2005 Michael L. Printz Honor Book.

Before We Were Free. Julia Alvarez. New York: Alfred A. Knopf, 2002.

Anita, 12, lives in terror in the Dominican Republic under the dictatorship of General Trujillo during the 1960s. The American Library Association (ALA) says, "Powerful and at times intense, this book will take readers on a frightening journey of fear and anguish that will cause them to pray for the rescue of Anita and her family." Winner of ALA's 2004 Pura Belpré Medal.

The Box Man. Kobo Abe. New York: Vintage, 2001.

An ambitious read for motivated, thoughtful readers willing to work for their rewards. Abe explores the nature of identity in this tale of a man who takes it to the extreme: He puts a box over his head and takes to the streets of Tokyo. Prepare teens for the fact that the book will probably befuddle them until they all put their heads together to make sense of it. The ultimate read-and-discuss book.

Bucking the Sarge. Christopher Paul Curtis. New York: Wendy Lamb Books, 2004.

Likeable Luther T. Farrell is determined to break free of his mother The Sarge, a ruthless slum landlord and shady dealmaker. This is the hilarious and sometimes sad story of how Luther succeeds—in a way no one could foresee. In a touching and often overlooked passage, Sarge explains to Luther why she behaves the way she does—a reminder of the devastating effects of racism on individuals. The brief moment barely interrupts the madcap tale, but it can easily spark an involved discussion of life choices versus life chances.

The Curious Incident of the Dog in the Night-Time. Mark Haddon. New York: Vintage, 2004.

Amazon.com describes this book as "a murder mystery of sorts—one told by an autistic version of Adrian Mole." Sure to raise questions about the disconnect between who we are inside as opposed to how we appear to the outside world, the nature of "real" life, and autism.

Fault Line. Janet Tashjian. New York: Henry Holt, 2003.

Becky's nearly perfect life takes a turn when she falls head over heels for Kip Costello, who shares her talent for improv comedy. When Kip's violence puts Becky in the hospital, she must confront how such a thing could happen to her. Young men and women alike will engage in wondering: Could such a thing happen to me (as victim or perpetrator)?

Heaven. Angela Johnson. New York: Simon Pulse, 2000.

The *School Library Journal* review of this book opens with: "What makes a person who she is?" Can there be a better question to launch a teen book discussion? Marley, age 14, has to figure out the answer for herself when she discovers that the parents she lives with are not her birth parents. Teens will find much to explore in the relationship of family to self.

Sammy and Juliana in Hollywood. Benjamin Alire Sáenz. El Paso, TX: Cinco Puntos Press, 2004.

It's 1969 in the barrio of Hollywood, New Mexico, and Sammy has just lost his first love. That's just the first in a long string of losses. Grim and realistic in its portrayal of poverty, racism, the Vietnam War, petty local rules, and their effects on the spirit of individuals and a community, this book offers plenty to talk or write about, to research, to translate into art, or to use as a springboard for community service.

The Truth. Terry Pratchett. New York: HarperTorch, 2001. (Discworld series #25.)

Believe little of what you read . . . In this hilarious skewering of everything journalistic, Pratchett asks us all: How do you know what you know is true?

Weetzie Bat. Francesca Lia Block. New York: HarperTrophy, 1999 (10th anniversary edition).

It's the stuff of science fiction: An incurable killer virus sweeps the world, devastating vast segments of the human population. That's the world Block makes achingly personal in this fable of 1989 Los Angeles, when love truly was a "dangerous angel." And that's the least of it, as Block magnifies the meaning of family and hits identity, meaning, and connection squarely on the head.

As the judges of ALA's 2005 Margaret A. Edwards Award put it, "Block encourages teens to celebrate their own true selves, helping them discover what time they are upon and where they do belong. . . . In Block's Shangri-L.A., there is pain and sadness, but love, magic, and hope prevail." If this novel doesn't move your teens to tears and to action, they need heart/soul transplants.

Note: If you're going to buy books for the club, buy the three-in-one volume titled *Dangerous Angels,* because teens who enjoy *Weetzie Bat* will clamor for the entire series.

READERS INTO LEADERS

What it is. Teens develop habits of thinking and acting based on discovery, reason, empathy, and respect. (See chapter 10.) They shoulder responsibility for organizing the club and conducting meetings, and they pull together to get the work done. This club focuses on how teens look at the world and think about it, handle feelings and thoughts, and relate to other people. All of those things come into play during lively conversation, which is why book club is the perfect setting to learn leadership.

Purpose. Emotional intelligence, knowing what sets you off and controlling your reaction, is a prerequisite of leadership but it's hardly a teen's strong suit. If clubbers learn nothing more than to suspend their emotions as they read and converse *civilly,* they've gained plenty.

How it works. Teens read a book, then come together to discuss it, just as in a read-and-discuss club. The difference is in *how* teens do it. To begin, you introduce core leadership qualities (e.g., knowing yourself, managing your emotions, developing empathy, thinking, communicating, doing). You challenge teens to keep those qualities in mind as they read and discuss and as they select books and take care of club business.

Advantages

- This can be the most rewarding type of book club. Teens grow into new roles, new ways of thinking and being, before your very eyes.
- Teens pocket the one tool they need to survive the next 10 years: emotional self-control.
- Because leadership begins with self-awareness and radiates outward to encompass others, it goes straight to the heart of teens' concerns with identity, meaning, and connection, making this one of the most appealing types of clubs.

Disadvantages

- This club is demanding for teens and for you. Preparation is time-consuming.
- Progress is slow. You're planting seeds here.
- It may take several tries to get this club right. Try it for a few months and if it doesn't work, ask teens if they'd like to try another type of club. Every year or two, try again. The more you practice, the better it gets.

Measures of Success

- Teens increasingly catch themselves in the midst of a heated moment and calm themselves down.
- Teens bring critical thinking, open-mindedness, empathy, and self-control into book club discussions.
- Teens can describe a wide variety of leadership acts and qualities of leadership. Teens can explain how they live (or strive to live) those qualities, and what small or large acts of leadership they have performed.

Tips

- Step back when teens don't really need you (e.g., they forget to bring discussion questions or food). Likewise, let them answer the tough questions.
- Jump in when teens do need you (e.g., when heated discussions get carried away or a teen seems about to reveal something he or she will later regret).
- Stay focused on books. In this club, leadership comes through books.

Note: To get a better grip on how recognizing and managing emotions *must* precede leadership, read Daniel Goleman's classic *Emotional Intelligence* and the more recent *Primal Leadership: Realizing the Power of Emotional Intelligence.* Although these books have been around long enough to take on the patina of old news, for teens, it's all new.

Teens Lead! Essential Reading for Finding the Leader Within

The Alchemist. Paulo Cohelo. San Francisco: Harper, 1995.

The subtitle, "A Fable about Following Your Dream," says it all. With life lessons and wise words sprinkled liberally throughout, *The Alchemist* speaks to teens where they are and offers tools they can use to build a bridge to their future. Discussion may be difficult for teens who don't wish to share their dreams. Focus narrowly on book and Santiago's experiences until teens feel free to reveal themselves.

Daniel Half Human and the Good Nazi. David Chotjewitz. New York: Atheneum, 2004.

In 1930s Germany, Daniel is an enthusiastic member of Hitler Youth—until he discovers he is half-Jewish. His best friend, Armin, also a Nazi, is torn between loyalty to friend and duty to country. Alternating scenes of Daniel's youth with his later return to Hamburg as an Allied solider in 1945, the book raises one question after another about personal and cultural identity, duty, and friendship.

The First Part Last. Angela Johnson. New York: Simon & Schuster Children's Publishing, 2003.

Bobby, age 16, is sensitive and intelligent—and a dad. This poetic novel tells the riveting story of his struggle to raise his infant son, culminating in a tragic revelation. Bobby's story may prompt teens to think more deeply about what leadership means. Is it possible that leadership is more personal than public, more about responsibility than recognition? Is it leadership then, or is it something else?

Winner of the 2004 Michael L. Printz Award, and a good example of a young African American man/leader not involved in sports or the hip-hop lifestyle.

Godless. Pete Hautman. New York: Simon & Schuster, 2004.

Jason, age 15, makes up his own religion—and comes to believe it wholeheartedly and unrepentantly, even in the face of serious consequences. Exploring the nature of belief, Hautman appeals to teens' questions about faith, religion, and the role of family or culture in determining our beliefs. 2005 National Book Award for Young People's Literature.

Jackie's Nine: Jackie Robinson's Values to Live By. Sharon Robinson. New York: Scholastic, 2001.

Nonfiction. From teamwork to justice, the author describes the principles that she observed as guiding the life of her father, legendary baseball player and civil rights icon Jackie Robinson. The book will spur teens to define, describe, and rank qualities of leadership.

Lives of Our Own. Lorri Hewett. New York: Puffin Books, 2000.

Shawna Riley, wealthy, intelligent, and African American, faces racial prejudice and casual segregation in a Georgia high school. Determined to effect change, and refusing to give up her right to free speech, she becomes a target as well. The key question here is not whether one person can make a difference—but at what cost?

The Lord of the Rings trilogy. J.R.R. Tolkein. Many editions available.

This trilogy, and every book in it, is packed with incidents of "ordinary" folk evolving into leaders—reluctantly, gradually, and with much bumbling. From small sacrifices to acts of magnificent heroism, every member of the company has a chance to shine. Teens will enjoy pointing out their favorite acts of leadership and how their favorite characters gradually grew into the leaders they were destined to be.

The Prince. Niccolo Machiavelli. New York: Penguin Classics, 2003. Many editions available.

A must-read for all would-be leaders, if only so they know what the term *Machiavellian* means! The trick is not to take it too seriously. Skim it, pick out the shocking bits, and let the games begin: Can you be a Prince *and* a humanitarian? Can you be a Prince *and* adhere to your religious beliefs? Can you be a leader and not a Prince? Amazon.com has the review that will pique teens' interest in this treatise on cold-blooded strategy.

Seedfolks. Paul Fleischman. New York: HarperTrophy, 1999.

Take one vacant lot in a troubled urban neighborhood. Plant one seed. Watch a garden community bloom as neighbors from many races, cultures, and walks of life come together (or are thrown together). This book looks at varieties of leadership and prompts the question: Do you have to set out to accomplish great things in order to be a leader?

Whale Talk. Chris Crutcher. New York: Laurel Leaf, 2002.

You don't need to be perfect to do good in the world. Tao Jones is a hotheaded smart-mouth, but he knows how to reach out to others with compassion, to inspire and engender hope in them—from the school's "losers," to a mixed-race girl tortured by her racist father, to his own father. And, in the end, for himself.

Warriors Don't Cry: A Searing Memoir of the Battle to Integrate Little Rock's Central High. Melba Patillo Beals. New York: Washington Square Press, 1995.

"In 1957, . . . I was escaping the hanging rope of a lynch mob, dodging lighted sticks of dynamite, and washing away burning acid sprayed into my eyes." If teens think school violence is scary now, put them in the shoes of one of the nine African American students who integrated Little Rock's Central High School. In honest, low-key prose, Beals tells it like it was: the bad and the good, including the encouragement she received from both white and black people.

This is just one example of the wealth of biographies and autobiographies of leaders in all walks of life, from Florence Nightingale to Malcolm X, from Cesar Chavez to Lance Armstrong. Consider this: For one session of readers-into-leaders book club, the whole club goes to the shelves, browses the biographies/autobiographies, and then returns to the meeting room to spread out the books. Teens can pick one to read. Next meeting, each teen talks about the book he or she read, and then the club can talk about the road to leadership and qualities of leadership.

BOOK BYTES

What it is. Tantalize teens with daily e-mails containing brief consecutive excerpts of a featured book. Chapter-a-Day club takes all the work (and copyright hassles) out of the equation. With the typical model, each week a new book begins. Emails may include the text itself or a link to a Web site where clubbers can read the passages. Of course, they also include a link to circulation so teens can reserve the book!

Purpose. Book byte clubs boost circulation of the featured selection. Along the way, they broaden teens' reading horizons by introducing new books, authors, genres; and they spotlight the library's recent arrivals or perennial favorites.

How it works. The library contracts with a vendor. Turnkey services handle all the logistics and may even help with recruiting, promotion, and evaluation. Custom services give you more control over book selection and list distribution.

Advantages

- Turnkey systems require minimal involvement.
- Book byte clubs attract readers who enjoy variety and surprise.
- What can be more convenient than having bits of books delivered to your email every day?

Disadvantages

- It's strictly one-way. Readers are passive and isolated.
- Teens may buy the book or get it from their school library, which does nothing for your circulation statistics.
- There's no good way to reach teens who lack easy access to computers.

Measures of Success

- Increased circulation of the featured book or related books. (If the club is small, blips in circulation also will be small.)

- Growing club membership.
- Cost-efficiency in terms of dollars per touch (e.g., 20 kids $\times$ 20 touches/month = 400 touches/month; Vendor fee of \$100/month = \$.25/touch).

Tips

- In recruiting and promotion emphasize variety, convenience, and curiosity.
- If the vendor allows, append a personal touch to every excerpt (e.g., a list of readalikes, author/book trivia)—and of course, your contact information.
- Host quarterly special events for clubbers to solidify the club's ties to the library and encourage checkout.

Best for Book Bytes

It's best to work through a vendor to set up this program. The vendor will provide you with a list of titles to choose from, and the vendor will obtain the publishers' permission to use the excerpts in this way. Unless you have the time to track down such permissions yourself, it's best to stick with what the vendors offer.

THREE-OF-A-KIND

What it is. This club meets three times only. Teens read and discuss a trio of related books, focusing on similarities, continuities, and connections.

Purpose. This club encourages consistent attendance. The combination of low commitment, short time frame, and related books creates safety, urgency, and continuity. That's a classic marketing tactic for motivating "customers" to buy.

How it works. The success of a three-of-a-kind club depends on great theme and book selection. Before you jump in, use the tips from chapter 3 to investigate what real teens find really interesting.

Advantages

- Tight time frame creates a sense of urgency and excitement.
- Focus on related titles yields insights that grow from thinking over time.

Disadvantages

- You may lose dedicated clubbers who don't find a particular trio appealing.
- Even three meetings is too many for some teens.

Measures of Success

- Number of new faces—and number of new faces that become familiar!
- Teens learn to look for readalikes.

Tips

- As you select books for each trio, go for variety. (A trio of books by Lauren Myracle is a good choice because each of her books is very different.)
- In recruiting and promotion focus on the niche and the "limited-time offer."

Three-of-a-Kind Sets

Series: Sisterhood of the Traveling Pants

Read these for fun with girls alone or with their mothers, and enjoy clubbers' own stories about barging and bumbling their way through adolescence.

Sisterhood of the Traveling Pants. Ann Brashares. New York: Delacorte Books for Young Readers, 2003.

Second Summer of the Sisterhood. Ann Brashares. New York: Delacorte Books for Young Readers, 2004.

Girls in Pants. Ann Brashares. New York: Delacorte Books for Young Readers, 2005.

Amazon.com says, "Full of homey platitudes about life, love and the pursuit of perfect jeans, *Girls in Pants* occasionally reads like a lengthy *Chicken Soup for the Teenage Soul* entry. But often that's precisely the kind of friendly reassurance female readers are looking for." That's true of every book in the series.

Series: The Abhorsen Trilogy

Lovers of fantasy deserve the best. Here it is.

Sabriel. Garth Nix. New York: Eos, 1997.

Lirael. Garth Nix. New York: Eos, 2002.

Abhorsen. Garth Nix. New York: Eos, 2004.

From Sabriel's quest to save her necromancer father and the Old Kingdom; to Lirael, only Sightless woman in a community of clairvoyants; to an ensemble cast on a quest that brings the series to a stunning close, this is simply one of the best high fantasy series in print. Beautifully written, intricately plotted, steeped in meaning—and still easily accessible—this series will inspire teens to plumb its depths and scale its heights.

Theme: Silencing Teens

In each of these books, troubled teens refuse to speak. Encourage teens to explore that aspect: Is withholding speech about control and personal power?

self-effacement? both? Are teens silenced in our society? How does silencing themselves serve these teens? In what ways do you silence or efface yourself?

You Don't Know Me. David Klass. New York: HarperTempest, 2002.

John's life spirals downward as the abuse mounts at home (violent stepfather) and at school. Though John speaks only in monosyllables as his world grows darker, he finds the bright spots and holds on to hope. Beautifully told, John's story is sure to spark discussion about whether life is "in the end, a love song."

Silent to the Bone. E. L. Konigsburg. New York: Aladdin, 2002.

Branwell calls 911 but can't speak to describe the crisis that results in the death of his infant sister—or to defend himself against the charge that he abused her. This is a middle-grade book but contains enough psychological insight and suspense to hold the attention of older teens. Good for a mixed book club, and a lighter interlude between two intense books.

Speak. Laurie Halse Anderson. New York: Puffin, 2001. (Paper.)

High school freshman Melinda loses her ability to speak in the aftermath of a summer party in which she was raped. Ostracized and ridiculed, she achieves a hard-won metamorphosis. Pay close attention as the discussion unfolds and intervene if necessary to prevent excessive self-revelation, gossip, or silent trauma.

Theme: The Inner Life of Soldiers

Three historic wars, three coming-of-age tales.

Fallen Angels. Walter Dean Myers. New York: Scholastic, 1989.

Myers's tale of young men in battle withstands the test of time. Combining adventure, camaraderie, humor, and shocking (though not graphic) events, Myers follows two young men on the path from innocence to world weariness.

This book could make a good counterpoint for girls who have recently read the Sisterhood of the Traveling Pants series. They can compare how male friendships differ in style and effect from female friendships. And of course, the key question applies to both books: Can friendship save your sanity—or your life?

Private Peaceful. Michael Morpurgo. New York: Scholastic, 2004.

British author Morpurgo gives teens a realistic and suspenseful glimpse at a war that receives short shrift in history courses and popular consciousness. As Thomas Peaceful, a wounded soldier, awaits imminent tragedy, he reflects on the events, brutal and sweet, that have led to this moment and the loss of his beloved brother, Charlie. Winner of the British Red House Children's Book Award (2005) and short-listed for the Whitbread Children's Book Award (2004).

A Soldier's Heart. Gary Paulsen. New York: Laurel Leaf, 2000.

As searing an antiwar story as *The Red Badge of Courage,* which inspires the spirit of the book, Paulsen raises questions about duty, cowardice, and all the various costs of war. Luminous and true, teens will feel they are living the book as they read it. The challenge in facilitating discussion is to keep the focus on the book—Charley, the inner lives of soldiers, and the situations presented—rather than allowing the discussion to devolve into a political debate on the world's war du jour.

Authors: Jerry Spinelli (good for younger teens)

Two fables and one heartrending World War II story, all about identity and survival.

Stargirl. Jerry Spinelli. New York: Knopf Books for Young Readers, 2002.

Maniac Magee. Jerry Spinelli. New York: Little, Brown, 1991.

Milkweed. Jerry Spinelli. New York: Knopf Books for Young Readers, 2003.

Authors: Julie Ann Peters

With sensitivity and compassion, Peters portrays teens living true to themselves, whatever their sexual orientation.

Keeping You a Secret. Julie Ann Peters. New York: Megan Tingley, 2003.

Luna. Julie Ann Peters. New York: Megan Tingley, 2004.

Far from Xanadu. Julie Ann Peters. New York: Megan Tingley, 2005.

A few other authors good for three-of-a-kind clubs include David Almond (masterpieces of surrealism), Lauren Myracle (as mentioned previously, no two books remotely alike), Walter Dean Myers (young men in trouble), and J.R.R. Tolkein ('nuff said). Genres, subgenres, and themes are a natural choice for three-of-a-kind clubs: think time-travel romance, science fiction, humor, teens in trouble, and postapocalyptic dystopia. You'll find a list of genres and subgenres in chapter 5; to find suitable books for these groups, see Diana Tixier Herald's *Teen Genreflecting* (2003).

BLOGGER

What it is. An online read-and-discuss club. There are lots of ways to do an online read-and-discuss club. We chose the blog because it addresses issues around privacy, security, and control.

Purpose. Encourage reading and thoughtful discussion using a popular medium.

How it works. Clubbers read the book, then email their comments to you. At least once a day, you check for new messages and read them for relevance, content, and language before posting them on the library's Blogger Book Club Web page. When things get slow, you post a provocative question. Teens select books to read by suggesting titles and voting on them. Each month, archive the old blog and start a new one.

Advantages

- Compared to chapter-each-day, blogger clubs offer more opportunity for building relationships among teens.
- Though constant, the time commitment is light. You can review and post messages in a few moments here and there. Most months you'll spend less time moderating a blog than you would preparing for, facilitating, and cleaning up from a book club meeting.

Disadvantages

- The time commitment is ongoing. Someone needs to cover you on your days off.
- Blogs tend to be invisible. Other than the link on the YA page, how will you let people know it exists? It must be promoted relentlessly.
- Security is huge. You must take measures to prevent adults disguised as teens from joining your club. (If your records include birth date or age, you can do this by requiring each person registering to give their library card number and then checking the number against the teens' record. An even safer bet is to require teens to register in person at the library.)
- Be sure teens use screen names and edit their messages to eliminate personal information (including where they go to school). You'll also want to ensure a single teen can't join under three different screen names.
- Censorship goes against the grain of many librarians. To decide for yourself if it's necessary, visit a few unmoderated teen chat rooms.

Measures of Success

- The number of hits on your blog site, how long each visit lasts, and how many minutes accumulate each month.
- The number of clubbers (but watch out for teens using multiple identities).
- Lively give-and-take. This is next to impossible on a blog; if you get a lively exchange going, give yourself a gold star!
- Circulation figures for the featured title and others by the same author for as long as the blog lasts.

Tips

- Every month invite the author to post a message or two. The Roselle (IL) Blogger Book Club has had great success with this with younger children, but the idea applies equally well to teens! (http://www.roselle.lib.il.us/YouthServices/BookClub/Bloggerbookclub.htm)

- Be visible! Post banners on the YA home page. Hang signs with photos of authors who have blogged with you. Print out the best months' blogs and hang them on the ends of the YA stacks.
- Resist the temptation to go to live chat. Security issues are insurmountable.
- Pose thoughtful questions. Don't let the conversation become superficial or wander too far afield.
- Follow up on what people say so they don't feel they're speaking into a void.
- Be prompt. Post every comment within 24 hours.

Books for Bloggers

Suggest teens try novels in verse, and you may find teens responding in kind. If poetry on the page intimidates teens, send them to the audio books.

Aleutian Sparrow. Karen Hesse. New York: Margaret K. McElderry, 2003.

The heartrending, little-known story of war and internment in the Aleutian Islands during World War II. Told in unrhymed verse, with many thought-provoking moments and ending on a hopeful note. Hesse has written several novels in verse, including *Witness* (the KKK comes to Vermont) and *Out of the Dust* (see description following).

Birdland. Tracy Mack. New York: Scholastic, 2003.

Poetry and prose poems take front and center in this novel, as Jed makes a documentary film based on the poetry journal created by his late brother, Zeke. Mack creates such a strong sense of place that the East Village becomes a character in its own right.

Keesha's House. Helen Frost. New York: Farrar, Straus and Giroux, 2003.

Sestinas and sonnets tell the stories of several teens sharing a safe house. Among them are Keesha, seeking refuge from a violent father; Stephie, pregnant at age 16; and Harris, thrown out of his home because he is gay. Each teen tells is or her own story, and none of it reads "like poetry."

Frenchtown Summer. Robert Cormier. New York: Laurel Leaf, 2001.

Cormier uses spare, haunting blank verse to reveal the secrets of post–World War II Frenchtown through the observations of Eugene, a young loner. Softer but no less intense than his other works, *Frenchtown Summer* captivates readers to the end.

God Went to Beauty School. Cynthia Rylant. New York: HarperTempest, 2003.

God comes to Earth as a man, trying to live a normal life but caught up in the craziness like the rest of us. Funny, touching and respectful, God as a modern guy comes across as compassionate and loving.

Learning to Swim. Ann Turner. New York: Scholastic, 2003.

The beauty of the language can't dull the shock and pain of a young child's sexual abuse perpetrated by a neighbor boy. Free verse carries the narrator from shock to silence and fear and finally to voicing the hurt and beginning to heal.

Make Lemonade. Virginia Euwer Wolff. New York: Scholastic, 1994.

True Believer. Virginia Euwer Wolff. New York: Simon Pulse, 2002.

Two teenage girls—one the mother of two and the other her babysitter—struggle to better their lives in the groundbreaking work *Make Lemonade,* which kick-started the whole novel-in-verse phenomenon. It took Wolff eight years to publish the sequel, following LaVaughn, the babysitter determined to escape the projects, on her quest to go to college.

Out of the Dust. Karen Hesse. New York: Scholastic, 1999.

During the Great Depression, Billie Jo is trapped in Oklahoma. In simple, spare free verse, Billie Jo survives a young life wracked by dust storms, poverty, and the anguish of watching her father disintegrate, physically and mentally, before her eyes. Ostensibly for younger children, the length makes it a good choice for teens as well. Winner of the 1998 Newbery Medal.

Shakespeare Bats Clean Up. Ron Koertge. New York: Candlewick, 2003.

When mono strikes, what's an MVP first-baser to do? Write poetry! With boyish energy, charm, and humor, 14-year-old Kevin Boland experiments with many types of poetry, writing to make sense of his life, his family, his girlfriends, and his problems.

Who Will Tell My Brother? Marlene Carvell. New York: Hyperion, 2004.

Evan Hill, who is part Mohawk, protests against his high school's use of Indian mascots. In free-verse vignettes, he chronicles his battles against classmates and the powers that be. Teens may wonder, "What's the big deal?" and that's fruitful ground for discussion.

BE THE CHANGE

What it is. Volunteer service adds a personal, meaningful dimension to book club. Teens experience the book more fully by experiencing life more fully—or is it vice versa?

Purpose. Ultimately, by connecting reading to reality to action, teens live the truth that literature can change the world.

How it works. You create book displays around social issues or services. Clubbers pick a topic, select a book from the display, and choose a service project. After reading and discussing the book, they spend at least half a day tackling the problem.

Advantages

- Connects reading directly to life.
- Appeals to active and altruistic teens.
- May fulfill service learning requirements or enhance a teen's college application.

Disadvantages

- Logistics can be daunting. Depending on the project, you may need at least one adult to drive teens to the project site and help with the project.
- There's a tendency to steer teens to no-brainers like bake sales, book drives, or cooking for the homeless. Help teens think large.
- The meaning can be lost if service is done in a vacuum. Follow up with a debriefing session and keep teens posted on the lasting effects of their efforts.

Measures of Success

- The quality of the project and its lasting effects.
- Teens' enthusiasm and participation in the project.
- Expressions of thanks from the organization or people teens helped.
- Teens' insights following the project.

Tips

- Right after the project, take teens out for pizza so they can talk about their expectations and experience, and revisit the book.. Debriefing helps teens examine their thoughts and experience before busy schedules propel them in other directions.
- Encourage teens to take on projects that require substantial effort and produce sustainable results. After reading *A Child Called "It,"* for example, motivated teens can organize a public forum at the library and (if they think it's called for) a petition drive calling for stricter penalties for child abuse.
- Follow up with thank-you letters to each teen, documenting what the group did, praising the teen's contributions, and commenting on insights the teen shared during the debriefing session. Give two copies to each teen: one for their school (to satisfy volunteerism requirements) and the other to accompany their college applications.

Books for a Better World

Autobiography of Malcolm X. Malcolm X. New York: Ballantine, 1987.

Autobiography of Martin Luther King Jr. Martin Luther King Jr. New York: Warner Books, 2001.

Two pillars of the U.S. Civil Rights Movement, one reviled and feared, the other posthumously beloved. Here, teens can discover these two icons for themselves, tracing their actions and their evolving spiritual philosophies. Most important, teens may answer in their own words and actions this question: What is the proper response to intransigent social injustice?

Buddha Boy. Kathe Koja. New York: Puffin, 2004.

Justin is an average kid who just wants to stay out of the school bullies' way. Jinsen is a deeply devout Buddhist, which means he brings out the worst in his narrow-minded classmates. Teens who have had anti-bullying messages pounded into their heads since kindergarten may find a fresh message here—and the impetus to do something about it.

A Child Called "It." David Pelzer. Deerfield Beach, FL: Health Communications, Inc., 1995.

Teens love this true account of how the author weathered a storm of abuse at the hands of his alcoholic mother. (Other books in the series follow the author's growth and recovery.) Teens will find plenty to do, either to promote prevention and punishment or to support the victims.

Doing Time. Rob Thomas. New York: Simon & Schuster Children's Publishing, 1997.

Ten intertwined vignettes about high school teens doing community service reveal much about the teens themselves. Should spark discussion about commitment, attitude, motivation, and teens' relationships with the many types of people that society labels as "Other."

Pay It Forward. Catherine Ryan Hyde. New York: Pocket Books, 2000.

What would happen if, every time someone did something nice for us, we did something nice for someone else? In this fable, the results are not always what you'd expect. This novel has moved people of all ages to quietly "pay it forward."

Persepolis: The Story of a Childhood. Marjane Satrapi. New York: Pantheon, 2004.

Persepolis 2: The Story of a Return. Marjane Satrapi. New York: Pantheon, 2004.

The first book of this gripping "memoir-in-comics" describes Satrapi's life in Iran, from the Islamic revolution of 1979 through the onset of the Iran–Iraq war, when her parents sent her to Austria for her own safety. The sequel describes her return to her family and her adjustment to living under a fundamentalist regime. This duo puts a human face on a country that U.S. leadership has labeled as Evil.

Slumming. Kristen D. Randle. New York: HarperTempest, 2003.

Three older teens each take on one outcast student as an improvement project. The do-gooders quickly lose control as they enter the world of their subjects. All gain painful understanding of the varieties of personal experience and both the futility and harmfulness of imposing one's own ideas on an objectified "Other."

The Storyteller's Beads. Jane Kurtz. San Diego: Harcourt Brace, 1998. Gulliver Books, 1998 (paper).

Ethiopia in the 1980s is all starvation and violence. As Sahay and Rachel (who is blind and Jewish) flee to a refugee camp in Sudan, they overcome generations of prejudice. *Publishers Weekly* said, "The story pays tribute to survivors who find the strength and courage to help others reach freedom." It may inspire teens to do the same.

Stray Dog. Kathe Koja. New York: Farrar, Straus and Giroux, 2002; Speak, 2004.

Rachel, high-school misfit and animal shelter volunteer, finds instant kinship with Grrl, a feral collie. Thinking she can tame the dog, she hatches a plan to save it. Rachel's attitude and wit make this a darkly funny novel about alienation and connection. Even teens who don't especially like animals may find themselves inspired to collect blankets or food for their local shelter (or better, launch a spay/neuter public relations campaign).

Thinner Than Thou. Kit Reed. New York: Tor Books, 2004.

Forget those three-hanky cautionary tales about anorexia and body image. In this funny, grown-up satire, anorexic Annie must be rescued from Reverend Earl's "convent," where anorexics are taught to eat—and think—correctly. A fresh take on body image, which may inspire teens to mount a "real bodies, real beauty" campaign. 2005 Alex Award.

Reference

Herald, Diana Tixier. 2003. *Teen Genreflecting.* 2d ed. Westport, CT: Libraries Unlimited.

5

◇✖◇　◇✖◇　◇✖◇

LET'S GO CLUBBING SOME MORE! SEVEN MORE TRADITIONAL AND INNOVATIVE BOOK CLUBS

Why settle for a half dozen book clubs when you can have a half dozen (plus one) more? This chapter builds on chapter 4 by offering more of the same: more ideas to build more book clubs to meet more teens' interests. If you are seeking to be teen-centered, you'll need all the variety you can get as the membership of your clubs shift over time. (Changing book club formats keeps you engaged and interested, too.)

THEME OR GENRE

What it is. Book selection defines the theme club: Every book the club reads belongs to a specific theme.

Purpose. Attract and retain clubbers with a steady diet of what they love.

How it works. You or the teens choose a theme. Only books that belong to that theme can be considered during book selection. Because they are open-ended, theme clubs lend themselves to combinations: A sci-fi blogger club. A read-and-discuss mystery club. A fantasy book/movie club. An animal stories/be the change club.

Here are just a few themes you can choose from:

Adventure	Folk tale	Nonfiction on any topic, from self-help to rocket science
Animal stories	Graphic novels/manga	
Biography	Historical fiction	
Chick lit	Horror	Picture books
Essays	Humor	Poetry
Fairy tale	Mystery	Realistic fiction
Fantasy	Nature	Romance

Science fiction	Sports	Thriller
Short fiction/Flash fiction	Suspense	Verse novels
Siblings	Teens in trouble	Work and career

Advantages

- Theme clubs are an easy sell. With a popular theme and solid promotion, your club will fill right up.
- Over time teens will make connections among books, noticing patterns, similarities, plot devices, and the like. The repetitive plots of genre fiction make it especially easy to watch the author at work.
- Popular theme books are readily available in paperback.

Disadvantages

- Theme clubs promote narrow reading interests, and genre fiction in particular fosters lightweight reading habits. That's OK. Teens can read Great Literature in school.
- You may tire of the theme long before teens do. That's OK too, as long as the teens don't find out.
- Fans of a theme may reject any book that doesn't fit the formula exactly. (Compare the popularity of fantasy novels based in pseudo-Europe with those based in historic America.)

Measures of Success

- Attendance and enthusiasm.
- Circulation. But beware: Serious genre fans devour books; it's possible they were reading as many books as their schedules allowed *before* joining the club. So circulation figures may not change.
- In genre clubs, teens become savvy about literary techniques typical of the genre.

Tips

- Push the limits on book selection. Urge mystery buffs to try a Ray Chandler. Pair traditional fairy tales with modern ones. Shock your "problem fiction" fans with a story that ends happily!
- Because genre books are formulaic, traditional discussion questions fall flat. Ask questions that go behind the scenes to expose the genre's assumptions: Why does justice always win the day? (mysteries) What's the difference between romance and love? (romance) Why do we love to hate big business/the government? (thriller) Surface the assumptions and play with them. It's like having your cake—and eating steak, too.

Great Theme in Literature: Teens in Trouble!

Behind You. Jacqueline Woodson. New York: G.P. Putnam's Sons, 2004.

Jeremiah's soul looks down on his body as two policemen realize they have killed the wrong person. Told in several voices, this lovely, sad story explores how the grieving must accept death and go on living. Then Jeremiah can "begin the long, slow walk into the next place."

Chandra's Secrets. Allan Stratton. Toronto: Annick Press, 2004.

Chandra, age 16, struggles against a fate that is almost unimaginably bleak, with poverty and AIDS the blight of her family and community in sub-Saharan Africa. According to *Publisher's Weekly*, "Strong language and frank description are appropriate to the subject matter." A 2005 Michael L. Printz Honor Book.

Emako Blue. Brenda Woods. New York: Putnam Juvenile, 2004.

Emako's friends paint a loving picture of her in life and after her death in a drive-by shooting in South Central Los Angeles. Raw and honest, this book will leave teens struggling with questions about choice versus circumstance, including race, self-determination, powerlessness, and fate.

How I Live Now. Meg Rosoff. New York: Wendy Lamb Books, 2004.

Troubled Daisy moves to rural England in the near future just before the country is invaded and a years-long occupation begins. Thrust into the hardships and deprivations of war (including separation from the cousin she loves), Daisy rises above her own troubles to care for others. This searing story is described by reviewers as riveting, brilliant, and frighteningly realistic. Winner of the 2005 Michael L. Printz Award.

Lizzie Bright and the Buckminster Boy. Gary D. Schmidt. New York: Clarion, 2004.

Turner Buckminster, a white teen, becomes friends with Lizzie Bright, an African American teen who lives on Malaga Island off the coast of Maine. To make way for tourists, racist town elders force all island residents to relocate to an institution for the mentally ill. Sad but tinged with humor, this novel combines fiction with little-know local history.

Looking for Alaska. John Green. New York: Dutton Juvenile, 2005.

Miles, age 16, goes to boarding school, where he is drawn into the orbit of lovely, reckless Alaska. Teens will bond deeply with both Miles and Alaska as they struggle with the darkness that haunts her. The book's theme, language, and treatment of sexual situations make this a book for mature teens. Winner of the 2006 Michael Printz Award.

Monster. Walter Dean Myers. New York: Amistad, 2001. (paper).

In a fast-paced format alternating between screenplay and journal, Steve documents his own murder trial and explains how he came to be accused. Myers exposes the dilemma of felony murder, forcing readers to consider questions of choice and circumstance, responsibility and intent. Winner of the 2000 Michael L. Printz Award.

Shattering Glass. Gail Giles. New York: Simon Pulse, 2003.

An Ugly Duckling story goes bloodily awry. Rob decides to remake geek Simon Glass into a popular guy. Soon, the new Simon shows a cruel streak that leads to disaster. A fast-paced thriller posing provocative questions about the ability of power to corrupt.

Sisters/Hermanas. Gary Paulsen. New York: Harcourt Brace, 1993.

Two girls, one an illegal immigrant from Mexico and the other a wealthy Texan, live parallel lives. The story skates on the surface, but teens will find plenty to talk about in exploring the girls' similarities. Two editions, English and Spanish, in one volume.

Tree Girl. Ben Mikaelsen. New York: HarperTempest, 2004.

During the civil war in Guatemala, most of the people (particularly the men) in Gabriela's village are killed by both sides in the conflict—native guerilla fighters and the U.S.-backed army. Garbriela befriends a mute girl, sets out for the refugee camps, and rebuilds her life there.

BOOKCHATTERS

What it is. Think of bookchatting as booktalking's laid-back cousin. Booktalks are polished performance pieces designed to sell readers on books. Bookchats are more like show-and-tell.

Purpose. Bookchatting clubs let teens share their enthusiasm for what they've been reading. Bookchatting throws open the doors of book clubs to *all* readers, regardless of reading interest or ability. "Tell us what you've been reading" is an invitation few readers, even poor or reluctant ones, can resist. Bookchatting also introduces teens to new authors and genres in the best possible way—by enthusiastic peers.

How it works. This club runs itself. Arrange the room, set out snacks, and ask, "Who's read something good lately?" Teens will do the rest.

Advantages

- This is, without a doubt, the easiest book club to put together. Better yet, it's one of the most popular, fun, and worthwhile!
- Over time teens pick up on one another's reading tastes and recommend books. It's not unusual to hear, "I saw this book I knew you'd like. I wrote down the title. . . ."
- For poor or reluctant readers, bookchatting is a generous gift: It makes them conscious of how much reading they do successfully every day.

Disadvantages

- Bookchatting rarely does more than scratch the surface. For depth, switch to a read-and-discuss club.
- If you have a large club or loquacious clubbers, time may run out before every teen gets a chance to speak. Break into smaller groups to give everyone a turn.

- Teens may talk about titles that are unavailable. Enthusiasm may wane before you can deliver the book.

Measures of Success

- Because bookchatting is an end in itself, the only measures of success are attendance, participation, and enthusiasm.
- Teens check out the books mentioned at the bookchat.

Tips

- Teach bookchatting by example. At the beginning of each meeting, talk about a few of your favorite recent reads (which you happen to have in hand if anyone would like to check them out).
- Don't let teens give away endings. Remind them, warn them, interrupt them if you must!
- Bookchatting is spontaneous and free-form, with teens sparking off one another. Ride the chaos, within reason.
- Have paper and pens on hand so teens can write down the titles of books that appeal to them.

Best for Bookchatters

Because bookchatters don't join to read the same book, you don't need a booklist for them. Best to come with an armful of great finds from the New Fiction and Nonfiction stacks. Also, be sure they keep a written (or electronic) record of books they love, so they can check out one another's favorites when they are looking for something good to read.

INTERGENERATIONAL UP: TEEN–ADULT

What it is. Teens mix it up with adults (parents, grandparents, guardians, others). Mother–daughter clubs are popular among younger teens. (Some intergenerational book clubs pair teens with younger children. Usually as a school or volunteer project, teens conduct story times with prereaders or mentor/tutor young readers. We detail these types on clubs in the following section.)

Purpose. Teens and adults use books to bridge the age gap. This club is as much about relationships as it is about books.

How it works. Any kind of club—book/movie, read write (described subsequently), three-of-a-kind—can be intergenerational. Just be sure that books and activities appeal to the club's youngest members. Safety is key: Adults and teens alike must feel free to speak from their experiences, vulnerabilities, doubts, and inconsistencies. To create a place where they can do that, keep book club values (see chapter 8) front and center. Don't let adults (or teens) fall into reminiscing, storytelling, censoring, advising, or pronouncing judgments, or slip into accusatory dialogue or personal arguments. Use the discussion leader tips in chapter 11 to prevent this from happening or to address it when it does. In intergenerational book clubs, adults and teens act as peers, *exploring* ideas together.

Advantages

- Speaking as fellow clubbers (rather than as authority figures and their subjects) frees teens and adults to explore topics that might otherwise prove explosive.
- Teens and adults often surprise and delight one another.
- As teens and adults get to know one another better, they may grow closer.

Disadvantages

- One age group may dominate while the other yields out of a sense of propriety.
- It may be difficult to find books that reflect the realities of teen life without creating a sensation among the adults.
- Many adults feel compelled to define what is appropriate for teens, from limiting book choices to censoring what people say to making pronouncements. If clubbers can't subscribe to book club values, this might not be the best program for them.

Measures of Success

In a club that is all about relationships, quantitative measures of success take a backseat to qualitative ones:

- Willingness to let go of age-defined roles and assumptions to engage as "thinking partners" and emotional companions.
- Appreciation and admiration for wisdom on either side of the age divide.
- Growing respect and affection between teens and "their" adults, which both will carry into the years ahead.

Tips

- All adults must be accompanied by a teen.
- Recommend books about issues that cut across all ages—for example, *Green Eggs and Ham* (peer pressure) or *The Clock* (the tyranny of schedules). Don't worry about recommending easy reads; a good booktalk ending with a provocative question will pique clubbers' interest.
- Mix it up! Just because teens come with an adult doesn't mean they have to sit together all the time.
- To help clubbers speak freely on sticky subjects, break up teen–adult units. Pair each teen with an unrelated adult or form two groups—teens and adults. Pairs/groups talk among themselves, then report back to the club. Ideas get out, and no one's the wiser.

Books to Share with Mothers and Friends

One of the most common types of intergenerational-up book clubs is the mother–daughter club, so that's what we highlight here, with a multicultural bent. See Patrick Jones's connectingya.com or John Scieszka's guysread.com Web sites for suggestions for a father–son club.

Bad Medicine. Portia Toples. Boonsboro, MD: Hilliard and Harris, 2004.

Corporate attorney Naomi Wells must stop the flow of psychoactive drugs from the factory to Detroit teens. Meanwhile, she balances an array of rich personal relationships, with all of their ups and downs. Though most of the drug users are punished, this is a nonpreachy route into discussions about drug use by teens and adults. (Full disclosure: Constance and the author are friends.) A *Forbes* magazine book club selection.

Cuba 15. Nancy Osa. New York: Delacorte Books for Young Readers, 2003.

Violet Paz is an all-American girl whose Cuban grandmother insists that Violet have a grand *quinceanero*, an elaborate coming-of-age ceremony that involves, among other things, a tiara. Family craziness, including love, laugher, and power struggles ensue in this hilarious romp that proves family love trumps it all.

Go and Come Back. Joan Abelove. New York: Puffin Books, 2000.

Alicia, a Peruvian Isabo teen, narrates a year in the life of her village as it comes under the study of two American grad students. In describing the book as a "startling, vibrant read," *Booklist* said, "readers will learn about a community with views on life, death, sex, and marriage that are so different from their own that they will be pulled up short."

God Don't Like Ugly Mary Monroe. New York: Kensington Books/Dafina, 2000.

Up to the age of 13, Annette's life has been a living hell (the worst of which is sexual abuse). Then she meets Rhoda, who decides the abuse must stop. Set in the racist South of the 1950s and 1960s, this is a story about two wonderful friends who build hope together in the face of extreme hardship. (And the author has a fascinating story herself.)

Leaving Home: Stories. Hazel Rochman, ed. New York: HarperTrophy, 1998.

Fifteen leading contemporary writers (e.g., Amy Tan, Toni Morrison) trace the transformation from child to self. More than simple variations on the coming-of-age theme, these poems and stories explore what it means to grow into yourself. Teens and their parents will be prompted to examine, and possibly share, their own life stories. Starred review in *Publishers Weekly.*

My Sister's Keeper. Jodi Picoult. New York: Washington Square Press, 2005.

All her life, Anna's body has been farmed to provide body parts that might help prolong the life of her older sister, who has cancer. On the eve of a kidney transplant, Anna hires a lawyer for a medical emancipation suit. Teens and mothers may not see eye to eye on this one … and you might be surprised who sides with Anna, or not!

My Soul to Keep. Tananarive Due. New York: HarperCollins/Eos, 1998.

Get spooky! Investigative reporter Jessica discovers her husband is immortal—and he wants her to join him. With compelling relationships, humane characters, and African-rooted supernatural elements, this soft horror/dark fantasy is a good "beginner" book for moms to get a taste of a genre their daughters may well love.

Pierced by a Ray of Sun: Poems about the Times We Feel Alone. Ruth Gordon, New York: HarperCollins, 1995.

From the opening line—"Am I the only person on Earth?"—this poetry anthology speaks straight to teens' hearts—and to the sense of isolation that persists even into motherhood. Teens and mothers alike may be surprised to find how much they have in common.

The Spirit Line. David Thurlo and Aimee Thurlo. New York: Viking, 2004.

Crystal, a Navajo teen grieving her mother and questioning her cultural identity, must examine herself and her beliefs as she searches for the thief who stole the rug she was making to use in her coming-of-age ceremony.

Year of Secret Assignments. Jaclyn Moriarty. New York: Arthur A. Levine Books, 2004.

A teacher's bright idea to build goodwill between rival boys' and girls' schools spins crazily out of control when one of the boys threatens one of the girls. The girls declare all-out war on the boys, and the mayhem begins! A fun read that will give everyone a chance to laugh together.

INTERGENERATIONAL DOWN: TEEN–CHILD

What it is. Teens become role models and reading mentors to young readers at school or at the library. School-based clubs are popular, in which middle school students spend time with preschoolers or high school students read with elementary schoolers. Usually as a school or volunteer project, teens conduct story times with prereaders or mentor/tutor young readers.

Purpose. Teens make a difference in a young person's life, and younger children gain positive role models with "teachers" who aren't adults.

How it works. Teens may conduct story times, do lap sits, read with or to children one-on-one, or tutor young children in reading. The tutoring is strictly informal; teens generally don't receive formal training in reading instruction. Participating in this type of club may fulfill a teen's service learning requirement.

As with other intergenerational clubs, safety is key: Teens must curb their sarcastic selves and be gentle with young readers. This type of club is best for teens who are wholeheartedly enthusiastic about it. Although it may seem like simple fun-and-games, it can be quite draining (and boring) for some teens.

Advantages

- Teens and younger children cross the lines that normally separate them in school and socially.
- Teens see firsthand how simple volunteerism can affect a real person in an immediate and tangible way.
- It's a great excuse for teens to reread and share their childhood favorites! Teens get to experience the great joy of turning a younger person on to a book that they loved.

Disadvantages

- Teens may dominate the children, simply reading for them rather than with them.
- Unless they have a fondness for children or children's books, teens may quickly grow bored.

Measures of Success

- Teen mentors motivate children to read.
- Teens begin to develop a sense of the value of volunteerism and their role in the civic arena.
- Working with children who are open and accepting (even admiring) can give teens a much-needed personal boost.

Tips

- Recruit teens to help the library staff with lap sits and story times. Who doesn't need all the help they can get?
- Give teens a few tips for reading with children. For the youngest readers, this might include: Use voices. Read slowly. Point to pictures. Stop to ask questions. For mid-grade readers it might be: Listen quietly. Sit still. Don't be too quick to help; give children a chance to figure out the difficult words.
- Don't force the activity. If you've taken the whole book club to an elementary school, and after about 15 minutes one of the teens quickly becomes bored and retreats to a corner with his own book—don't panic. He's modeling solitary reading—and soon a young friend or two may join him in the corner!

Books to Read to or with Younger Readers

For lap sits turn teens and kids loose to choose their own books. When that's not possible, or you need a read-aloud for a group, here are a few terrific picks.

Africa Dream. Eloise Greenfield. New York: HarperTrophy, 1991.

In her dreams, a young girl travels back to Africa, where she sees the wildlife, visits the marketplace, and returns to the village of her ancestors. A visual and auditory "dream" that will delight readers of all ages and races.

Ella Sarah Gets Dressed. Margaret Chodos-Irvine. New York: Harcourt Children's Books, 2003.

Crazy outfits and lots of word repetition make for a party of sight and sound. Great for all those kids who like to express themselves through their clothing, whatever their age!

A Gift from Papa Diego/Un regalo de papa Diego. Benjamin Alire Saenz. El Paso, TX: Cinco Puntos Press, 1998.

Love knows no borders, including the one dividing the United States from Mexico. Any child who longs to visit loved ones far away will delight in Diego's wishful thinking—and the surprise ending.

Green Eggs and Ham. Dr. Seuss. New York: Random House Books for Young Readers, 1960. Many editions available.

A book and a game, all in one! Readers and listeners love the rhyme and rhythm. Teens can amuse themselves by reading it fast and by asking kids to fill in the repetitive bits.

I Love My Hair! Natasha Anastasia Tarpley. New York: Megan Tingley, 2003. Board book.

A disproportionate share of a girl's self-esteem is tied up in her hair. Here, mother and child celebrate natural hair as beautiful watercolors bring the words to life. Teen girls get the message along with the kids.

Knuffle Bunny. Mo Willems. New York: Hyperion, 2004.

A treat for eyes and ears. Sepia-toned photographs with hand-drawn "comic characters" pair with tongue-twisting baby talk in this Laundromat near-disaster.

Owl Moon. Jane Yolen. New York: Philomel, 1987.

A young girl and her father bundle up and go looking for owls on a magical winter night. A good quiet-time read.

Please Baby Please. Spike Lee, Tonya Lewis Lee. New York: Simon & Schuster Children's Books, 2002.

Want to squelch teen thoughts of parenthood? Give them this book and a roomful of energetic toddlers. Baby wreaks havoc all day long (but in the end love wins).

The Stupids Step Out. Harry G. Allard. New York: Houghton Mifflin, 1977.

The Stupid family and their dog, Kitty, have a day of side-splitting adventures. The book's age compounds the fun—get a load of dad's tie!

Where the Sidewalk Ends. Shel Silverstein. New York: Bantam Dell, 1986.

Teens likely remember this from their own childhoods and will delight in sharing their old favorites with a new generation of readers.

READ WRITE

What it is. Reading and writing are two sides of the same coin; read write clubs flip that coin over and over. Journaling, poetry, short stories, reviews: Anything goes in this club, as long as it relates to the book at hand.

Purpose. Celebrating language and personal expression, read write clubs spotlight the very things that attract readers to books. In recreational settings, they're all about personal expression and word play. In educational settings they offer a drill-free leg up on literacy.

How it works. All clubbers read the same book, write their responses, and read what they've written aloud. Or they read different books. Or they write in response to what another clubber has written. Or they use the setting or language as a starting point to create something entirely new. In the best read write clubs, it's no holds barred.

The easiest way to share teen writing is to take turns with each person reading or saying "I pass" in turn. Establish ground rules for sharing writing (see the "Tips" section). If time allows, ask whether any new ideas bubbled up during the read-aloud. That's all there is to it. Teens will carry the ball.

Advantages

- Answers teens' drive to express themselves creatively and share their creations.
- Puts teens in the author's seat. Many teens who love to read also love to write. This club indulges both their passions.
- The more people read and write, the better they get at both.
- This club is great for curriculum support.

Disadvantages

- Many teens fear writing. This club's focus may narrow your pool of potential participants. Keep the focus on writing games and they'll come around.
- Some teens may reveal embarrassing information and later regret it. Caution them about that before they write and before they read aloud. They can always keep a private journal, but what they share in club should be OK to go public.

Measures of Success

- The number of teens writing and reading their works aloud. When teens read their works aloud, they're saying they feel safe in book club and they trust you.

- In recreational clubs, it's pure pleasure. In educational settings, it's pleasure mixed with all of the typical anxieties.
- Practice, practice, practice. Reading and writing are like any sport; the more you do, the better you get.

Tips

- Share your own writing. Teens find it encouraging and entertaining to hear adults' authentic thoughts.
- Create three simple ground rules: (1) Anyone can say "I pass" when it's their turn to read aloud. (2) We all clap for everyone, whether they read or not. It sounds corny, but it makes teens feel great. Make sure they clap when you read, too. (3) What's said here stays here; book club is confidential.
- Look at some writing workshop books to get ideas for great writing games. Try *Panning for Gold in the Kitchen Sink* (Smith and Greenberg 1999) or *Pencil Dancing* (Messer 2001).

Reading the Greatest Writer

Since this is a writer's club, why not read works inspired by the master, Shakespeare? Along the way, slip in a bit of the real thing.

Blue Avenger Cracks the Code. Norma Howe. New York: HarperTempest, 2002.

It's always a wild ride with the Blue Avenger, aka David Schumacher. Here it's all about theft and code-cracking: Who really wrote all those great plays? Will Blue's buddy Louie get credit for his video game idea? Who stole Grammy's dog? And will Blue ever gain his true love's heart? Propose this scenario: A teen dashes into the library, snatches the clock off the wall, then dashes out again. What's up? Give them 10 minutes to write a stream-of-consciousness of the thief's thoughts. (Bonus brownie points to the writer who works in a code or a cipher.)

Dating Hamlet: Ophelia's Story. Lisa Fiedler. New York: Henry Holt, 2002.

Sooner or later, they're going to read *Hamlet.* Be ready when they do with this funny and feminist take on Ophelia's master plot to help Hamlet make his move. It's best if clubbers read the original first, because (1) they will enjoy this story more and (2) after they read this, Ophelia's original role is bound to disappoint. Writing in Ophelia's voice, teens can voice Ophelia's response to being set free (by Fiedler) from her role in Shakespeare's original script.

A Midsummer Night's Dream. William Shakespeare. New York: Washington Square Press, 2004. Folger Shakespeare Library.

Get teens' feet wet with Act V, Scene 1, in which even the Wall gets in on the act! Then have teens script a scene along the line of "if these walls could talk…"

My Father Had a Daughter: Judith Shakespeare's Tale. Grace Tiffany. New York: Berkley Trade, 2004.

When Judith Shakespeare thinks her father has used their family's tragedy to create a new play, she disguises herself as a boy and tries to infiltrate his acting troupe. Shakespeare loved cross-dressing disguise (a theme repeated in novels like Terence Blacker's *Boy2Girl*). Ask teens to imagine this scenario: They have reason to suspect the coach of the lacrosse team is fixing games. To discover the truth, all they need to do is join the team. Just one catch: The team is for the opposite sex, so they have join in disguise. What happens next?

Othello. Julius Lester. New York: Scholastic, 1998.

This novel that has everything the original play had and more: intensely beautiful language, deep insights into the human spirit, and an all-African cast. By eliminating the racism from the central plot, Lester can shine the light on universal questions of the heart. Teens can pose questions as a group and then choose one to answer in a free-writing exercise.

Romiette and Julio. Sharon M. Draper. New York: Simon Pulse, 2001.

In this tale, the lovers aren't so much star-crossed as cross-cultural, and that's bad news in Cincinnati, Ohio. Love, gangs, and family all enter into this sometimes obvious retelling. (Obvious is good when your clubbers—teens and parents alike—probably remember little more than the highlights of the original play.) Draper gives the story an upbeat ending. Tell teens the original ending, then challenge them to create an ending of their own.

The Shakespeare Stealer. Gary Blackwood. New York: Puffin, 2000.

Something for the youngest teens, young Widge is pressed into service to attend many performances of *Hamlet* and transcribe the script for a rival theatre company. Play audio passages from *Hamlet* to give teens the full flavor of the language, then turn them loose to make their own music.

The Slaying of the Shrew. Simon Hawke. New York: Tor Books, 2002.

The title ought to lure readers in. Shakespeare and his bumbling sidekick Smythe are a sleuthing team à la Holmes and Watson (but funnier) in this, the second in the Shakespeare and Smythe series. Alternate realities is a popular sci-fi genre. Ask teens to choose another profession (or hobby) for Shakespeare and then write about what happens.

Thirteenth Night. Alan Gordon. Carmel, IN: Crum Creek Press/The Mystery Company, 2004. (Reprint of 1999 title.)

Cleverness. Witticisms. Local color. Misdirection. It's another Shakespeare extension, "full of sound and fury and a fair amount of juggling," according to the publisher. Duke Orsino is murdered, and it's up to the jester, Feste, to find out whodunit. Have teens stage an improv murder trial, where the antics and wordplay continue.

Will. Grace Tiffany. New York: Berkley, 2004.

Fact and fancy combine in this "boisterous" (*Booklist*) novel of William Shakespeare's evolution from young boy to driven playwright, written by a professor of Shakespeare and Renaissance Drama. Ask teens: What makes a writer? Thinking into the future, what would it take to make them into writers? (Many writers simply say a writer is a person who writes every day. Are the teens in your club already writers?)

A Winter Night's Dream. Andrew Matthews. New York: Delacorte Books for Young Readers, 2004.

Teens fall in love with the wrong people, get into comic messes, and eventually find one another. Does the title sound familiar, too? A British import with "fast, frank talk about friends, family, snogging" (*Booklist*). Matthews' language offers lots of pleasant startles. Ask teens choose an emotion and freewrite on it until they startle themselves.

BOOK TO MOVIE/MOVIE TO BOOK

What it is. Teens look at a story from two angles: print and film.

Purpose. Most book/movie clubs claim to have no ulterior motives. They're entertainment, pure and simple. Part of the entertainment is comparing the book to the film, and that's where ulterior purposes sneak in: By making comparisons, teens become savvier about each medium and better able to match the right one to their needs or mood.

How it works. Which comes first, the book or the movie? Traditional clubs always put the book first; the movie is a reward for doing the "real work" of reading the book. Afterward, everyone complains that the filmmaker left out the best the parts and agrees the book is better.

It might be time to rethink that: In an age when teens' first language comprises television and film, it might make sense to reverse the order of things. Seeing the movie first changes the dynamic; instead of looking for what the film left out, teens look for what the book adds. Focusing on the book's greater depth, detail, and character highlights the strengths of each medium and shows how authors and filmmakers must create their art within the constraints of the medium. Reading a book after seeing the movie proves that there's more to it than plot.

Scheduling depends on your approach: In some clubs, teens read the book, then meet to watch the movie. In others, teens read the book, then meet to discuss it. The following month they watch the movie at home, then meet to discuss it. (If you watch the movie during the meeting, there's no time left to discuss it.)

Advantages

- The movie may pique the interest of readers reluctant to dig into a slow-moving book. A great example is *Jane Eyre.*
- Book to movie clubs are perennial favorites, and they are easy to set up and deliver.

- Getting a handle on what each medium does best (and worst) and why helps teens choose between them for various purposes. And that's a key information literacy skill.

Disadvantages

- Discussions tend to be superficial.
- Even when they are thoughtful, discussions tend to focus on style and technique rather than understanding and insight.
- Teens may skip the book and show up only for the movie.

Measures of Success

- Entertainment! (Attendance.)
- Teens become savvier media critics and consumers.
- Seeing filmmaking techniques in action helps teens spot and understand their literary equivalents and vice versa.

Tips

- If teens resist reading a book after seeing the movie, send them on a treasure hunt: Tell them to find three things in the book that aren't in the movie.
- Follow library policy on copyright/licensing. *Never* charge admission, even to cover the cost of refreshments. That may move you into the zone of commercial use.
- If you're watching the movie as a group, make sure the screen is large enough for everyone to get a good view. If you need to limit attendance, choose teens who have read the book (or promise to). Be sure to arrange the seating so everyone can see *before* you start the movie.
- Unless the cleaning crew is due in shortly, *don't serve popcorn!*

Read the Movie! See the Book!

Half of the book/movie combos featured here are classics, because teens may be unaware of these new-to-them favorites. For new and forthcoming movies, keep your eye out on Listservs and scan book-to-movie Web sites like the one from the Skokie (Illinois) Public Library (http://www.skokielibrary.info/s_audiovisual/av_lists/Movies/teens.html).

Akira. 6-vol. series, numbers 1–6. Katushiro Otomo. Dark Horse, 2000–2002.

Akira. Katushiro Otomo. Pioneer Video, 2001. DVD. English subtitles with Japanese and English audio tracks.)

A massive and massively popular manga series set 38 years after World War III. Two teenagers in a motorcycle gang run into what looks to be a child with an old man's features. From there's it's all high-speed adventure with plenty of violence, car chases, mayhem, and sex. The artist spent two years creating the film version, which is a hit among anime fans. Both print and film versions are graphic enough to get you into trouble with some parents.

Animal Farm. George Orwell. New York: Signet, 1996. Many editions available.

Animal Farm. John Stephenson. Hallmark Home Entertainment, 2000. Animated. DVD.

Teens love the satirical voice, identify with the powerless, and can certainly tell plenty of stories about how they've seen absolute power corrupt absolutely. Good news: Everyone thinks its theme applies only to "the Others," so it's easy to steer discussions clear of political debate and stick with the universal theme. The animated film is mostly true to the original, and the DVD includes a segment on historical background.

Dracula. Bram Stoker. New York: Tor, 1992. Many editions available.

Dracula (starring Bela Lugosi). Tod Browning. Universal Studios, 2001. DVD. Many editions available.

You know they'll love it—if they stick with it. Plan it for a two-month read, September/October. A lively discussion in September will inspire reluctant teens to get started or stick with it through slow-moving passages. Show the Bela Lugosi movie for a campy October meeting. (Alas, we can't recommend the 1992 Francis Ford Coppola version because it's rated R.)

Ella Enchanted. Gail Carson Levine. New York: HarperTrophy, 1998.

Ella Enchanted. Tommy O'Haver. Miramax, 2005.

This one is just for fun and just for girls (young girls). It's nothing but mind candy, great for times when homework loads are heavy. Consider it book club bonding time.

Eragon. Christopher Paolini. New York: Knopf Books for Young Readers, 2005.

Eragon. 20th Century Fox, 2006 (forthcoming).

High fantasy fans will have read both *Eragon* and its sequel, *Eldest,* long before the movie is released (scheduled for summer 2006). That's all right; they'll read it again. That's because this story has it all—dragons, a quest, evil powers struggling for control of the world, and a young rube destined for greatness.

Fahrenheit 451. Ray Bradbury. New York: Del Ray, 1987.

Fahrenheit 451. Francois Truffaut. Universal Studios, 2003. DVD.

Who needs reading when they have big-screen televisions and never-ending reality shows? In a world where readers are enemies of the state (the equivalent of terrorists), a few hardy souls insist on print—to their peril. A fun, scary, must-read for every book club! The 1966 film is suitably creepy, includes an audio track in English as well as subtitles in Spanish and/or French. It also includes a discussion with Ray Bradbury and a segment titled "The Making of Fahrenheit 451." Everything you need to build a great, two-part book-to-movie series!

Inu-Yashi. 2d ed. Rumiko Takahashi. San Francisco: VIZ Media, 2003.

One fan calls Takahashi "the Steven Spielberg of Japanese comics," because of the warmth and passion of her work. That's certainly evident in this time-travel story, in which a Kagome, a high school girl, is transported back to feudal Japan to save the world. High fantasy, humor, and romance come together in this saga.

To Kill a Mockingbird. Harper Lee. New York: Warner Books, 1988.

To Kill a Mockingbird. Collectors Edition. Robert Mulligan. Universal Studios, 2002.

This is one of the few books teens have to read for school that they also gladly read for pleasure. Common human decency does battle with the evil of racism in the Depression-era South. In print and on film, the timeless message shines through with a quiet artistry that transcends Hollywood's typical flash-and-dazzle. Teen readers love the book, and the movie will mesmerize them as well.

Romeo and Juliet. William Shakespeare. New York: Dover, 1993. Dover Thrift Edition.

Romeo + Juliet. Baz Luhrmann. Twentieth Century Fox Home Video, 2002. DVD.

Shakespeare was meant to be viewed, not read, and movies really help teens make sense of the work. This version, starring Leonardo di Caprio, may not be the best version (it was widely panned for what critics called its MTV sensibility)—but it is rated an acceptable PG-13, and it *is* for an MTV generation.

Speak. Laurie Halse Anderson.

Speak. Jessica Sharzer. Showtime Entertainment, 2005.

High school freshman refuses to speak; over time, we learn why. That summary doesn't hint at the emotional impact of this book. Ask teens which hits them harder—the book or the movie? Does the movie make you see things differently or more vividly than the book? Does it raise a new set of questions?

CURRICULUM SUPPORT

What it is. Whether it's a formal intervention program staged by librarian and reading specialist during summer school or a simple three-of-a-kind club complementing a middle school unit on invertebrates, book club is a natural for curriculum support.

Purpose. In a recreational curriculum support club, teens explore a topic from an unexpected angle in a nothing's-at-stake environment. In an instructional club, teens build knowledge and develop literacy skills in a casual setting. Both types of clubs promote reading for pleasure.

How it works. For direct instruction or literacy intervention, collaborate with the classroom teacher or reading specialist. Keep in mind that direct instruction should be handled by the educator. You collaborate with the educator (classroom teacher or a specialist) to choose topics and books; then you play a supporting role during instruction.

For supplemental support clubs, simply find out what is being taught when, and plan a book club around it. Keep it short; curriculum moves quickly. One or two sessions are plenty if you meet monthly. (Of course, you don't need to stick to the monthly format; Constance's summer-school literacy club met three days a week for three weeks.) A book/movie club on the Civil War might read *Soldier's Heart* (Paulsen) and watch *The Red Badge of Courage* (Crane). A two-of-a-kind club to prepare for physics might read *Zero: The Biography of a Dangerous Idea* (Seife and Zimet) and *Einstein's Dreams* (Lightman).

Advantages

- Book club helps teens ease into a new topic. With a little prior knowledge under their belts, teens are relaxed and primed to learn.
- In a casual atmosphere teens follow their interests, discovering new information and surprising perspectives not covered in class.
- Teens learn that no matter what topic catches their fancy, the library is their conduit to a lifetime supply of materials about it.

Disadvantages

- Collaboration isn't easy. If curriculum support appeals to you, befriend teachers. Most often collaboration happens when friends work together.
- Scheduling can be a problem. If you can't find out from teachers when certain topics are covered, ask teens for a peek at a syllabus. Take notes; curriculum schedules tend to remain the same year after year.

Measures of Success

- Thank-you letters from teachers you work with. (You'll write to them, too.)
- Feedback from teens. During the last club meeting, distribute survey forms asking teens what things they learned in book club helped them in class and how. Blockade the snacks until teens complete their forms.
- If teens do the club before they start a new unit, invite them back for a party. (See previous bullet for how to gather feedback.)

Tips

- Toss the brainiac questions. This is still book club. Keep it personal, exploratory, and low-key.
- Approach topics from oblique angles. If the subject is history, download magazines from the relevant time frame. If the unit is human health, read *Stiff: The Curious Lives of Human Cadavers* (Roach 2003).
- Serve food. Even if it's in school. Even if you're reading *Stiff.*

A Personal Look at the Vietnam War

Teens will get the names and dates in class. These book selections help them fill in the gaps with personal accounts and the stories surrounding the war, as it rippled out to affect teens far from Vietnam in time and place. Some of the books are quite long; it might be useful to focus on the short stories and oral histories, allowing those with a special interest to delve deeper.

Bloods: An Oral History of the Vietnam War by Black Veterans. Wallace Terry. New York: Ballantine, 1985.

Twenty African American men tell the story of the Vietnam War as they experienced it. Race is an often-overlooked aspect of the Vietnam-era military experience; this was the first war in which the Army was integrated. These soldiers share a diversity of views regarding the 1960s civil rights movement and other race-related issues. A *New York Times* Notable Book.

Dispatches. Michael Herr. New York: Vintage, 1991.

This classic war correspondent's documentary is not for the faint of heart. *The New York Times* said, "Nothing else so far has even come close to conveying how different this war was from any we fought—or how utterly different were the methods and the men who fought for us."

Felon for Peace: The Memoir of a Vietnam-Era Draft Resister. Jerry Elmer. Nashville, TN: Vanderbilt University Press, 2005.

During the 1960s and certainly since then, the lines between all the various anti-establishment movements became blurred; this book clearly separates peace activists from counterculturists (hippies) and other political activists (Students for a Democratic Society, Weathermen). The author publicly resisted the draft, burglarized draft offices, served his time, and continued to work in the peace movement for 20 years before finally attending Harvard Law School. He argues passionately for nonviolence, including nonviolent resistance.

Fortunate Son: The Autobiography of Lewis B. Puller, Jr. New York: Bantam, 1993.

Following his famous father into the military, Puller experiences the horror of the Vietnam War. He loses much of his body to a booby trap but overcomes the resulting disabilities (mental and physical) to run for Congress. This 1992 Pulitzer Prize–winning autobiography ends on a hopeful note, but three years after its publication, Puller killed himself.

Home before Morning: The Story of an Army Nurse in Vietnam. Linda Van Devanter. Amherst, MA: University of Massachusetts Press, 2001.

A patriotic woman enlists as a nurse, experiences the horror and brutality of war, and is saved by the support of her fellow soldiers. She loses that support when she returns home to her patriotic family which is not interested in her stories and an Army establishment that denies her experience to assign her menial duties.

She survives by purely personal strength in this suspenseful, healing book. A *much* better choice than Ellen Emerson White's romanticized war novel *The Road Home*.

How memorable is this book? Constance read it 20 years ago, and it still stands out as one of the most riveting and emotionally memorable books she has ever read.

In Retrospect: The Tragedy and Lessons of Vietnam. Robert McNamara. New York: Times Books, 1995.

The author was Secretary of Defense during the escalation of the Vietnam War under Presidents Kennedy and Johnson. His memoir shows a man struggling to remain loyal to his nation's leader yet extricate the country from the war. As with any memoir, McNamara benefits from hindsight and strives present his best face to posterity. Still, teens wondering what it was like to be on the inside track when crucial decisions were made will find this book revealing.

Strange Ground: Americans in Vietnam, 1945–1975: An Oral History. Henry Maurer. New York: Henry Holt, 1989.

Sixty-five Americans from many walks of life (most *not* combat soldiers) share their experiences living and working in Vietnam during the years leading up to, through, and until the end of the Vietnam War. It's too long to read in its entirety. Ask each teen to read one entry, then use book club to compare/contrast the experiences.

The Things They Carried. Tim O'Brien. New York: Broadway, 1998.

A series of interconnected short stories showing brief glimpses of Vietnam moments, building to a coherent whole. O'Brien's first work, *If I Die in a Combat Zone,* is his memoir; this is his truth. The opening paragraphs of the first story are pure art, haunting and rich enough to spark a week of rumination. *School Library Journal* says this collection could be used to support short story curriculum, and indeed, Constance has used it for both short story and essay.

Vietnam: A Portrait of Its People at War. David Chanoff and Doan Van Toai. London: I. B. Tauris, 1996. (Available through amazon.com.)

Oral history interviews of ordinary people in both North and South Vietnam (collected from refugees) paint a picture of the Vietnam War rarely seen. *Library Journal* highly recommends it. This is a good complement to other oral histories, including Al Santoli's *To Bear Any Burden,* oral histories of participants from many walks of life (Bloomington, IN: Indiana University Press, 1999), and Keith Walker's *A Piece of My Heart* (New York: Presidio Press, 1997), the oral histories of 26 women who served in the war.

When Heaven and Earth Changed Places. Le Ly Hayslip. New York: Plume, 1993.

As a child, Hayslip was caught in the middle of the Vietnam War. She worked in jobs ranging from Vietcong courier to hospital aide; she was physically and sexually abused by North Vietnamese, South Vietnamese, and Americans alike. This is her account of her life until age 20, and her return to her homeland nearly 20 years later. In the end, she eloquently pleads for both countries to put the past behind them.

BOLDLY GO!

Role-play. Meet-the-author. Self-help. Brainiacs. Great Books. Whatever your teens' interests, you can craft a book club to suit them. These days, Constance's specialty seems to be hybrids: She is organizing two clubs: a Dr. Seuss readers-into-leaders literacy-building club for middle schoolers and a theme-based intergenerational readers-into-leaders three-of-a-kind club for teens and adults.

Grab a pencil and start letting your ideas flow. Try out these clubs, or come up with your own. Then write to us! Let us know what works and what doesn't. We'd love to hear from you—and your teens! (Write to us at: chardesty2@yahoo.com).

References

Messer, Mari. 2001. *Pencil Dancing*. Cincinnati, OH: Writers Digest.

Roach, Mary. 2003. *Stiff: The Curious Lives of Human Cadavers*. New York: W.W. Norton.

Smith, Michael C., and Suzanne Greenberg. 1999. *Panning for Gold in the Kitchen Sink*. Chicago: NTC Publishing.

6

◇🁢◇　◇🁢◇　◇🁢◇

WORD OUT! WAYS TO TAKE YOUR CLUB PUBLIC

Now that you have gotten to know teens, set up the framework for the club, and scheduled the first meeting, it's time to attract some clubbers! While you're at it, you'll also be "selling" the club to gain the support you need to keep it going strong.

Marketing is everything you do to kick-start your club and to keep it going and growing strong. It's selling the library up the chain to directors, administrators and funding agencies. It's recruiting and retaining club members. It's telling your story to the public to gain visibility and support. It's anticipating questions and expectations and fulfilling them before anyone asks. It's anticipating objections too, and answering them before they're voiced. It's everything you do to keep everyone feeling good and talking good about your club.

That's the bird's-eye view. This chapter zeroes in on what we typically consider marketing: What you do and say and *how* you do and say it to create excitement and support for your club.

In a sense, this book revolves around marketing. *Teen-centered* is a marketing concept. Listening to the teens you serve, building the club just for them, delivering what you promise, repeating that cycle again and again: It's all marketing. In this chapter we look at three nitty-gritties: recruiting/retention, increasing awareness, and building support. We'll start with a few broad principles; then we'll hit several quick ideas and tips to choose from for recruiting and promoting your club . . . and to have fun doing it!

Marketing Basics

Recruiting: Get teens to join the club.

Retention: Keep clubbers coming back for more.

Promotion: Shorthand for publicity *and* building support.

Publicity: Make a name for your club.

Build support: Get influential people on board.

Slant: Address your audience's interests and concerns.

Spin: Make straw into gold (*not* slant).

WHATEVER YOU DO, DO THIS . . .

For all its wit and flash, marketing is a *process* based on *principles*. You'll save yourself eons of time if you build these principles into your process before you create your first poster, recruit your first teen, or approach your first funding prospect. Standing on principle keeps your marketing efforts on track.

1. **Keep teens front and center.** If you hold teens foremost in your mind and double-check your thinking against theirs, your recruiting can hardly miss. Creating promotional materials that keep teens front and center reminds influential people that the bottom line is not numbers, but service to teens.

2. **Know your audience.** Knowing your audience equips you to address their interests and concerns, use words and visuals that appeal to them, and deliver your message using the most effective medium. Chapter 3 is all about getting to know teens; use the same strategies to learn more about your other audiences, from community partners to city council members.

3. **Get people talking.** Word of mouth is absolutely the best way to build enthusiasm—especially when it comes to teens. This chapter is devoted to ways to get people talking—teens, library staff, and community members.

4. **Be honest.** If you don't deliver on your promises, teens will leave never to return, and they'll tell all their friends to steer clear too. Ditto for funders, bosses, and other potential allies.

5. **Deliver an** *amazing* **book club.** Without a great "product," you have nothing to market. Create a book club that is so surprisingly terrific people flock to support it. Make every meeting a showcase. Never assume you own your clubbers; earn their loyalty by delivering richly rewarding programs month after month.

6. **Know thyself.** Every serious marketing campaign begins with this question: What are we offering? Look beyond the concrete; remember your purpose. Are you offering books or friendship? Service learning credits, doing good in the world, or connecting as humane beings?

Answer the question meaningfully; then build your recruiting and promotion around it.

7. **Build your brand.** Every single message you put out and every single action you take should, in every single way, let people know exactly who you are. This takes the mystique out of marketing. Instead of cobbling together a cacophony of buzzwords, you speak simply and from your heart.

8. **The medium is the message.** Pay attention to the look and feel of your marketing messages, and the medium you choose to deliver them. These form the subtext of your message, and subtext speaks louder than words. (A single-page, single-spaced annual report stapled to the back of the director's report sends a much different message than a freestanding report with an attractive design, or even a PowerPoint presentation.)

9. **Stay one step ahead.** Short-circuit questions and objections by answering them before they are voiced. The more obstacles you clear from the road, the easier it is for teens and others to say yes.

10. **Document your success.** When you know what your different audiences care about, you can collect statistics *and stories* that speak to their interests. Don't skimp on this; the most effective marketing programs are built on statistics and stories.

Those are our general principles for book club marketing. Hold fast to them as you get into the details. Whenever you feel intimidated or overwhelmed by a marketing task (e.g., making a presentation, writing the annual report, making a poster), take time out to reflect on to the principles as they relate to the task at hand. Start with your feet on solid ground, and you'll discover you don't need fancy footwork to get the job done.

RECRUITING AND RETENTION

Consider these strategies for recruiting and retention:

Know your teens better. By now, the strategies in chapter 3 should have helped you get to know the teens in your community. If what you learned helps you recruit new teens, that's great. If not, go back to the well for the specifics on what motivates teens to join book clubs, what stands in their way, and what emotions or other factors drive their decision to join (or not).

Get personal. If you know that Chantal is often in the library on Wednesdays, loves to read difficult books, and frequently looks bored, talk to her about the challenging Wednesday after-school book club. If you notice Doug chatting up Ria every chance he gets, you can casually mention to him that she's joined the club. If you see that Justin is always borrowing fantasy novels, tell him about the fantasy book club you're trying to organize, and ask him if he's willing to help lead.

Cast your net wide. Make a conscious effort to reach out to *all* teens, not just the most likely prospects. The greater variety, the better the conversations! Use the library Web site and newsletter, booktalking stints in the schools, and flyers placed in community facilities that serve youth to spread the word.

Button . . . or buttonhole. Wear a button that says "Ask me about 13/15!" (meaning the book club for teens ages 13–15). If no one asks, buttonhole teens and ask, "Have you heard about our book club?" Then launch into a 20-second speech that answers the questions: What is book club? What does it do? What's in it for you (the teen)?

Reach them in school. If you are convinced the best place to recruit teens is in school, place paid ads in the school newspaper. Or work through your outreach coordinator to bring the school library media specialist on board.

Schedule teen attractions. Every three to four months, plan a special event—an author visit, manga workshop, strategy game night, for example—that attracts new teens to your club. Wear your "Ask Me about 13/15!" button, hand out flyers, and invite visitors to sign up.

Recruit teen recruiters. No one will talk up book club like loyal members! Give them "Ask Me about 13/15!" buttons and flyers the size of business cards, and send them forth.

Remember: It's easier to hold on to existing clubbers than to recruit new ones.

Offer goofy prizes. You will get more returns with a goofy prize than with cheap trinkets. Here's one that works for the playful and minimally fit: Promise you'll do a cartwheel for every friend teens bring to book club. You don't have to be able to do cartwheels, you just have to be willing to look goofy. You'll certainly end up with a free-for-all as all the teens show you how to do cartwheels right.

Pile on the positives. In lieu of tangible rewards, build esprit de corps. Have clubbers' pictures published in the local newspaper, invite them to exclusive events, post their signed book reviews online or on the walls, and give them first dibs on those advance readers copies that have been piling up!

Encourage teens to bring a friend. Encourage teens to bring friends to book club. When you introduce the book for the next meeting, ask clubbers if they know anyone who might enjoy the book. Then, suggest they invite that person. Once or twice a year, challenge everyone to bring at least one friend to the next meeting.

WOM (Word of mouth) happens. After the first few meetings, the club will develop a personality. Clubbers will spread the word and recruit friends who will enjoy the atmosphere.

Who You Calling *Teen?*

Younger teens (ages 13–14) don't mind being called *teens* and *teenagers*. But don't try putting those labels on older teens. And don't use the term *young adults,* either. So, if you can't call them teens or young adults, how do you say, "This club's for you"?

Make it obvious in the language, colors, design, and delivery who you're targeting. Use splashy, upbeat language and fashionable colors—the ones you see teens wearing. Deliver messages via email, on kiosks, on posters in the YA stacks. Run your flyers by teens to be sure you're getting it right. Or have teens design the flyers.

Leave teens wanting more. End each meeting with a teaser. Say something like, "I've invited a mystery guest to our next meeting. All I can tell you is that you've all heard of her." Give just enough detail to whet their curiosity, and feed it every time you see them.

Go with the flow. Note patterns in attendance. If you can't beat them, don't try. You'll never recruit marching band members during fall. If attendance consistently ebbs and flows in a three-month cycle, change to a short-term club (see chapter 5) with breaks in between.

Go to the source. Ask loyal clubbers why they attend. Ask other teens why they stopped coming. Use their feedback to make the club more appealing.

Build bonds ASAP. Clubbers are sociable people. Help them connect right from the start with icebreakers, team-building games, and casual conversation over snacks.

Like your clubbers and let them know that you do. Liking the librarian is one reason teens give for participating in library activities.

Bookmarks, Flyers, Posters, Invitations, and Announcements

As you develop your marketing materials, keep these suggestions in mind:

Clear beats clever. We admire advertisements that are cool and clever, but most are brief and straightforward...almost prosaic. Why? Because clarity sells.

Be specific. Instead of "If you want to join book club, come next week" try "What they don't teach you in drivers ed.... This month, book club reads Stephen King's *Christine.* Join us Wednesday, March 3, 4 P.M.... and plan to *walk* home!"

"A library should produce nothing, no booklist or flyer or sign, for teens without teens passing judgment over it" (Jones and Shoemaker 2001).

The same goes for recruiting strategies, distribution, and follow-through.

Ask for what you want. The point of marketing is to get people to do things. Disseminating information doesn't get the job done. Always include a "call to action," a direct appeal that tells your audience what to do...now!

Create a simple, consistent look. Simple equals high impact. A distinctive logo, consistent color palette (three to four colors) and standard fonts (two or three) simplify designs and create a look people can recognize at a glance.

Use teen talent. Ask artistic teens to create posters, flyers, bookmarks, the Web site, public service announcements (PSAs), and other promotional materials. Don't limit yourself to clubbers. Grab any teen with the talent you need.

More! Simple Tactics

Don't forget about these tried-and-true promotion methods:

Bookmark it. Insert bookmarks or flyers promoting the club in books when teens check out. Leave a few scattered about the stacks, on study tables, and near computers and self-check-out kiosks.

Display book club favorites. Create bookmarks in three colors: past picks, current reads, and future choices. Put the appropriate color bookmark in each book. For a fast, no-fuss display, park a book cart loaded with club picks near the YA stacks. Affix a label, "Teen Book Club Picks," to the side of the cart.

Use tabletops. Create simple table tents to publicize book club and recent reads. Use them in the library and distribute them to eateries teens like.

Give that book a star! Put a gold foil label on every copy of titles the club reads. Purchase blank labels and print them yourself.

Wallpaper the world. Hang flyers in the young adult stacks, near the reference and circulation areas, near the computers and bathrooms and coffee bar . . . anywhere teens congregate. While you're at it, ask for permission to hang flyers in coffee shops, eateries, and convenience stores near teens' schools. If you like, also hang them in other teen gathering places.

Contribute to community calendars. Each month, send announcements of book club meetings to community calendars in every media outlet. Be sure to include an invitation (call to action).

Speak to teens. When you give booktalks, always include your 20-second speech and hand out flyers or bookmarks.

Go on the air. According to Harris Interactive (2003), teens aged 13–15 years spend 14.4 hours per week listening to the radio (just 1.5 hours behind television!). Place PSAs on the stations teens like. Ask the radio station to help you create the PSA.

The other PSAs. Create small classified ads (three lines) or space ads (one column wide by one inch tall) for newspapers to use as fillers. It's the print media's version of PSAs. This is all you need:

Like sci-fi? Join the club.
Public Library, June 12, 4 P.M.
13–15 year olds only

Collect teens' email addresses. Keep signup forms at the reference or teen desk, and ask for email addresses when teens register for summer reading programs. Get parental consent to contact teens if library policy requires.

Just for school libraries . . .

- Create announcements to be read during homeroom.
- Stuff teacher and staff mailboxes with book club flyers to post in classrooms.
- Ask the student newspaper to run descriptions of upcoming book club titles.
- Develop a book club Web page and link it to the school's or the library's homepage.
- Collaborate with teachers or the reading specialist to create a book club that supports curriculum directly or indirectly (see chapter 5).

INCREASING AWARENESS

Whatever medium or tactic you use, be sure to keep increasing awareness as your primary goal.

Be everywhere all at once. People respond to the familiar. Putting book club in front of as many people as you can as often as you can creates a sense of familiarity and the impression that book club is well established and reliable. You can build on that when you're ready to recruit or ask for active support.

Tailor your message. When you're increasing awareness, you're addressing adults. Speak to their interests; they want to know that book club serves larger purposes. What do teens get out of book club? Why is it worthwhile? What you say will depend on the club you've created. Most often you can speak to the ways in which reading *and* sharing ideas about what they've read help teens explore their identity, connect with their own humanity as well as with other individuals and the larger world, expand their horizons, and think more deeply about why they are here on earth. Some adults will want you to address educational issues, including literacy. In this case, you can speak to both the beneficial effects of book club for both reading skill (more reading makes better readers) and for developing lifelong habits of reading for learning and pleasure.

Establish a Web Presence

Use the Web for more than just conveying information about when the club will meet:

Create a book club page linked to the library's teen page. Include sections for recruiting, increasing awareness, and building support. Call them "13/15 Only!" "For the Media," or "For Friends and Partners."

Recruit teens. Include reviews of the current and past picks; The List (a record every books the club has read or seriously considered reading); photos of book club in action; upcoming meetings and special events; bookish trivia and brain teasers; links to cool sites related to authors, graphic novels, book-to-movie connections, and so on; and of course, an invitation to join the club!

Increase awareness. Create a separate section for press releases, book club annual report, statistics, links to reports on the benefits of reading and book clubs, a brief presentation on book club (the Web version of your 20-second speech), brief summaries of club activities, and what teens get out of book club.

Build support. Create a page for current and prospective supporters. Include your annual report and update it frequently.

Get your link on other sites. Brainstorm a list of likely sites (e.g., supporters' Web sites, community sites). Email Webmasters a brief introductory note with link; then follow up to encourage them to use it.

Online community calendars. Send book club announcements and invitations to community calendars online. Create a teaser line with a link to your recruiting page.

Mass Media

Mass media is so . . . well, mass . . . you'll need to focus your efforts on the media that appeal most to teens. The easiest ways to do that are to ask and observe. Do teens pick up the free alternative weekly in the library lobby? Does anyone actually read the school newspaper? Are teens plugged in while doing homework? What are they listening to? Do they all log on to a certain blog? Do they wiki?

To expand your research to teens you can't ask or observe directly, do some basic research. Gather demographics from local radio stations to find out which ones appeal to teens.

Don't forget about parents. For all the talk about the generational divide, teens and parents do talk, and many times teens follow their parents' advice. So be sure that in addition to teens' media you put your notices in parents' media, too. Generally, mass media include the following:

- Newspapers (city, suburban, and rural dailies and weeklies, classified-ad freebies and alternative weeklies, school newspapers)
- Radio and television stations (network, cable, satellite, Webcast, community access, school)
- Specialty publications for teens and parents (literary magazines by teens, parenting magazines)
- Community Web sites

Pitch it! Create a 20-second speech to explain *for the media* what book club is and what teens get out of it. Give it a hook—something interesting and right-now the editor can use as the basis of an article. Infuse it with your own passionate belief in the value of reading. Practice it on colleagues and friends, and then start calling editors and news directors at community newspapers and local radio stations to share the news. If you live in a small community, contact the general news editor. If you're in a large metropolitan area, look for the local news director or lifestyles editor.

A 20-second speech might go something like this:

I'm AJ Murphy, the young adult librarian with the Service Learning Book Club at Public Library. I've got six outstanding teens who've racked up 100 hours of community service this fall because they are so affected by what we're reading they can't stand to leave it behind when they finish the book. These kids are fearless; they've taken on projects from homeless war veterans to animal rescue. Would you be interested in announcing/visiting our next meeting?

Or

I'm AJ Murphy, the young adult librarian at School Library. We've just gotten our test scores back—and the results show that our Literacy Now! book club boosted readers' scores by 10 percent. Would you be interested in an article about that?

Or

I'm AJ Murphy with the Books Are Better Club at Public Library. About a month ago, I made it my personal mission to pry every teen boy I see away from his electronic toys. I'm batting less than .300 right now, and I could use your help. Would you post an announcement about our next book club meeting, please?

Create a fact sheet. Keep it brief, simple, and low-cost. Explain what book club is, what its ultimate purposes are, how it works, how long it's been in existence, a selected booklist, and quotes from teens about how book club serves them well in school, family, and life. This is for the media and community supporters, not teens.

Be prepared. Have plenty of fact sheets on hand in the library. Carry the fact sheets with you on off-site trips you make on the library's behalf. Be ready to launch into your 20-second speech and hand out a fact sheet whenever the opportunity presents itself.

Share your strengths. Work book club into current outreach efforts. If the director has a monthly newspaper column, give her some tidbits to include in each one. The outreach coordinator is your point person for community partnerships. If staff members share booktalking duties, give everyone a copy of the 20-second recruiting speech and a handful of flyers to take on their rounds.

Visuals are worth 1,000... When your club plans to do something visually interesting, such as painting a mural or placing every book they've read in the last six months end-to-end, let local media know well in advance. Or ask the school's video club to record it. If you have the skill, do it yourself. For photos, write a caption, including the names of everyone in the picture (left to right), and send them to the local newspaper with copies of signed releases from the teens and their parents.

Here are some tips for creating a great press release:

- Send it on library letterhead.
- Include the release date at the top in a big, bold font. If there is a date after which the material is no longer useful, include that too.
- Include your contact information in a big, bold font at the top of the page.
- Keep it short and to the point. That includes sentences (no more than 10–15 words), paragraphs (four lines max), and the release as a whole (75 words for a simple announcement, up to one page for a year-end review).
- Leave no question unanswered. Busy editors like to use press releases as is.
- Write a headline, even if it's not the best. The editor will rewrite it if there is time.

SAMPLE PRESS RELEASE

FOR IMMEDIATE RELEASE (to August 6, 2010)

For more information: CONSTANCE HARDESTY, 555-555-5555

BEYOND THE BOOK

Teens get up close and personal with fallen angels

Vietnam is history. For teens and their parents, it's nothing more than a tourist destination, complete with boat tours of the Mekong Delta. That is, until the Mother–Daughter Book Club at Public Library took on Walter Dean Myers' acclaimed teen novel *Fallen Angels.*

Reading the book opened the women's eyes to a history still very much alive for veterans of the war, particularly those who were left with lifelong physical or psychological damage. And that raised the question: How are they faring today?

To find out, the club visited the Fitzwallace Veterans Hospital last week, spending the afternoon reading to veterans, sharing their stories, and learning what life is like when war won't let you go.

"My grandfather died in Vietnam, but that was before I was born, so I never really thought about it," said Saide Thomas, 14. "Now that I know some of the things he lived through, I wish I could give him a big hug. It gave me a new goal, to work for the United Nations to make peace in the world."

For more information about the book club, please contact Constance Hardesty, 555-555-5555.

Personal Appearances

You are the book club's best promoter; leave no stone unturned in your quest for publicity. Don't forget the following:

Speak up the organization ladder. Speak at least once each year to the board of directors and friends of the library. Speak every three to six months at city council or school board meetings. Give a few quick highlights: One to three minutes is good. You want them to ask for more information.

Speak to community groups. Speak to community groups like Rotary Club to explain how book club serves the community directly (through volunteerism) and indirectly (by building developmental assets).

Booth presence. If the library has a presence at book festivals, community fairs, or other local events, keep the booth stocked with flyers and bookmarks. If there is room, create a small book club display.

Invite questions. Always wear your "Ask me about 13/15!" button.

BUILDING SUPPORT

Support comes in many shapes and sizes. The following suggestions should help you keep in mind a wide variety of possibilities:

Aim for the support you need. Do you need donated snacks? funding to buy books and supplies? speakers? commitment from the library and its sponsoring organization? Keep those things in mind as you build support for the program.

Create an annual report. Showcase book club for directors, friends, city council, granting organizations and donors, and community partners. Keeping their interests and concerns in mind, make the case that book club is worthy of their support. In eight pages or less, highlight a few of the following:

- Book club's purposes and how book club serves the community
- Measures of success
- Recruiting and retention efforts
- Statistics on attendance: per meeting, cumulative for the year, and number of teens who attended consistently
- A list of all titles and teens' reviews or comments about them
- A summary of activities, including pictures; highlight activities showing teens learning something important or serving the community
- Teens' testimonials on the benefits of book club
- Research on the benefits of reading and book club, including developmental assets
- Resources required for the program
- Promotional efforts
- Community partnerships, donations, or sponsorships, with testimonials from sponsors about why they support book club
- Wish list of specific things book club needs (e.g., books, snacks, sponsorship for special events or volunteer projects)

Get the word out! Print the annual report individually or as part of a larger library report. Post it on your book club Web site. Distribute it to everyone on your list of influential people (e.g., donors, directors, sponsors, friends). Be sure to send copies to prospective supporters to increase their awareness of book club before you ask for their support..

Choose your prospects carefully. Your Friends of the Library group is a natural first stop for book club support. Treat it as you would any other funding organization, presenting a sound proposal to back up your request for funding.

Community-based organizations, including family foundations (which have proliferated in the past decade) may be interested in supporting teen reading or associated projects. For example, the Binning Family Foundation in Littleton, Colorado, recently awarded funds to the Bemis Public Library to help teens develop a teen Web page.

Community leaders may be delighted to become involved in your program. Adapt an idea from Mayor Daley's Book Club (http://www.mayordaleysbook-club.org/funding.html) and bring in a community leader to be Honorary Book Club Member for a day. A person who agrees to accept the honor is likely to support the club and may recruit his or her peers to supporting the club, too.

You'll find many organizations willing to give donations. Contact grocery stores or bakeries for food, office supply stores for pens and sticky notes, bookstores for gift certificates, and other businesses for cash donations. With imagination and teen legwork, you may find your club fully supported!

Whatever organization you decide to approach, begin by discovering their interests and concerns and ruthlessly weeding out all that don't align with book club. Ask those that remain to support book club, being sure that your appeal addresses the grantor's interests and concerns (e.g., this is a local teen-development opportunity; this is an educational opportunity; this is a marketing opportunity for your organization. . . . you get the idea).

Cultivate relationships. Send annual reports, press releases, and other materials to prospective supporters so they can get to know you before you ask them for help.

Make support a give-and-take. Show supporters that book club "gives back" to the community by supporting bookish events. When an author visits a local bookstore, have book club read his or her book and attend his or her reading or signing. Encourage teens to help out at used book sales, book drives, book fairs, and literary festivals. Take pictures everywhere!

Collect testimonials. Always collect testimonials from teens, sponsors, community partners, and others involved in or benefiting from book club activities. Keep them on file to use again and again in annual reports, Web pages, grant proposals and so forth.

Give it time. It can take months for word to spread. Enjoy your small group, encourage clubbers to invite their friends, and keep putting the word out. Your club will fill up. Meanwhile, remember you're not alone; everyone struggles with drawing enough teens to justify the program and gaining the funding and support to make it great.

> ### Once a Year, Make a Big Splash!
>
> Have book club host a special evening gala event, organize a high-profile service project, perform a Book Club Revue, or coordinate a citywide book conference. If you do it for three years in a row (so that it becomes an established event people begin to recognize), you'll reap enormous benefits for recruiting, awareness, and support. Here are a few ideas:
>
> **Host a book gala.** Invite influential people to attend a special evening "gala" meeting of book club. Serve fancy snacks, decorate the room with book club posters and art, and encourage teens and influential people to meet and mingle. You'll need to act as hostess to keep teens and adults from separating like water and oil.
>
> **Work together.** If teens enjoy service work, encourage them to take on a large event that connects the book to the real world in a very tangible way, like organizing a blood drive at the library. Invite influential people to work with teens, to give blood, or donate their time. Or invite local personalities or visiting authors to participate in book club activities; be sure to invite the media to cover these events.
>
> **Song-and-dance routine.** If your teens are hams, suggest they create and perform a five-minute Book Club Follies highlighting titles and activities. Let them draw you into the fun. Perform the Follies at the annual meeting of directors or friends, a city council meeting, or the book club gala.
>
> **One city, one club for one day.** Host a citywide book club conference. See http://www.mayordaleysbookclub.org/funding.html for Mayor Daley's Book Club conference.

PICK AND CHOOSE, OR CREATE YOUR OWN

There are enough ideas in this chapter to fuel several years of recruiting and promotion. Some are suitable for small libraries; others are better for large library systems. Choose three or four ideas that work for you, or use them as a springboard to create tactics that work even better. Don't worry about covering every base right from the start. Marketing is about doing the most with what you have, where you are. As book club develops, so will marketing and promotion.

References

Harris Interactive, Inc. 2003. "A Brave New Media World," *Trends & Tudes* 2 (10).
Jones, Patrick, and Joel Shoemaker. 2001. *Do It Right! Best Practices for Serving Young Adults in School and Public Libraries.* New York: Neal-Schuman.

PART TWO

◈■◈　◈■◈　◈■◈

The Nitty-Gritty Book Club Guide: From First to Final Meeting

You've done the prep work. You know the teens you serve, you've created the support structure, and you've settled the major planning issues. With plenty of publicity, you've recruited a crowd of teens who are eagerly awaiting the first meeting. Now what?

Chapter 7 gets you off to a good start with a comprehensive walk-through of the first meeting, beginning one week before the meeting and ending with day-after follow-up. Chapter 8 leads you through book selection, offering plenty of time-saving options, various perspectives on several important selection issues, and advice about difficult situations, like vetoes and challenges.

With books chosen, we get to the heart of book club. Chapters 9, 10 and 11 offer general discussions, guidelines, tips, warnings, advice, and many reproducible handouts you can use to help teens create scintillating discussions and unforgettable activities. Chapter 9 focuses on preparation: reading for discussion, researching the book and author, and creating provocative discussion questions. Chapter 10 explains the art and practice of great book discussions, centered on critical thinking, civil discourse, and joint exploration. Chapter 11 describes activities that build meaning, understanding, perspective, and connection.

Chapter 12 returns to the administrative arena. Whether, when, and how you evaluate the program has everything to do with whether teens will continue to come and whether the larger community will continue to support it. With innovative ideas for evaluation, chapter 12 helps you to both troubleshoot the club and document its successes.

7

◈■◇　◈■◇　◈■◇

IT'S CLUB TIME! CREATING
A GREAT FIRST MEETING

First meetings are problematic. Do you spend your time planning or doing? In our model, you've done the basic planning already. Based on listening to learn (chapter 2) or a planning meeting with teens, you've established the basic structure of your club: what type of club you'll have, when you'll meet, and where. You've promoted the club in every way.

After all this preparation . . . at last, it's time for the first meeting.

First impressions are the ones that last. Here we'll look at ways to set up your club for success. (See "First Meeting Checklist" and "What to Cover in the First Meeting.") All of this preparation may appear daunting in print. In practice it's quite simple: Set the ball in motion, give it an occasional nudge, and the momentum will keep it rolling.

ONE WEEK BEFORE . . .

Plan the Meeting

Create a time line for the first meeting. This is just a planning tool, a loose outline of steps and activities to choose from. The top three things to accomplish in the first meeting are as follows:

Create the atmosphere
Establish group dynamics
Engender the feelings you want teens to walk away with

What do those priorities look like in action?

Get to know one another
Step aside so teens can take charge
Talk about books

FIRST MEETING CHECKLIST

One week before. . .

- ☐ Create and distribute invitations
- ☐ Make timeline
- ☐ Recruit teens to make
  - –Posters and decorations
  - –Directional signs
  - –A talking stick
- ☐ Buy or acquire
  - –Journal or scrapbook and pen
  - –Inexpensive clock with timer and toy horn
  - –Materials for games or activities
  - –Portable whiteboard or large sheets of paper and pens
- ☐ Start a box to store journal, toys, and materials

A few days before. . .

- ☐ Double-check the room reservation
- ☐ Practice your opening and closing
- ☐ Make directional signs
- ☐ Acquire food and paper products

A few hours before. . .

- ☐ Post directional signs
- ☐ Prepare the food
- ☐ Set up the room

Just before teens arrive

- ☐ Set out the food
- ☐ Bring all materials to the room
- ☐ Check the room

Get into the spirit

FIRST MEETING CHECKLIST (CONT'D)

What to Cover in the First Meeting

With your top priority for the first meeting being to create an atmosphere and allow teens to connect, the last thing you want to do is rush through an overfull agenda. From the following list, choose two to four activities most important for your group and table the rest.

- ☐ Welcome
- ☐ Icebreaker
- ☐ Booktalks
- ☐ Club structure, format, and logistics
- ☐ Book selection
- ☐ Book club behavior
- ☐ Book club roles
- ☐ Eat!
- ☐ Announcements about teen activities between now and next meeting
- ☐ Closing

Get to Know One Another

Building bonds among teens is your number-one priority. The more you can help them make friends (around books), the more committed they will be to the club. Help them to include everyone—and lay the groundwork for teen leadership—by including activities and games that require teens to think and work together. Team building and leadership activity books offer many activities; you'll find a few of our favorites in chapter 11.

Teens in Charge

Stand back as teens make decisions about how the club works. For older teens, suggest that one person bring up each topic for consideration while another person makes sure everyone has their say. Younger teens may look to you to lead the discussion and offer advice.

Talk about Books

Casual chat about books and authors, even when it seems to devolve into minutiae, is the best bond-building activity you can hope for. Give teens time and free rein to do that. Your role is host. Encourage teens to talk among themselves. Observe and, if you see someone on the fringes, orchestrate their integration into groups—much as you would do if you were hosting a party.

Putting It All Together

Time is always an issue in book club, especially in the first meeting. Prepare to focus on the priorities, keep a casual eye on the clock, and stay attuned to the discussion so you can help move it along if it becomes bogged down. Decide ahead of time which activities can be cut on the fly, so if the meeting begins to run long you can unobtrusively skip an activity or two. Remember, the time line is only a sketchy outline; the reality may look quite different. If you feel pressured to accomplish an agenda, label each item *optional*.

Set the Stage for Teens Taking Charge

To demonstrate for teens that this club surely is by, for, and about them, give them a rundown of decisions that need to be made; then stand back as they decide:

- What kind of club do we want to be? (see chapters 4 and 5)
- Is this a good place to meet?
- Can people come if they haven't read the book? Will we avoid spoilers (giving away the ending) for people who haven't read the book?
- How will we come up with discussion questions?
- Do we want to do things other than talk about books, like watch movies, invite guest speakers, perform service projects, play games, have parties,

or do activities? (Brainstorm and record their ideas. Do they seem to prefer activities to discussion? Revisit what type of club they want to be.)

- Do we need ground rules?
- What is the adult's job in book club? What are teens' jobs in book club?

Teens can do all of the decision making at once (the Big Slug approach), or they can intersperse decision making with other activities (the Eyedropper approach). Whatever approach they choose, if discussion goes on and on, ask teens if they'd like to recap what they have decided, table the rest, and move on to the food and picking a book for the next meeting.

These early discussions set the group dynamics in motion and establish the tone for future meetings. Subtly (or directly) intervene to encourage a lively give-and-take in which everyone participates and teens freely exchange diverse ideas, disagree without arguing, and make decisions by consensus.

Remind Teens about the Meeting

Several days before the meeting, make a point of inviting (or reinviting) all teens who might be interested in book club—in person, by email, by telephone, or by mail. (If you use snail mail, you'll need to send them out a week ahead.) Don't assume certain teens are so interested or uninterested that they don't need an invitation. A personal invitation builds excitement, reminds teens of the date, and makes them feel truly welcome. And it may encourage undecided teens—or those who never considered themselves book club types—to give it a try.

Create an invitation or attractive postcard, print or digital. In addition to details about time and place, include graphics and a message that sparks curiosity or enthusiasm:

- **Provocative quotes:** "An idea isn't responsible for the people who believe in it."—Don Marquis
- **Fascinating questions:** You're stranded on a deserted island with a character from any book. Who is it?
- **Brain teasers:** Chris and Tom are found on the floor in a locked room. Nearby are a broken bowl and a puddle of water. How did they die? (Chris and Tom are goldfish . . .)

During the first book club meeting, as the icebreaker or closing activity or while waiting for teens to arrive, ask teens to respond to the message on the invitation.

A FEW DAYS BEFORE . . .

Buy the Food

Simple snacks, like chips and soda are standard for teen groups. If your schedule, budget, and refrigerator storage allow, try following teens' lead to healthier finger foods like cheese sticks, grapes, crackers, sports drinks, and flavored waters or teas. Don't forget to buy paper products (i.e., cups, lots of napkins, snack plates).

> **Tip!**
>
> Use the invitation in many different formats and venues to get the word out as broadly as you can:
>
> - Send the invitation via snail mail, email, or instant message (IM). Snail mail gives teens a physical reminder they can put in an obvious place, but IM is becoming standard. Lacking an address, and if library policy allows, call the teen.
> - Make a poster-sized version of your invitation and hang it in as many places as you can within the library and throughout the community.
> - Buttonhole teens as you encounter them in the library. Smile warmly as you put an invitation in their hands.

Make Signs, Posters, and Other Decorations

You'll want signs to direct teens to the meeting room, as well as posters with catchy quotes and cool graphics to decorate the meeting room. Recruit teens to make them for you, make them yourself, or buy them.

The Readers' Bill of Rights makes a great poster and discussion starter. Here are a few ideas, adapted (with a few items just for teens) from *Better Than Life* by Daniel Pennac (1999):

You have the right to read *anything*.
You have the right to read ahead.
You have the right to listen to the radio while you read.
You have the right to stop before you finish.

Practice Your Welcome and Closing

Encourage cohesiveness by addressing the group as a whole. Keep both welcome and closing short and on target. Practice them aloud a few times, and time yourself until each is no more than one minute.

A FEW HOURS BEFORE . . .

Prepare the Food

Put the food on a tray and, if it's not individually wrapped (like cheese sticks), cover the tray with plastic wrap. Find a box and put the paper products and nonperishable food in it. When it's time to set up the room, add the refrigerated food to the box and carry everything you need in just one trip.

Set Up the Room

Decide how you want to handle the food during the meeting and arrange a setup: Sitting around a table tells teens they will eat their way through the meeting. Placing a table at the side of the room and setting out snacks midway through the meeting creates a welcome break. Sitting in chairs with snack plates and cups in hand is a disaster waiting to happen—and it won't wait long.

When you arrange the chairs, think outside the circle. Constance has had great luck placing chairs at random and letting teens arrange themselves. They rarely form a circle but usually clump together—and they don't feel the need to sit in the same chair at each meeting.

Put on the Finishing Touches

Recruit teens to help you with finishing touches. This is a good opportunity to fold tweens or younger teens into the club as they work with older teens on an activity they can easily share. Decorate the room.

- **Arrange a book display.** Showcase teens' favorites (which you note as you speak with teens) along with readalikes or first books by favorite authors. This shows teens you really do listen to them, pay attention to what they read, and value their choices. It may also help jump-start book selection. (One good first-book/famous-book pair: Nicholas Sparks, author of teen favorite *A Walk to Remember* (2000), first wrote *Wokini* (Mills and Sparks 1999), a self-help book, with runner Bobby Mills, the first Native American to win an Olympic gold medal.)
- **Set yourself up.** Set up the easel or large sheets of paper for note taking. Place The List of Books (a decorated scrapbook or journal) in a prominent place. Place props and other supplies where you can easily reach them.

JUST BEFORE TEENS ARRIVE . . .
Organize the Food

Fetch the food. Don't forget what's in the refrigerator. Keep temptation out of sight: If you don't intend to serve right away, hide the food box in a corner or under a table with a table skirt.

Check the Space

Run a last-minute check to be sure directional signs are in place, colleagues know where to send teens looking for book club, there are enough chairs, and you have all the materials you need, including your timeline.

Breathe!

You've done everything you can do. Now, relax and get in the spirit. If you send out anxious vibes, teens (who take everything personally) may misread them as dislike. In contrast, if you put a smile on your face, teens wandering around the library just might decide to find out what you're up to.

AS TEENS ARRIVE

Greetings!

Welcome each teen personally with a warm smile and greeting. Look them in the eye. Use their names. If you don't know a name, ask for it and then greet the teen again using his or her name. Say, "It's good to see you. I'm glad you made it." You're not simply making each teen feel welcome; you're making a statement about the kind of space they're entering.

Once you've greeted them, let them talk among themselves. If they need help getting started, model small talk: Ask about their weekends, hobbies, pets.

DURING THE MEETING

Welcome the Group

Start on time. Tell them how much you're looking forward to the club (i.e., plant commitment in their minds). Acknowledge each teen individually, and let them know you're happy to see them. Briefly remind the group this is a teen-centered book club, and that means you'll be playing a supporting role: They are the stars.

Name the Club

Teens may want to name the club. You won't need to help much with this. You probably won't even need to suggest it. A word game is a good icebreaker/ team building activity. Write many words on cards (think: magnetic poetry), then ask teens to walk around to get out of their seats and arrange the cards on the floor, table, or whatever. Offer several blank cards and pens so teens can add their own word cards.

To make semipermanent cards, which can be used in a variety of similar activities, laminate the cards (including the ones teens make), put a dot of sticky-gum on the back, and use a tabletop or painted wall as the playing field. (Check out the wall first, to be sure the sticky dots won't tear the paint off!)

Help Teens Get to Know One Another

Start building those peer connections right away. Play a game that brings teens together. Chapter 11 includes several icebreaker and team games.

Teens Talk Books

After the preliminaries, you can devote the rest of the meeting to a leisurely conversation or play a fast-paced bookchatting game. Here's how the game works:

Allow each teen 30 seconds to name their favorite book or author or anything they've read lately. Pass around the timer and toy horn. When each teen's time is up, whoever is holding the timer and horn beep-beeps. The idea is to create a lively give-and-take.

Because this activity exposes individual interests and draws on teens' shared enthusiasm for books, it makes a great connecting/bonding activity. Be sure to ask teens to write their favorites in The List (a journal just for this purpose). And, if teens enjoy bookchatting, ask them if they'd like to make it a part of every book club meeting.

Select Books

If the club follows an all-read-one format (all club members read and discuss the same book), clubbers will need to decide how to select books to read. Offer some options (see chapter 8) and let teens decide. Remind them they can experiment with different selection methods each month. Then ask them to choose one method to use next month.

The Pesky Perennial Problem: Choosing the First Book

If teens want to read and discuss books in the very first meeting, you'll have the challenge of choosing the first book. Try this: As you do your initial research (see chapter 2), ask teens to make a wish list of books they'd like to read for book club. Choose a book that's frequently mentioned, and you'll have as good a chance as any of getting it right. For more quick-and-easy ways to select books, see chapter 8.

Book Club Behavior

Chances are by the time kids reach adolescence they've established ground rules so many times they can do it in their sleep. What they're missing is a deep grasp of why ground rules matter. Ground rules exist to reinforce book club values. So why not start with book club values and ask teens for ground rules that affirm them, rather than outlaw certain behaviors? Book club values as outlined in Appendix A are as follows:

- Respect is more important than agreement.
- Exploration is more meaningful than conquest.
- No one has the right to an unfounded opinion.

These values give rise to many of the same ground rules teens would rattle off if you asked them to. By starting with values, you help teens see the larger significance of their behavior. It's not really about controlling your tongue; it's really about building a safe environment where everyone, even the timid, can feel free to speak their minds. If you want teens to engage in thoughtful discussion *and* to think about their behavior, introducing book club values is all you need to do.

What Shall We Talk About?

Teens come to book club to connect with one another around books. If they don't get enough of that in the first meeting, they may never come back. Unfortunately, there may not be time for an in-depth discussion of a single book during the first meeting.

Try this: Read aloud something aloud that's quick and discussable. *Green Eggs and Ham* is perfect, because it's an insightful take on peer pressure, a subject teens know all too well. Then throw out a few questions: Would you want Sam-I-Am for a friend? Was the nameless guy smart when he tried green eggs and ham? Even if it turned out well in the end, was it a good decision? Have you had a green-eggs-and-ham experience?

The Positive Alternative

Ground rules tend to be negative. If you want to accentuate the positive, create a Book Club Constitution. The Constitution states what clubbers will do rather than focus on what they won't. Here are a few examples:

We welcome all ideas for discussion.
We speak our minds and we listen carefully when others do the same.
We think—and talk—beyond the book.
When we disagree, we stick to the point.
We look at situations in book and topics in discussion from every angle.
We look for evidence to back up our ideas and opinions.
When we get angry, we stay quiet or leave the room until we cool off.
Everyone is welcome, even if they haven't read the book.

Once written, ask volunteers to make a poster of it. Calligraphy is great. So is the image of a group signing with fancy feathered pens. And if your teens want to take it to the nth degree, let them pose a playful Constitution-signing picture (think Howard Chandler Christy's *Scene at the Signing of the Constitution of the United States*) for the scrapbook.

> **Tip!**
>
> Use That Picture!
>
> Get the marketing most out of your Constitution photo. Send it digitally with the invitation to the next book club meeting. Publish it on the Web site. Submit a copy of the photo with a caption to the library newsletter, city newsletter, and local newspaper.

If You Must . . .

Groups typically generate ground rules by brainstorming or by asking each person to name one rule and then combining or eliminating duplicates.

Minimalism is good. So is humor. Figure 7.1 is the Sulzer (Chicago Public Library) Read 'n Rap 2000 Ground Rules poster—a great example of not only keeping it short but making it fun.

An even more minimalist list looks like this:

Listen.
Think.
Speak your mind.
Respect yourself, respect your friends.
Come to book club even if you didn't read or like the book.
What happens in book club stays in book club.

What's a rule without enforcement? Some groups impose silly penalties, like jumping up, spinning around three times while saying "I will not be vulgar," and then sitting down again. Let teens create the penalties.

Delegating Roles

There are two types of roles in book club: Some enrich the discussion and others support book club behind the scenes. In this part of the meeting, teens look at the various roles and decide which ones to take on.

Sulzer Read 'n Rap 2000
GROUND RULES
[Andrew Medlar, Chicago Public Library]

THOU SHALT NOT ARGUE OR BACKTALK.

One person talks at a time and everyone listens to
what they are saying with rapt attention and anticipation.

IT IS OF DIRE IMPORTANCE TO RESPECT OTHER
PEOPLE'S IDEAS AND FEELINGS, BECAUSE IT IS ONLY NATURAL
THAT WE WANT FOR THEM TO RESPECT OURS.

KEEP IT CLEAN, PEOPLE!
NO SWEARING!!

SUFFERING IS OPTIONAL!

Food, as it is necessary for human survival, is welcome,
but cannot leave the read 'n rap room.

*No one will speak negatively about, or laugh at, another member of
the group, lest they shall be spoken about negatively or laughed at.*

WHAT IS DISCUSSED IN READ 'N RAP STAYS IN READ 'N RAP, WHAT
HAPPENS IN THE OUTSIDE WORLD STAYS OUTSIDE. THIS INCLUDES
DISAGREEMENTS WITH FAMILY MEMBERS, ESPECIALLY SISTERS!!

Ground Rules for the Librarian

Start on time. Never cancel.

Be prepared. Always have backups.

Affirm teens every chance you get.

Don't rescue, but mediate serious conflicts outside book club.

Breach book club confidentiality if a teen seems to be in danger, is doing something illegal or excessively risky, or poses a threat to others.

Make up a simple handout listing some roles and their responsibilities, or use figure 7.2, a reproducible handout for teens. For discussion roles, adapt from Harvey Daniels' *Literature Circles: Voice and Choice in Book Clubs* (2001). Though literature circles are quite different from book clubs, it may be fun for teens to take responsibility for things like looking up odd words or creating games or activities based on the book.

Ask teens to decide which roles are important and which can be discarded. That's all you need to do for now. Until attendance becomes regular it doesn't pay to plan ahead; the best approach is to ask for volunteers as teens arrive. As patterns of regular attendance emerge, you'll know which teens you can count on to show up. Those teens can take on roles that require advance preparation, like book or author research. In the meantime, teens can volunteer for specific roles at the beginning of each book club meeting.

Encourage teens to take on a different role each month; part of being in a teen-centered club means taking responsibility for making it work. For setup and cleanup, you might want to sweeten the pot: Give the crew a special treat or let them take home the leftover refreshments.

Make Announcements and Close the Meeting

Teens who come to book club are your best prospects for other programs and Teen Advisory Group. While teens scarf down the last of the snacks, make announcements about upcoming events and remind teens of all the ways they can find out what's going on in the library: Web site, library newsletter, email updates (if you provide one), and asking you, of course!

To close, tell teens something you learned from them today or compliment them on something they did well. Tell them again how happy you to see them. Remind them to check out the book for next month. And promise them the next meeting will be all about books!

AFTER THE MEETING

Say Goodbye

While your cleanup crew gets to work putting away chairs, say good-bye to departing teens at the door. Comment on something they said or did during the

FIGURE 7.2
Behind-the-Scenes Roles Make Book Club Run Right

Go Behind the Scenes Roles with
These Roles that Make Book Club Run Right

Greeter

- You'll say hello to everyone who comes in the door.
- When new people come, you'll introduce them around.

Time Tracker

- You'll make sure meetings begin and end on time.
- During the meeting, you make sure all the segments (like passing the food) don't run too long.
- And you get to make sure no one talks too long during discussions!
- You'll get a clock, a timer and a noisy toy horn. When the facilitator says someone has 1 minute to finish their thought, start watching the timer. When it gets down to 40 seconds, say something polite like "Please finish your thought now" or "Twenty seconds to go." If they don't stop on time–use that horn!

Keeper of The List

- You'll create a big poster or scrapbook to keep track of all the books we read or like. The List includes all the books we read and who recommended them.
- In a separate section of The List, everyone names books they like, even if the club doesn't read them.
- Leave lots of blank space. Everyone in book club can write in reviews of books we've read and thoughts about what we've discussed.
- Between book club meetings, we'll keep The List on display in the library. But at every meeting, we'll have it back here so we can add more to it.

Set-Up/Clean-Up (Don't be frightened! These jobs are easy and quick.)

- Arrange chairs/Put chairs away.
- Bring in The List/Put The List back where it belongs.
- Hang posters/Take posters down.
- Bring in the food/Clean up the food.
- Set out supplies/Collect supplies.
- You get the idea. And there might be a treat waiting for you when you're done.

meeting (e.g., "Good question about . . . Nicole," "Let me know how you like that book, Justin. I haven't read it yet.") And be sure to say thank you.

Keep it brief and positive. But don't let them get away without it.

Takeaways

It's always nice to give teens something to walk away with. Sticky notes make a nice giveaway because teens can use them to mark passages in the book. (Chapter 9 suggests what passages to mark.) Offer a basket filled with small sticky notes in lots of colors and let teens take one or two.

Listening and Thanking: Core Leadership Skills

Leadership begins with listening and ends with saying thank you (DePree 2004, p. 1). On its face that observation seems disingenuous, coming as it does (by way of adaptation) from Max Depree, chief executive officer of Hermann Miller, once one of the country's most successful companies. But a second look reveals Depree's deeper meaning: Leadership doesn't begin with power and end with achievement. It begins and ends with respect.

There can be no better starting point for a teen-centered book club. Leadership begins and ends with respect, for one another and for the club itself.

Follow Up with a Card

If you can possibly manage it, send each book club member a message or card the day after the meeting. Reiterate your appreciation for their thoughts, sense of humor, helpfulness, and so on. Make this part of the message personal, because you can bet that teens will compare them.

Tell teens you have already started next month's book and you're looking forward to hearing what they think about it. If they haven't checked out a copy, remind them to do that.

This will take about a half hour, but it will reward you many times over in increased commitment to book club.

References

Daniels, Harvey. 2001. *Literature Circles: Voice and Choice in Book Clubs & Reading Groups*, 2d ed. Portland, ME: Stenhouse.

Depree, Max. 2004. *Leadership Is an Art*. New York: Currency.

Hunter, Kaye. 2003. "Literature Circles and Book Clubs: Variations on a Theme," *FYI* (Winter). Published online by the School Librarians Association of Victoria (Australia). Available at: http://www.slav.schools.net.au/fhyback/winter20031.htm.

Mills, Bobby, and Nicholas Sparks. 1999. *Wokini: A Lakota Journey to Happiness and Self-Understanding* Carlsbad, CA: Hay House.

Pennac, Daniel. 1999. *Better Than Life*. Portland, ME: Stenhouse Publishers.

Sparks, Nicholas. 2000. *A Walk to Remember*. New York: Warner Books.

8

❖✦❖　❖✦❖　❖✦❖

THE FINE ART AND METICULOUS SCIENCE OF BOOK SELECTION

When time is at a premium, as it always is in teen book clubs, choosing books is a blessing and a curse—a blessing because avid readers enjoy poring over and debating the choices, and a curse because it eats into discussion and activity time. You can't go wrong if you follow these general principles:

1. Keep teens at the center of the selection process.
2. Cast the net wide to generate a broad list of book choices.
3. Narrow the field, creating a short list of four to five books.
4. Stand aside as teens make their choice.

Simply put, teens discover likely candidates, read the dust jacket and a few reviews, rule out the duds, describe each book's fine points to one another, and choose. The whole process can take as little as 10 minutes of club time (when teens do research during the interval between meetings), or up to 30 minutes (when teens do the research and evaluation during club time).

This chapter first describes some shortcuts for selecting books, then walks through the full selection process, and finally touches on the pros and cons of online selection. Encourage teens to experiment with different methods. Over time they'll figure out what works best for them.

BALANCING TIME AND TEEN CHOICE

Book selection can easily eat up all a club's time if teens do it at every meeting. Some teens enjoy that. If your club is all about choosing books to read, ask them if they'd like to become a bookchatters club, as described in chapter 5. But if they'd really rather be reading, offer suggestions for streamlining the process:

Book Selection: What's in It for Teens?

In a teen-centered club, book selection is about taking choice to a higher level. The more teens know about their preferences and dislikes—and the more they know about the universe of what's available—the better informed choices they can make. Book selection helps teen readers choose books better as they:

- Learn more about their personal likes and dislikes
- Expand their reading interests and tastes
- Take a chance on the unknown
- Become their own readers' advisor and learn how to effectively ask a readers' advisor for help
- Recognize what makes a book a dud

And that's not all. Book selection gives teens plenty of practice in leadership skills like speaking to a group, influencing others, negotiating, and building consensus. It serves them well now and gives them practice using a model of informed decision making that will serve them well all their lives.

Take turns: Skip every step in the process and let individuals name the club's next book. Go alphabetically, by birthdays, by random drawing, and so on.

Leave it to chance: Everyone writes their favorite title on a slip of paper. Put them in a bowl and pick one.

Leave it to chance—almost: Do a random drawing (see previous). The teen who recommended that book talks about it, then the club decides whether to read it. No? Draw again.

Pick from the known: Each teen recommends one book they have read. They briefly booktalk it and say why it's a good book club book. Then the group picks one to read. (If a teen recommends a book she hasn't read, don't reject it out of hand. Tell teens if you know the book is a dud, but otherwise why not take a chance?)

Copycat: Go online to find another club's list. Use that as your short list.

Go for the gold: Read your way through the year's award-winning books. Judges have done all the work for you.

Adopt an author: The club chooses an author; then each teen reads any book by that author. Next month, compare the books.

My own top two: When you invite teens to the first meeting, ask them to bring the titles of their two favorite books. Compile their favorites to cast your net wide.

Adult does it: Teens may delegate some or all steps in the process to you. For example, you may create a broad list of books for them to choose from (cast the net wide); or you may create the short list of likely candidates (narrow the field); or you may review and booktalk the

> **Time Matters**
>
> If you do book selection at every meeting, allow two-thirds of club time to respond to books and one-third of club time to choose future reads.
>
> If you choose two (or more) books at once, devote one-third to one-half of one meeting to book selection; then devote all of the following meetings to the books themselves.
>
> It's almost impossible to do all the steps in the book selection process during club time. Teens will let you know how they'd like to divvy up tasks and time—or, if they don't seem to understand that that's an option, you can suggest it.

short list (apply selection criteria) so that all teens have to do is make the final selection. Be aware, however, that the more teens delegate to you, the less teen-centered the process is—and the less invested teens are in the outcome.

Minimize Club Time: Choose Several Books at Once

Some clubs choose two or more books at once. Then they can devote their time to reading. On the one hand, this approach has advantages:

- The club spends less time choosing books, more time discussing them.
- You can structure your marketing around the chosen books. Announcing books months in advance gives time for word of mouth to develop and builds excitement as teens look forward to favorite books.
- You have plenty of time to acquire and distribute books.

On the other hand, as months pass between book selection and reading, teens involved in the initial book selection may drop out of club—and new clubbers may not want to read books that previous clubbers chose. Also, over time, tastes and circumstances change. If too much time elapses between book selection and book reading, teen interests may have moved on.

We recommend teens choose no more than two books at a time. This gives time for word of mouth to build, allows you to time to acquire and distribute the titles, and ensures that choices will reflect current circumstances and members' tastes.

The easiest way to choose several books at once is to have a vote. The winning book appeals to most club members; the runners-up (it is hoped) appeal to teens who didn't vote for the winner.

1. KEEP TEENS AT THE CENTER OF SELECTION

Teens decide how to select books, they carry out or delegate every step in the process, and they bear ultimate responsibility for the selection. That said, teens don't make their selections in a vacuum. You, parents and other adults, and the library itself are in position to influence the club's book selection.

Plan Ahead

If the club chooses it's "next" book two months in advance, you'll have plenty of time to acquire and distribute it. Here's how it works: The club choose its March book in January. During the month of January, you acquire/collect multiple copies of the book. You distribute them at the February meeting. Teens read and come ready to discuss in March.

This works for clubs that choose their books one at a time. For clubs that choose more than one book at a time, you'll need to compress the acquisition/delivery schedule to one week. It works like this: In January, they pick books for February and March. In the week following the January book club you acquire the February book and let teens know it's available. They read it in the remaining three weeks before the next meeting. Meanwhile, you are acquiring the March book, which you make available at the February meeting. With this system, you'll always have one "crash course" in acquisition/delivery alternating with one more leisurely schedule.

If your teens read ebooks, and you have a budget for them, acquisition and distribution become a piece of cake.

You can veto book choices that are not deliverable or that violate library policy (e.g., a school library might disallow interlibrary loan [ILL]). You cannot veto a book based on content unless the veto is tied to library policy (e.g., certain schools might not allow teens to ILL books published by The Hemlock Society).

Teens have the right to challenge your veto. Respond as you would to any book challenge, with documentation and well-reasoned argument. Perhaps teens' challenge will reveal flaws in your thinking, and your veto will fail. More likely the discussion will spark ideas about ways to overcome the library's objections. If your veto stands and teens are adamant about overriding it, they'll have to take discussion of that book elsewhere. It's a tough fact of life that the sponsoring organization gets the final say.

Parents and other adults in teens' lives may challenge a book choice, but their ultimate power of veto is limited to pulling their children from the club or initiating a formal challenge. If that happens, help teens understand that a challenge is simply part of the process. And make sure your library's policy on challenges applies to teen book club selections.

Boldly Go ... Out of the YA Section

The book's classification as children's, young adult, or adult doesn't matter for book discussion. It goes without saying that teens will read up—that is, venture into the adult section. It's less known that teens also enjoy a variety of children's books, from Dr. Seuss to J. K. Rowling, from *Harold and the Purple Crayon* to *Breadwinner*.

2. CAST THE NET WIDE

This step can be done in 10 minutes or less, although some teens never want to quit.
One of the things book club does best is throw open the door to the unknown, from the outer reaches of the universe to the deepest recesses of the human mind. Casting the net wide is how that open-endedness begins. Capitalize on their proclivity to experiment and to explore the unknown by encouraging them to make risky reading choices. At this stage of the game it's all about possibilities. Here are some ideas for getting started:

Listen: Ask teens "What are you reading?" "What's in your backpack?" "What have you been wanting to read?" Don't limit yourself to book club members; ask every teen you encounter. During club meetings, offer up the more unusual ideas.

Inundate them with booklists. The world is filled with booklists on every subject imaginable. To help teens generate lots of ideas, inundate them with suggestions. Pull from Diana Tixier Herald's *Teen Genreflecting,* 2d ed.; ALA's *Best Books for Young Adults,* 2d ed.; YALSA's Quick Picks list; and other lists you'll find on the Web or in YA bibliographies (see "YA Books Mentioned in the Chapter" and "A Sampling of Sources for Book List Ideas: Bibliographies, Book Lists, and Reviews"). For lists tailored to your type of club, see chapter 4, which includes book lists for 12 types of book club.

Go shopping! Send teens to the stacks for books they have never read. Give them 10 minutes to bring back likely candidates. This bumps up variety and provides much-needed physical activity for this active age group.

Do it with food: Cover a large table with a paper tablecloth, toss out colored pens, and ask teens to brainstorm every book they've ever wanted to read. Meanwhile, set out the food.

Research: Go online to find favorites of teens in other parts of the country or world. Research teens' picks awards. Ask professional colleagues at the ALA listserv yalsa-bk and at local schools and libraries what their teens have been reading.

Keeping Track of All Those Books

Record teens' picks in The List, a record created just for this purpose. The List can be a scrapbook, highly decorated journal, loose-leaf notebook, or digital file. Every month a different teen plays Keeper of the List, updating The List with new favorites.

With a little imagination, you'll find many uses for The List for book selection, promotion, and marketing. Chapter 6 offers some suggestions.

> **Tip!**
>
> Teens may look to you to kick-start the process. Don't do it. Suggest ways they can get started, but let them have the first word. You can help by tossing out titles, but don't take the lead.

Think outside the novel: Encourage teens to consider short stories, folk tales, poetry, plays and screenplays, picture books, humor collections, graphic novels, and nonfiction (even magazine articles). If the book club label constrains teens' choices, change the label.

Go for the gold: Mine lists of award-winning books. Find teen picks from other countries, other decades. And don't forget the runners-up, many of which have as much staying power as the winners.

3. NARROW THE FIELD

This is a two-step process. Explore what makes a book good for book club (10 minutes), then test a handful of favorite titles against those criteria (20–30 minutes).

Talk to teens about selection criteria and how we use them to evaluate books. Then ask teens what makes a book good for book club. Ask them to brainstorm book club selection criteria. Feel free to add your two cents if teens overlook obvious criteria, like feasibility (availability, length, reading level). Finally, ask them to choose two or three of the most important criteria for book club books. Three key selection criteria are:

- **Deliverable:** Every library has its own capabilities in terms of time, budget, ILL, and the lengths it is willing to go to cater to special groups like teens and book clubs. As teens narrow their choices, keep in mind:
  - Are multiple copies readily available? Are they available in paperback or through ILL?
  - Can I buy used copies? Will my budget cover the cost? Can I get a funding? Might teens be willing and able to purchase their own books?
  - Does my work schedule allow time for me to collect and distribute copies? Can I distribute copies quickly enough that teens will have enough time to read it?
  - Will providing this book violate any library policies?
- **Engaging and wide ranging:** YA materials should "reflect young adult interests and concerns about the world and their place in it" ("Teen Edition"). In short: identity, connection, and meaning. The more immediately and intimately a book engages teens on these levels, the better. This is true whether the book deals with the themes overtly (*Luna*), subtly (any of *The Lord of the Rings trilogy*), or to all appearances, not at all (*Spiders in the Hairdo: Modern Urban Legends*). Although no single book may appeal to every reader in the club, the *range* of choices should offer something for everyone.

- **Well-written and discussable:** The characteristics that define *well-written* are the very things that make a book discussable. The Washington Center for the Book at The Seattle Public Library puts it this way: "Good books for discussion have three-dimensional characters who are forced to make difficult choices, under difficult situations, whose behavior sometimes make sense and sometimes doesn't. . . . Good book discussion books present the author's view of an important truth and sometimes send a message to the reader."

What Makes for a *Bad* Book Club Book?

Book club gurus often ban formulaic, plot-driven books. These types of books present the world in simplistic terms, and the authors make free use of stereotypes and cultural assumptions to move the plot along. As a result, conventional wisdom says, there is nothing to discuss.

We disagree. To spark a lively discussion, zero in on the stereotypes and assumptions. Ask: Is the author right? Is the author being fair? What message is the author trying to sneak into your head? What does he or she leave unsaid? What are the assumptions? Some books make this ridiculously easy: Think Harlequin romance. But you can find stereotypes and unspoken assumptions among well-written, thoughtful novels as well.

Many teens love formulaic, plot-driven books. Book club needn't deny them their favorites. Question those caricatures, challenge the dominant paradigms, explore issues of identity and meaning—and you've just turned a bad book club book into a star.

Choose a Few Likely Candidates for Your Short List

You've cast your net wide; now it's time to narrow the field. Each teen (or pair of teens) simply chooses a book that seems good for book club. Teens evaluate the book in light of the book club criteria they just named, discarding any that don't make the grade.

Most book club criteria boil down to: Do you find the book intriguing? Do you think other people will? Try to find books with broad appeal, or clubbers simply may skip the next meeting (and the next…and the next). That said, if an occasional book selection misses the mark, it's not the end of the world. Good discussions can occur when there are strong differences of opinion. Will the book give the club something interesting to talk about?

The following reproducible ranking form helps teens answer these questions. Some will judge the book for themselves. Others will check out the blurbs and reviews on Amazon.com, Teen Matrix, and other sites (see "A Sampling of Sources for Book List Ideas: Bibliographies, Book Lists, and Reviews" at the end of this chapter). If teens need a place to start Web research, it's easy enough to pull together some links and post them on the book club Web site.

IS THIS A GOOD BOOK CLUB BOOK? YOU BE THE JUDGE!

1. **Do you like the book?**

   Judge the book by its cover.

   What does the front cover tell you? How about the back cover? The jacket flaps?

   Publishers work hard on that cover copy to make you feel something about the book, not just to tell you about the plot. Does the cover make you want to read the book?

   First impressions are the ones that last

   Read a few lines on random pages. Are you intrigued?

   Fan through the pages of the book. Do you like the way it looks?

   Ask around

   Read a review of the book online. Does the book seem to measure up to its first impression? Are you hooked?

   Question:
   Would you read this book? Yes __ Maybe __ No __

2. **What's the book *really* about?**

   Read the book cover again. Does the author have something to say? What makes you think so? Question: Is what the author has to say interesting, important, or controversial?

   Question:
   Does the book give you anything to think about? Yes __ Maybe __ No __

3. **Does the book give you anything to talk about?**

   Based on the little bit you know about this book, do you think you would want to talk about it in book club?

   Question:
   Name up to three things you could talk about in book club after you read this book.

   Scoring:

   Did you answer any question "No" or "Maybe"? The book is a book club reject, but it might still be good for reading on your own

   How many things could you name in question 3? If you could name at least one, the book is good for book club!

Teens can evaluate books during club meetings or on their own between meetings. If they're doing it during club time, be sure to reserve enough computers to go around. Schedule 20 minutes for getting to the computers, finding the info, completing ranking forms, and coming back together.

There's a tendency for people to use research to affirm their choices rather than evaluate them. This is especially true for "good kids" who want to perform well. You can short-circuit that thinking. Remind teens they're just making a quick pick to start; they're judging the book by its cover, more or less. Now they're going to find out if the book measures up. Help teens understand that "getting it right" means finding the truth.

Break Out of Your Comfort Zones

Daunted by the number of choices, teens may turn to what's comfortable. If you find teens choosing only safe reads (e.g., old favorites or familiar genres) or books that are very similar to one another (e.g., all female authors, all contemporary or Western settings), pick out a few unusual books to champion. Suggest teens try these more unusual books, and feel free to passionately express your views about the value of reading broadly . . . but let teens make the final decision.

Compare Results in Person or Online

Here's where those ranking sheets come in handy. After teens research their book, they can share the results in person during the book club meeting, or online between club meetings.

- **During a meeting:** Teens take turns presenting their results, referring to their ranking sheets. Listeners make notes. After everyone has their say, spread the ranking sheets out so teens can take a few minutes to remind themselves what was said.
- **Online:** Teens email the ranking sheets to you. You post them on the club's Web page. Doing it all online with tight deadlines, a touch of competitiveness, and plenty of IM ("I just heard from Shauntay. Looks like *Gossip Girl* is out! How about your book, *The Sparrow*—in or out?") keeps energy flowing. Encourage teens to check out one another's ranking sheets and IM about the books, so everyone is ready to choose at the next club meeting.

CHOOSING AT LAST!

Allow 5–10 minutes for teens to talk about the choices. They may easily come to consensus. If not, allow 1 minute to vote or as many as 30 minutes to come to consensus.

By this time everyone is impatient to get on with reading. If teens were ruthless about eliminating the duds, then every choice will be a good one, even if made hastily.

Start by giving everyone a chance to *briefly* share their views. Keep the conversation narrowly focused on why the book is good for book club. Then choose.

Take a vote: Voting is simple, quick, and familiar, but it has drawbacks. Teens can follow their immediate, knee-jerk reactions (or blindly follow a friend's lead) without thinking about or explaining their choice. And, voting fails to promote the essential book club goal of building connections. Teens vote in isolation, and there's no clear distinction between voting for/against a book and for/against fellow clubbers. Voting doesn't connect winners in any meaningful way, and it leaves losers out in the cold. If winners aren't truly hot on the choices voted upon, then winning the vote isn't sufficient motivation to read and return to book club. As for losers: without connection to fellow clubbers, without interest in the book selected, and feeling as if they have no voice, they have no reason to return to book club.

Come to consensus: Everyone agrees on the chosen book. Consensus means that teens agree they can live with the chosen book, even if it's not their first choice. Consensus embodies the book club value of exploration over conquest, encourages discussion, and strengthens bonds among clubbers. As teens share their ideas and preferences, the emphasis moves away from dominating the decision, toward contributing to the discussion. They get to know one another better, and they become intrigued by books' possibilities. In short, they connect—with one another and the book. The drawback? Coming to consensus takes time. It works best when the short list has no more than three titles, teens are mature enough to avoid insisting on having their own way, and there is ample time for discussion (even if that means taking it online or tabling it to the next meeting).

Go your own way: If, after a reasonable amount of time, teens remain widely divided on a particular title, help them step back from the selection process, rethink their assumptions, and brainstorm alternatives. Don't let them stop at their first thoughts; probe and leave silence so they can think. Must they choose only one book? Should they scrap the most contentious titles and consider others? Should the club become bookchatters for the next meeting only? Would one person from each camp be willing to read the title from the opposite camp and report back to the group? Would the group consider reading both books in one month? Could those who like each book read it, and then compare them at the next meeting? Teens might be surprised at the connections between two seemingly unlike books!

A final thought: It's too much to expect that everyone will share the same level of enthusiasm for a book. But it's important to work hard to find a book that everyone can minimally agree on. Teens do enough required reading already; they come to book club to read for pleasure. That's the promise of book club. When book clubs break that promise, they fail.

Why Collaborate in Person when You Can Do It Online?

With access to a few bookie Web sites and Instant Messaging or a moderated chat, teens can perform the entire book selection process online. What's good about this?

- Going online, you go where teens are. You may attract readers that your marketing efforts would otherwise miss.
- Online selection gives you more time for discussion and activities during meetings.
- Chatting online builds bonds among teens. (However, these bonds may not translate into attendance at meetings.)
- Teens may be more likely to participate online because there are fewer barriers to commitment and it's easy to disengage if they want to.
- Teens can access information on the fly without disengaging from the online chat.
- Having established the online component, you can use it for all book club purposes (e.g., recruiting; sending thank-you notes or reminders of upcoming events).

In short, everything that's good about online collaboration applies here. However, the same issues that plague all online collaborations present themselves:

- Some teens lack access to the Internet.
- Commitment online doesn't translate to commitment in person. Teens may participate in online book selection because it's interesting but with no intention of attending the club. These half-outsiders may unduly influence the selection process——but they are also prime targets for your future recruiting efforts.
- Online discussions are more difficult to facilitate than face-to-face ones. For example, you have no clues from body language.
- Online-only may undermine your purpose of hosting a teen book club, if you're trying to get teens into the library.

CONCLUSION

Choosing books is one of the great joys and frustrations of book club. It can swallow clubbers' time and energy, leaving them little opportunity to engage with the book or with one another. Unless your clubbers prefer book selection to discussion and other activities, help them streamline book selection for the club's reads—and promise to help them find other good books to read on their own!

References

Chicago Public Library. n.d. "Teen Edition: The Collection." Folder produced to introduce the YA collection.

Washington Center for the Book at the Seattle Public Library. n.d. "Starting a Book Club." Available at: http://www.spl.org/default.asp?pageID=collection_discussiongroup.

YA Books Mentioned in this Chapter

Breadwinner. Deborah Ellis. Toronto: Groundwood Books, 2001.

Harold and the Purple Crayon. Crockett Johnson. New York: HarperTrophy, 1981.

Luna. Julie Ann Peters. New York: Little, Brown, 2004. No paperback as of this writing, but reprints may be available as you read this.

Soldier's Heart. Gary Paulsen. New York: Laurel Leaf, 2000.

Spiders in the Hairdo: Modern Urban Legends. David Holt, et al. Little Rock, AR: August House Publishers, 1999.)

The Sparrow. Mary Doria Russell. (New York: Ballantine Books, 2004.)

Lord of the Rings Trilogy. J.R.R. Tolkein. Includes: *The Fellowship of the Ring, The Two Towers, and The Return of the King.*

A Sampling of Sources for Book List Ideas: Bibliographies, Book Lists, and Reviews

Bibliographies

Carter, Betty, Sally Estes and Linda Waddle. *Best Books for Young Adults.* 2d ed. Published in association with Young Adult Library Services Association. Chicago: American Library Association, 2000.

Gillespie, John T. and Catherine Barr. *Best Books for High School Readers.* Westport, CT: Libraries Unlimited, 2004.

——. *Best Books for Middle and Junior High Readers.* Westport, CT: Libraries Unlimited, 2004,

Herald, Diana Tixier. *Teen Genreflecting: A Guide to Reading Interests.* 2d ed. Westport, CT: Libraries Unlimited, 2003.

Online Booklists and Reviews

Amazon.com

Favorite Teenage Angst Books: http://www.grouchy.com/angst/

Teen Matrix, http://www.teenmatrix.org/books.htm

Teen Reads: teenreads.com

9

♦✖◊   ♦✖◊   ♦✖◊

BEFORE WE OPEN OUR MOUTHS: PREPARING FOR BOOK DISCUSSION

Every type of book club puts a different spin on discussion. Service learning clubs use the book as a jumping-off point to explore social issues. Book/movie clubs compare the effectiveness of the storytelling as told in various media. A readers-into-leaders club might use role-play instead of discussion to get inside character's heads. Whatever type of club you have, they all connect around books, and they preparation generally involves:

- Reading the book for discussion
- Researching the author and the book
- Creating questions or activities that explore the book and spark a lively exchange of ideas

Who does all that? You are already expending time and energy on managerial tasks like acquiring books, lining up speakers, promotion, evaluation, and so forth. It doesn't leave much time to research the author, collect book reviews, and create scintillating discussion questions. The good news is that you can (gradually) turn those tasks over to teens. As you model behavior, teach skills, and support teens in their learning, you build a cadre of experienced teens who can take over these tasks for you. Reward them with lots of attention, praise, and one-on-one time, and their confidence and enthusiasm will grow.

READING FOR BOOK CLUB

Reading for discussion is a different experience than reading for pleasure. When we read for pleasure, we go one-on-one with the book. Whether we passively consume it or grapple with every nuance, the reading experience is between us and the book. When we read for discussion, the whole book club joins the party. This calls for some serious multitasking. While one part of the mind just wants to become one with the book, the other part is self-consciously taking notes and anticipating what other people might think and say about the book—and about our opinion of it.

Reading for discussion is reading *as* reading. When we're moved, we notice what caused our reaction. Likewise when we snort in derision. We pause at unusual turns of phrase. We question. We think. And we jot down what's important, because we know that book club discussion is coming and we want to remember these things!

Most book clubbers vacillate between the two types of reading, and most books allow us to do so. Ann Brashare's *The Sisterhood of the Traveling Pants* doubles as a fun summer read and a thought-provoking exploration of teen girls' hearts. From *A Tale of Two Cities* to *Lord of the Flies*, classics are rollicking good stories when read simply for entertainment. And many rollicking good stories, like *Hoot*, can make us stop and think about who we are and our place in the world.

How to Read for Discussion

Clearly, discussions that explore ideas require careful reading. These types of discussions ask teens to make connections among the book, their lives, and the world. They allow for challenge and debate, and they require teens to back up their ideas and opinions with evidence from the book. But even with these greater expectations, book club is still all about reading for pleasure. Following is a reproducible handout for teens that offers some ideas of things to look for while reading for thoughtful discussion.

> **Tip!**
>
> When you're teaching teens to read for discussion, remember that many teens' (males, in particular) interests tend toward the concrete and informational. Make it clear that those kinds of insights and interests are as valuable as conceptual and emotional insights. One can build on the other to create greater understanding.

How to Read for Bookchatting

Bookchatting clubs don't discuss books so much as share them. What's *bookchat*? It's a phrase we coined as an alternative to *booktalking*. Booktalks describe or summarize a book in a way that makes people drool for it. They're carefully written sales pitches, polished and read or memorized. Bookchat is more casual, less sales-oriented: I'm simply telling you about a book I liked. Both share the cardinal rule: Don't give away the ending!

Bookchat is part book summary, part critique, and part recommendation. Preparation is easy: enjoy the book! To help teens organize their bookchats, remind them of a few basic things people generally like to know about a book. (Following is a reproducible teens can use to structure their chat.) Model good bookchatting by talking about the books you enjoy. Then sit back and let the teen facilitator gently nudge the long-talkers when their chats turn into lectures.

HOW TO READ A BOOK FOR DISCUSSION

While You Read

Use sticky notes to flag passages that

- you like or dislike
- are unclear
- don't seem to fit or make sense
- describe troubling events
- include things that seem to be symbols
- raise questions or interesting ideas
- support your opinions and ideas

Write reminders on the flags: ☺, ☹, HA! ⚲ It slows down your reading, but it helps later on—you won't lose your chance to speak at book club because you can't find the page you're looking for. Here are some things you might want to flag. Choose the ones that appeal to you.

- **Chase down the Big Idea.** Authors almost always have a message on their minds: Cheaters never prosper, revenge is sweet, love conquers all, might makes right, money can't buy happiness. . . . Find out what the author harps on, and flag clues that hint at the Big Idea. Do you agree with the author's Big Idea?
- **Get out of your head and into the book.** "Get out of your head" means don't assume that what you take for granted is right. See the world from the characters' points of view and figure out why they speak, think, or act the way they do. Does what they do make sense for them, even if it doesn't make sense for you?
- **Ask hard questions.** Think *how* and *why.* Think up questions you can't answer or that don't have one right answer. Flag the passages that made you think of those questions, and flag passages that give clues to the answers.
- **Watch yourself.** Keep track of your own reactions as you read. Flag passages that set you off. Think about what it is that sparks your reaction. Look for clues that tell you whether the author did that on purpose.
- **Find the author behind the book.** Look at some of the literary aspects of the book, like language and structure. Is the author a poet? a smart aleck? Flag passages where the language really stands out. Think about whether the author chose the best "tone of voice" for the book. Notice whether the author does anything unusual, like start every chapter with quotes or leave a mystery unsolved. Take a guess as to why he or she did that. Flag passages with phrases you like. Also flag passages that show or hint at why the author wrote the book the way he or she did.

- **Crack the code.** Symbolism is like a secret code. You might suspect something is a symbol without knowing what it means. Flag things that seem to be symbols. Then at book club, try to figure out what they mean. Some symbols have standard meanings—for example, red rose = love. Others have several meanings: A bird in flight symbolizes freedom and death (the soul taking flight). Sometimes an author creates a unique symbol, and the book itself gives you the clues you need to figure out what the symbol means. Sometimes a whole scene has a double meaning, like the train wreck at the beginning of Marilynne Robinson's *Housekeeping*.

After You Finish

- Reread the first chapter. Authors love planting clues; you'll be amazed what you see now that you know the end. (If you read the whole book again, you'll find all kinds of things you missed the first time through, including ironies, recurring ideas or images, and the way plots and subplots mirror or play off one another.)
- When you finish reading each day, write down a word or thought that comes immediately to mind. It might be "A Doberman could bite off a finger, but it wouldn't swallow it" or an outstanding word like *susurrus*.
- Pick your number-one favorite passage and write an X on that flag. You might get a chance to read it aloud at book club.
- Go back through your flags and pick out three questions or opinions to toss out in book club discussion. (Make sure you have marked the passages that support your opinion or answer your question.)

CREATE A FASCINATING BOOKCHAT!

While You Read

Flag passages that jump out at you—good or bad. It might be just one funny phrase or a half page of dialogue. Flag all you like.

After You Finish

- Go back through your flags and choose your favorite passage to read aloud at book club.
- Choose a few ideas from the following list of things to include in your bookchat.
- Make a few notes: You don't need to write down everything you want to say, just a few notes to glance at while you're talking.

What to Include in Your Bookchat

The best bookchats give it straight: What happened in the book and why you liked it. Here are things people usually like to know about a book. Mix and match these ideas to create a one-of-a-kind bookchat. You won't have much time, so just pick a few.

- What did you like about this book?
- No book is perfect. What didn't you like?
- What kind of book is it? Mystery, science fiction, war story, girlfriends story? Is it part of a series?
- In 25 words or fewer, what happens?
- What's the Big Idea? Many authors write because they have a message to get out. Others write for pure entertainment. Did you get a message?
- Who else would like this book? Who should *not* read it?
- Finish this sentence: If you liked this book, you'd also like _____.
- Rate the book from 1 to 10 and tell why.
- If you read the book because someone else in the group recommended it, thank that person. Compare what you like about the book to what the other person said they liked.

Warning: Don't give away too much of the plot! Tell what happens in the first few chapters and then offer a teaser: You have to read the rest of the book to find out if Tiffany escapes!

Uh-oh

It happens: The book you read was lousy. What now? Talking about a lousy book can be a lot of fun. Tell why you didn't like it and read some passages that show how truly awful it is.

Don't be surprised if someone in the group loves the book—including the same things you can't stand! It happens all the time.

From *The Teen-Centered Book Club: Readers into Leaders* by Bonnie Kunzel and Constance Hardesty. Westport, CT: Libraries Unlimited. Copyright © 2006.

What If Clubbers Can't Stand the Book?

No matter how popular the title or how well a book is reviewed, it's likely that someone is going to dislike the book that's been chosen for discussion. That's OK. Controversy makes for great discussions, and teens like everyone else, like to share their distaste.

If teens just can't stand a book—can't even finish it—encourage them to come to book club anyway, to talk about what they don't like. In this chapter you'll find a reproducible handout titled "How to Read a Book You Hate" you can give to teens early on, so they'll have it on hand when they encounter a book they just can't tolerate.

Meanwhile, a subversive dynamic goes to work: The act of discussing the book builds a sense of connection to it, and hearing what others liked often creates new paths into the book. Sometimes, teens who felt cool or cold toward a book will give it another look after book club.

RESEARCHING THE AUTHOR AND BOOK

Many book clubs start each discussion with a minilecture on the author and the book, including:

- Biographical information
- Book reviews and critiques
- Information about setting, time period, and historical characters or events
- If relevant, the aftermath of the book's publication

Chances are, you'll need to teach teens to do the kind of research that yields interesting and useful info-nuggets, and you'll need to support them as they complete and present their research. If different teens volunteer for the research job each month, you'll be working with new "trainees" every month. This is a great opportunity to pry teens away from Google, help them hone their information literacy skills, and introduce them to the wonderful worlds of subscription databases and standard research tools. It's also a time commitment. Track the time you spend; you'll use the figures later in documenting the value of book club and painting a realistic picture of the time it takes to implement.

You may find yourself, by choice or by default, the designated researcher for your club. There are many reasons why this happens, not the least of which is that teens are as pressed for time as the rest of us are. They may not have the time to do the research—and you may not have the time to help them each month. If you enjoy doing the research and the group prefers that you do it, you may feel there's no harm in accepting the job. Avoid the temptation! At most, you might perform the job for a few months to demonstrate its value. Then it's up to the teens to volunteer or go without (and discover whether the discussion actually suffers).

Researching the Author

Some facilitators believe author background can contribute much to one's understanding of a book. Interesting facts about how the author comes up with ideas, how long the book took to write, and so forth can pique interest and add depth to discussion. And it's interesting if you can find an interview (usually

HOW TO READ A BOOK YOU HATE

Make a list of all the things that annoy you. If you can clearly say what you don't like about the book, then you can start a truly interesting discussion. Flagging the parts you don't like is one way to enjoy a book. Here are some ideas of things to flag:

- The page when you first knew that you would never enjoy this book
- An especially horrible passage to read aloud at book club
- The boring parts
- The unrealistic parts
- Passages that show what you don't like about the characters
- Examples of things that don't fit or happen for no apparent reason
- Parts that make you mad, that you disagree with, or that offend you
- Passages where you feel the author talks down to you

Ask yourself…

- Is the book dishonest? Do you get the idea the author doesn't know what he is talking about? or sugarcoats difficult issues? or oversimplifies the solutions? Does she beat you over the head with the Big Idea?
- Is the book too difficult to follow? Sometimes, it seems as if authors are just showing off. If you think that's the case, flag passages in the book so you can bring them up the book club meeting.
- Has the author written other books you liked? Have you read other books that are like this one, but they were better? What is the difference between those books in this one?

Here are two ideas for turning a book you don't like into a book you can tolerate:

1. See the movie. It might fill in some blanks or untangle a confusing plot. If it's a good book, seeing the movie won't ruin the story.
2. If the book is just boring and irrelevant to your life, try reading an article on the Internet to find out why the author wrote the book or to hear about someone who lived through what the book characters are going through. It might make the story more interesting.

---

published shortly after the book was published) in which the author talks about the book's meaning or the reason for writing it.

Others feel that books stand on their own merit. Folks in this camp would say that unless the authors' life experiences have a direct bearing on their books (or vice versa), their life stories are superfluous to discussion of the book itself.

Which way to go? Ask teens. If they generally find author information interesting and useful, then by all means let them dig it up. *Contemporary Authors* and *Popular Young Adult Authors* are great resources for this, as are authors' Web sites. (Be aware that authors' Web sites are naturally biased, since their goal is to market the author.) The following reproducible handout for teens offers tips for researching an author.

Since readers often interpret books differently from authors, sharing the author's viewpoint with the group is almost like adding another member to the discussion. Some online book clubs take an extra step and invite the author to participate. A great example is Blogger Book Club, hosted by Roselle Library Kids' World (www.roselle.lib.il.us). You can invite authors to participate in your book club three ways: invite local authors, schedule out-of-town authors to visit book club when they are in town for other purposes, or connect with them via Web conference or audio conference. Even a direct phone call over speakerphone could bring an author into a small book club.

A good time to offer fascinating facts about the author is when you are (or a teen is) introducing the next month's book. Teens enjoy celebrity gossip as much as anyone, and dangling bits of juicy info before them is guaranteed to pique their interest.

Researching the Book

The book's setting in place and time, historical characters or events, and other elements can pique teens' interest when introducing a book. But that's only part of the picture. Authors often assume that readers have some prior knowledge about a setting, time period, or historic event. Making sure that your teens have that knowledge before they read the book enhances their pleasure and improves the odds they'll finish the book. Later, as they discuss the book you (or a teen) can monitor the conversation to be sure the background information doesn't become forgotten or distorted, and can offer more bits of interesting, relevant information.

Many YA novels are "issue" novels that deal with topics from war to gossip. In some cases it's impossible to fully appreciate the story and the characters' motivations and actions without understanding the world in which they're operating. Of course, it's the author's job to give readers enough sense of that world so that they can follow the story. But if more information would enrich teens' understanding of the characters, add a deeper dimension to the discussion or raise new perspectives—or if teens simply develop an interest in the larger social issue—you can help them learn more using the whole range of nonfiction resources available, from census statistics to online museum collections.

The following handout for teens offers tips for researching a book.

HOW TO RESEARCH AN AUTHOR

Read a brief bio of the author. Look for anything related to the book:

Why did the author write it?
Is there a connection between the author's life and the book? Anything in common (e.g., hometown, job, family situation, experience)?

Find some odd facts or trivia about the author.

Good places to start author research:

The back of the book—most books have a brief bio
The author's or publisher's Web site
Databases or reference books like *Contemporary Authors* (1962–present), *100 Most Popular Young Adult Authors* (Drew 1996), and *100 More Popular Young Adult Authors* (Drew 2002)
Web sites featuring author interviews like teenreads.com

If your research doesn't unearth any fascinating facts, email the author (via the Web site or through the publisher) and ask!

How to Use Your Author Research

- When the book is first introduced, tell the club something that will create interest in the book. It may be something to look for (the author said he exactly describes the seventh game of the 1941 World Series) or something interesting to think about (Stephen King said he wants to write books that give his readers the same feeling Stephen had when his mother told him about a time she bit a live moth in two).
- During the discussion, listen for places where it might be helpful or interesting to drop in some info about the author. For example, if people get stuck trying to figure out the Big Idea, you can tell them what the author said about why he or she wrote the book.

From *The Teen-Centered Book Club: Readers into Leaders* by Bonnie Kunzel and Constance Hardesty. Westport, CT: Libraries Unlimited. Copyright © 2006.

Views of the Book

Many book clubs read book reviews aloud before the discussion begins. As a matter of routine, that seems to work against the group's exploration and interpretation of the book. It never hurts to have a few insightful or provocative book reviews on hand to jog teens' thinking when they get stuck, or—after the discussion is well underway—to compare teens' thinking to the pros' thinking. But choose carefully. The standard review format (plot summary, comparison to other works, analysis of the author's competence) aren't sufficiently open-ended to spark lively discussion.

Share Research One Drop at a Time

After teens go to the effort to research an author or book, it's tempting to use all the info they find. Encourage them to be selective. A 10-minute info-dump at the beginning of the session may deplete energy that has been building for the discussion. Dropping in useful facts and insights as the conversation progresses is more effective.

CREATING QUESTIONS THAT SPARK SCINTILLATING DISCUSSIONS

It's easy to obsess over preparing for book club. The truth is, it's amazing how few questions you need to carry the day. That's because the really good questions—simple, straightforward queries that show genuine interest and push teens' talk buttons—spark a frenzy of free-association and creative conversation that meanders down a dozen different directions before exhausting itself.

Nevertheless, the club needs a place to start and teens need help creating provocative questions. So, what sorts of questions work best for book club, and where do they come from?

Standard Questions

Some book clubs run through a list of predetermined questions at each meeting. These questions usually address general literary elements—plot, character, setting, and so on. We don't recommend this approach. First, because general questions about literary elements are not likely to interest teens. Second, because the best questions specifically target the book in hand.

On the other hand, knowing what to expect can prove useful. Teens can anticipate the questions and develop answers as they read. They can mull over their answers and practice what they'll say. Even if they don't consciously think through the questions, their subconscious minds will be hard at work. We hope, of course, that all this ruminating will yield deeper answers than a spontaneous question-and-answer session does.

To help teens warm up for discussions, create three or four general questions that speak to their interests. Then stand back as the conversation takes off.

HOW TO RESEARCH A BOOK

Researching a book in its entirety is time-consuming and not really necessary. So how do you narrow it down?

Pick out one or two things that interest *you* and go for it. If nothing jumps out at you, try one of these:

Name one thing in this book that really caught your attention.
Name one thing that seems odd or unbelievable.
Name the most realistic thing about the book.
Name something the characters do that doesn't make sense.

If the content of the book doesn't grab you, look for some things about the book itself that are interesting, such as:

When was it published?
How many copies sold? Was it a best-seller?
Did critics hate it? Love it? ignore it?
Has it ever been banned?

Finding the Answers

Take the thing you just named and turn it into a question. Here's an example from the book *Weetzie Bat* by Francesca Lia Block.

> Weetzie Bat liked to eat cheese and bean and hot dog and pastrami burritos from Oki Dogs. Was that for real?

Figure out what you need to know to answer your question. Break it down into a series of smaller questions. This is your "research problem."

Is there a place called Oki Dogs in Los Angeles?
Was there ever a place called Oki Dogs in Los Angeles?
Does it or did it serve cheese and bean and hot dog and pastrami burritos?

Now, before you dive into databases or bookshelves, ask the librarian to look over your research problem. Why? Because an incomplete or misworded question will send you off in the wrong direction. Once you know you're on the right track, ask the librarian to point you in the direction of resources—databases, books, magazines, and so on—that will give you the best answers fastest.

Tip!

When it comes to research, think outside the library. The real questions about those cheese and bean and hot dog and pastrami burritos might be: What do they taste like? and If you ate one, could you keep it down? Make a cheese and bean and hot dog and pastrami burrito. Bring it to book club and see who's brave enough to try it.

From *The Teen-Centered Book Club: Readers into Leaders* by Bonnie Kunzel and Constance Hardesty. Westport, CT: Libraries Unlimited. Copyright © 2006.

> ### Great Questions Spring Directly from the Book
>
> The best questions arise straight from the book itself. They are so specific they can't be used with any other book. And, as always, they speak directly to teens' concerns about identity, meaning, and connection. Here are a few examples:
>
> For *Too Good to Be True: The Colossal Book of Urban Legends:*
>
> What kind of person starts an urban legend? Would you ever pass on one of these stories, just for fun, even if you knew it wasn't true? What's the difference between an urban legend and gossip? Would you ever pass on a lie about a person, just for fun? Would it make a difference if you knew the person?
>
> For *Running Out of Time:*
>
> At the beginning of the book, Jessie is trapped in cultural assumptions—that is, she assumes the whole world is like the place she lives. What assumptions do you live under? Do you and your family share the same set of assumptions? Do you share assumptions with your peer group? We live in a country that believes in freedom. If you're bound by all these assumptions, how free are you, really?
>
> These questions encourage readers to answer from their own life experiences and viewpoints. We often define good discussion questions as open-ended and leave it at that. These questions show that the initial open-ended question is just the kickoff. The best discussion question may not be one question at all, but a series of questions that build logically on one another.

Bad Question Makeover

If it's important to avoid rote questions about plot, setting, theme, character, and other literary or stylistic elements, what are you supposed to talk about? Do you abandon the book as literature? Is that even possible?

No. It's safe to assume that the teens in your club *want* to talk about the books they read—that's the immediate reason they joined the club. They *like* character, plot, and setting. They *love* theme. But they want to break out of the confines of schoolish thought, to move beyond identification and analysis. They want to ruminate, imagine, and feel—or, more accurately, they want to express the feelings that saturate their every waking moment. They want to talk about character, setting, plot, and theme in terms of their lives and the choices and situations they face. Very often, whatever the ostensible topic, they will talk about the issues that drive them: identity, meaning, and connection.

The trick is to frame and augment questions about the book so that teens can respond from their whole selves, their hearts as well as their minds, their emotions, intuition, and imagination as well as their understanding. The good news is, these types of questions occur naturally—more naturally than lit-analysis type questions. The bad news is, they're harder to put into words. Some makeover questions might be:

Not so good: Describe the circumstances surrounding each appearance of the apparition. (*Cliff's Notes, Turn of the Screw*)

Made over: Have you ever seen an apparition? What was it like? How did your experience compare to the governess's?

Not so good: *The Mists of Avalon* revolves around a number of dualities: male/female, Christianity/druidism, duty/desire. How are these dualities represented in the book? Can you think of others that were presented? (Reading Group Guides.com)

Made over: Before teens read the book, explain to them what dualities are, giving male/female and duty/desire as two examples. Give them adhesive notes and ask them to flag passages where striking dualities are at play. During discussion, ask, What are the most striking dualities you found in the book? Do you have any of those same dualities in your life? Let's take just one duality: duty and desire. If the characters in the book handled that the same way you do, how would the book have turned out? Now bring it home: If you handled duty and desire the way characters in the book do, how would your life be different? Is duality good?

No makeover needed: Define what you think *normal* means. Is everyone normal? Is normal the best way to be? Is normal the same for everyone? Who gets to decide?

Can't improve that one. Like most of the questions at the back of *Define "Normal"*, it's a terrific discussion-starter.

Who Should Make Up the Questions?

It's best when teens make up discussion questions. But feel free to ask questions when you are honestly curious about what club members think of some aspect of the book or you are confused by the book or find it impossible to take seriously. Some facilitators like to have a few open-ended questions or topics on hand, just in case the teens go into the discussion doldrums; our view is that, with judicious prompting or a few minutes of silence, teens will generate new, unexpected questions. Most people like to fill silence. If you prompt teens, then let the silence grow, you may hear some amazing responses. You might say, for example, "If you could ask Sabriel one thing, what would you ask?" "If you could ask Garth Nix one thing, what would it be?" "If you were a detective or an investigative news reporter, what would you ask?" You could also repeat a recent provocative question and ask, "What's the next logical question?"

How to Write Great Questions for Discussion

To help teens create good discussion questions, do a mini lesson during book club. Start by handing out copies of the "Top Tips" handout and briefly touching on what makes a good book club question. Follow up with group brainstorming for up to 15 minutes. The longer time frame allows teens to get past their first thoughts into the meaty ones. If teens need help getting started, throw out a creative question or two by way of example. When the brainstorming sessions starts, though, resist the temptation to fill pockets of silence. If you let the silence stand, someone will feel compelled to fill it, and the wheels will begin spinning again.

TOP TIPS AND TRICKS FOR CREATING DISCUSSION QUESTIONS

- Don't ask anything a teacher would ask.
- If you think better with a partner, get a partner.
- Skip the yes or no questions. Start with *why* and *how* instead of *who, what,* or *when.*
- Keep your questions open-ended—the kind that don't give away your opinion or reveal the answer.
- Ask about things that interest you.
- Ask questions you don't know the answer to.
- Ask a question that's impossible to answer.
- Find a part of the book where you can't figure out what's going on. Ask about that.
- Find a part of the book where you are *almost* 100 percent sure you know what's going on. Ask an open-ended question about it—one that doesn't give away your opinion—and see what others think.
- Make up a provocative statement—something that's sure to stir up disagreement. Then turn it into a question.
- Find something in the book you feel strongly about. Ask readers what they think.
- Ask the next logical question. And the next. And the next.
- Work from your gut. Speak from your own experience.

From *The Teen-Centered Book Club: Readers into Leaders* by Bonnie Kunzel and Constance Hardesty. Westport, CT: Libraries Unlimited. Copyright © 2006.

Brainstorming's shadowy opposite—rumination—is another way to generate thoughtful questions. It's a poet's way of getting at meaning and as you might predict, often the results differ not only in content but in texture from the results of a brainstorming session. Rumination yields questions that call more on intuition than reasoning, cosmic sense rather than common sense.

Here's how it works:

- As you are reading or soon afterward, close the book and just think about it for a few minutes. Many questions and thoughts will occur to you. Let them float through your mind, but don't get attached to any one concept.
- After a minute or two, write down one question or concept that stands out for you. Then let that thought go. Let your mind drift for another few minutes. Write another question or concept. After you do this several times, good questions and thoughts will begin to flow.
- When something resonates, ask yourself, What is it about this idea that rings true? If you discuss this idea in book club, what might you learn about it? What might you learn about other clubbers?
- Then write your questions to reflect your ideas and curiosities.

Encourage teens to let questions arise naturally from their own curiosity or confusion as they are reading. If teens can let go of the topics they feel they should address, their questions will reflect their own concerns, opinions, cultural background, assumptions—in short, their individuality. These kinds of questions cannot help but strike a responsive chord in their peers.

The Golden Rule of Discussion: Ask the next logical question.

A BAKER'S DOZEN BACKUP QUESTIONS

The best discussion questions rise straight from the book, but there are times when you could use a little backup. This section gives you that backup. You can use these questions in a couple of ways: If you have plenty of prep time and you need a little help getting started, select a few questions from the list and reframe them in terms of the book group's interests and the book under discussion. If you don't have that much time—say it's five minutes to club time and the question-asker hasn't shown yet—simply use them as is. They're generic enough to serve a wide range of clubs and books. As a matter of fact, you can prepare for emergencies in advance by writing the questions on cards and storing them in a container. When the emergency arises, pass the container and let teens draw out questions to spark their discussion.

1. Take a minute to just *feel* your reaction to this book. Don't use your brain so much as just your emotion. What do you feel? Where in your body do you feel it? Did it make your heart race? Did it make you antsy? Did it make you cry? What is it about the book that makes you feel that way?

2. What kind of story was this? (e.g., love story, adventure story, battle of good and evil) Does it make a difference to you what kind of book it is? If you knew in advance what kind of book it was, would you have read it?

3. Who did you like in this book? Did you like him or her right from the start? What made you like the character? Would like him or her in real life?

4. Pick the person you liked in this book. Did that person do anything you didn't like? When the character did it, did you like them less? Did you want to warn the character not to be stupid? Did you get over it? If you had been friends, would you have tried to stop your friend from doing it? If later in the book, you found out the character had good reason for doing what he or she did—how did that make you feel?

5. What one thing could have changed everything in this book? Let's say you wanted to change the way the book came out, what one change could you make to the action, the characters, or the setting that would do it?

6. What did you notice most about this book? (e.g., poetic language, setting, humor, descriptions, the way characters talk or think)

7. Think about this: Some people say that what we do *reveals* who we are. Other say that what we do *shapes* who we are. For example, some people would say that when you gossip, that shows your true nature—you are a mean-spirited person. Others would say that even nice people can gossip—*but* each time you gossip, you let mean-spiritedness take hold in your life and if you gossip enough, you'll *become* mean-spirited. So the question is this: When you look at people in this book, did their words and actions *reveal* or *shape* who they are?

8. Did this book change the way you look at the world? Sometimes, the way we look at the world changes, but our actions don't. Do you think this book will have any effect on your actions?

9. If the story happened somewhere else or in a different time, what would have to change? Would the characters' race have to change? their sex? their jobs? their personalities? their beliefs? How much does where and when a person live influence who they are? If where and when you live shapes who you are, then what say do you have in your life? Are you truly responsible for your actions—good or bad?

10. Read us your favorite passage in this book.

11. If you were going to write a title for this book, what would it be? (You can brainstorm the new titles now. If this becomes a favorite activity for your club, you can do it often and create a display of books with alternate titles.) What is a title supposed to do? Does the title of this book do that?

12. On the scale from Perfect to Big Disappointment, where does this book fall?

13. Could the book have ended any other way?

A Few Words about Prepared Reading Group Guides

You'll find prefabricated discussion guides in print and online. The implied promise of these guides is that you can scan the questions a few minutes before book club meeting and you're good to go. It just doesn't work that way. Take a moment to imagine the response you'll get if you ask a room full of teens, "What is this book's inciting incident?" or "What types of symbolism are used in this novel?" This is the stuff of lit class term papers. For purposes of the teen-centered book club, we'll just call them the Kiss of Death.

However, some guides break the mold, with insightful questions that teens can easily relate to. For example, *Define "Normal"* has great discussions in the back-of-book reading group guide (and because they're built into the book, motivated teens can actually give some thought to the questions before take their thoughts live in book club!). Bonnie had a good experience with the reading group guide created for *Shattering Glass* (Kunzel 2003). Questions from the guide sparked thoughtful, wide-ranging discussion among her readers. Still, teens found shortcomings with the questions.

In general, our advice is: By all means, refer to prepared readers guides. (And if your teens are formulating the questions, give them access to the guides.) Just don't lean on them. In the occasional instance when you need to come up with some book-specific questions quickly, these guides can be a good place to start.

CONCLUSION

Attentive reading, a little background research, and some thought-provoking questions lay the groundwork for good discussions, but they are only the beginning. Chapter 10 takes you into the heart of discussion, with some ideas for keeping the conversation flowing, on topic, civil, and fruitful.

References

Contemporary Authors New Revision Series. 1962–present. Detroit: Thomson Gale.

Drew, Bernard A. 1996. *The 100 Most Popular Young Adult Authors: Biographical Sketches and Bibliographies.* Englewood, CO: Libraries Unlimited.

———. 2002. *100 More Popular Young Adult Authors: Biographical Sketches and Bibliographies.* Westport, CT: Libraries Unlimited.

Kunzel, Bonnie. 2003. "Shattered By: *Shattering Glass.*" *VOYA* (April), p. 19.

YA Books Mentioned in This Chapter, Current Paperback Editions

Define "Normal." Julie Ann Peters. New York: Megan Tingley, 2003.

Housekeeping. Marilynne Robinson. New York: Picador, 2004.

Lord of the Flies. William Golding. Various editions available.

Lord of the Rings trilogy. J.R.R. Tolkein. Various editions available.

The Mists of Avalon. Marion Zimmer Bradley. New York: Ballantine, 2000. (Originally published by Del Rey in 1982.)

Running Out of Time. Margaret Peterson Haddix. New York: Aladdin Library, 1997)

Sabriel. Garth Nix. New York: HarperTrophy, 1995.

Shattering Glass. Gail Giles. New York: Simon Pulse, 2003.

Sisterhood of the Traveling Pants. Ann Brashares. New York: Delacorte Books for Young Readers, 2003.

A Tale of Two Cities. Charles Dickens. Various editions available.

Too Good to Be True: The Colossal Book of Urban Legends. Jan Harold Brunvand. New York: Norton, 2001.

10

◇✕◇ ◇✕◇ ◇✕◇

IN THE THICK OF THINGS: FACILITATING AND PARTICIPATING IN BOOK DISCUSSIONS

In person or online, sharing ideas and thoughts is the whole point of book clubbing. This is where you'll spend most of your time. It's where teens will hone their skills in critical thinking, civil discourse, and joint exploration—all key leadership skills. And it's where teams will forge connections to reading, to books, to one another, to you, and to the library.

What makes for lively discussion? Openness to new ideas is key. Just as readers must temporarily suspend their disbelief to enter into the world of the novel, so book clubbers must temporarily suspend their own beliefs and assumptions to enter fully into discussion. In addition to openness, lively discussions depend on solid communication skills, thoughtful participation, and good facilitation.

This chapter covers helping teens put into action the attitudes, skills, and roles that make discussion work, including:

- Opening the book club meeting and transitioning into discussion
- Practicing open-mindedness attentive listening
- Sharing responsibility for good discussion
- Managing the flow of ideas and keeping discussion on track
- Including everyone in the conversation and establishing and enforcing boundaries
- Keeping disagreements from escalating into arguments and calming the waters
- Closing discussions

Several reproducible handouts will help you explore these ideas with teens.

KICKING OFF THE DISCUSSION

Early on, your group will decide whether to begin meetings with some chit-chat or go straight into the book. We recommend the latter because meetings that begin with social chat may never go anywhere else. But there's another, more subtle reason for saving the social time until the end of the meeting: During discussions, tensions sometimes run high. Teens may need time to decompress, regain their equilibrium, and reaffirm their friendships. Social time at the end of the meeting provides a place for that to happen.

Rather than chat, consider starting each meeting with a standard opening or ritual. To help build connections among teens, focus on them as people. (Later in the meeting, they'll get to know one another as readers.) Ask a question or toss out a topic and let teens respond. For younger teens, tie it to pets, family, school, and friends. For older teens, ask about friends, sports or pastimes, cars and driving, aspirations, and so forth. Constance has had great luck asking younger middle schoolers to share their most embarrassing moments, tell jokes, or say one interesting thing they've read in the past month. Then transition into the meeting proper with a word of welcome, reminding teens which book is being discussed and opening the conversation. Following are some ideas:

- **Get personal.** Andrew Medlar, YA specialist at the Chicago Public Library, likes to start his book clubs with a brief check-in. Teens take turns talking about the good news/bad news in their lives. As teens talked (or later during book discussion), he would mention connections between their lives and the book they were discussing. Sometimes, he'd recommend other books that teens might enjoy, providing very informal readers' advisory/bibliotherapy.

- **Let's take turns.** Many clubs start with a structured response, like a round robin or passing a talking stick. The most popular starter question is: "What did you think of the book?" That question is too broad. Try asking: "What do you remember best about this book?" "What was the most interesting fact in this book?" "What didn't fit?"

- **Go for it!** Start with a free-for-all. Words fly fast and furious as everyone tosses their ideas into the ring. There's no sorting, no follow-up, no discussion at this point—just an initial mind dump. While that's going on, the facilitator or recorder jots down ideas for later discussion.

- **Talking head.** The facilitator or researcher talks for two to three minutes about the book or the author. Be sure to keep comments open-ended so the presentation sparks broader conversation; you don't want to create the impression that the research offers the authoritative answer.

- **Dramatic moment.** Read a passage from the book. Depending on time and interest, some or all of the teens can read their favorite passages, or the group can come to consensus about one favorite passage and who will read it aloud. Like answering an easy first question, this process helps the group settle in and brings the book freshly to mind.

In new groups or groups with high turnover in membership, early conversation tends to drag. No one wants to go first; no one wants to commit to a point of view. In these cases, break the ice with a game. Have teens draw a question from a hat and hand it to someone to answer. Have them write their answers to questions on a slip of paper and draw the answers from the hat to read aloud. Or, use a standard icebreaker: Pin a character's name to each person's back and have teens roam the room, asking each other questions that will help them figure out what name is pinned to their back.

THE ART AND PRACTICE OF GREAT BOOK DISCUSSION

If there's one thing teens know how to do, it's talk. As long as the conversation goes well, you can stay in the background. Monitor teens' discussion styles and conversational behavior, and step in with a little light coaching or instruction as the need arises.

The Art: Exploring Your Ideas As if They Were My Own

Book discussion is not about coming to a place where everyone agrees. It's about exploring diverse ideas. Ironically, the club can only do that when everyone buys into the same core value: Open-mindedness is good. This comes naturally to teens, when they are not hamstrung by their own narrow assumptions and rigid beliefs. Like all of us, teens sport a combination of taken-for-granted beliefs and free thinking. Openness is a skill, and like all skills, it can be learned through modeling, coaching, just-in-time correction, and practice.

Still, open-mindedness is not an end in itself, nor is it a one-way street. Like so much behavior it has unexpected effects. As we enter into others' ideas, thoughts, and opinions, we come to see the world—and ourselves—in new ways. That changes us, not only in what we see and know but in who and how we are—heady stuff for teens engrossed in creating identity. The following handout for teens offers some thoughts on open-mindedness.

ARE YOU OPEN-MINDED?

Occasionally during book club, people mistake themselves for The Keepers of Ultimate Truth. Whatever they say, you get the message loud and clear: "I have the only right answer." People who speak this way are suffering a delusion; bring them gently back to reality. Thank them for their opinion and enforce the ground rules.

Meanwhile, if you keep a few things in mind, you'll never mistake yourself for The Keeper of the Ultimate Truth:

- What makes an answer right? You can defend it. If you can clearly explain why you think or feel the way you do and you can point to places in the book that lead you to think or feel that way, then your answer is defensible.
- The same goes for everyone else. Opposing answers can be right, if they're defensible.
- What if, in defending your answer, you discover a flaw in your thinking or you realize that you misread what the author was saying? As *The Wee Free Men* say, "Nae problemo." Rethink your ideas and change your mind if you like. It shows you're open-minded, even with yourself.
- When you want to emphasize that you're expressing your own point of view, start with "I think . . . " or "The way I see it . . . " or "To me . . . " or "I don't see it that way."

From *The Teen-Centered Book Club: Readers into Leaders* by Bonnie Kunzel and Constance Hardesty. Westport, CT: Libraries Unlimited. Copyright © 2006.

The Practice: Attentive Listening

Listening makes the difference between conversation and the verbal equivalent of a food fight. We hear the difference most obviously in certain political talk shows, where no one even pretends to listen to one another. A more relevant example is news interviews, where you can easily spot the difference between a reporter running through a rote list of questions and an honest exchange in which each question builds on the previous answer.

Attentive listening is more than a skill; it's a value. Attentive listening is a visible act that indicates the underlying value of openness. As you teach, encourage, and reward attentive listening, focus on the value—*why* we listen—as well as the how. The following handout covers both points for teens.

LISTEN UP!

Until we perfect the mind-meld, trading words back and forth is the best way we have to learn about the Greatest Mystery of Life: what goes on inside another person's head. More often than not, it's the best way we have to find out what's going on inside our own heads as well!

Real listening takes concentration and practice. It's all about paying attention.

- **Listen for the message.** Separate *what* people say from *how* they say it.
- **Make eye contact.** Usually, we give more attention to what we see than what we hear. (That's why we can read and listen to music at the same time.) Keep your eyes on the speaker, and your mind will stay there, too.
- **Set aside your own thoughts.** All kinds of things will leap to mind while you're listening. You'll think of what you want to say next. You'll wonder what's for dinner. You'll remember what the ocean in Georgia smelled like on vacation last summer. Let them go. They'll be back.
- **Rephrase what the speaker says** to show you understand, even if you disagree. *Especially* if you disagree. Be sure you know what you're disagreeing with. Ask the speaker to rephrase a question or comment that isn't quite clear.
- **Make new friends, but keep the old.** It works with ideas just as it does with people. You can be open new ideas *and* hold onto what's important to you.

Bonus Tip!

Listen your way into a whole new world. The best way to see what something looks like is from the inside out. You don't have to adopt another point of view, but if you can try it on for a few minutes, you will *really* understand it. You might disagree 100 percent, but at least you'll know what you're rejecting. And, look out for that boomerang effect: Delving into another person's thoughts, you'll come away with a new perspective on your own ideas, too.

From *The Teen-Centered Book Club: Readers into Leaders* by Bonnie Kunzel and Constance Hardesty. Westport, CT: Libraries Unlimited. Copyright © 2006.

> **Tip!**
>
> The Zen of Conversation
>
> In meditation lingo, the phrase *monkey thoughts* refers to the myriad thoughts that leap to mind and scream for attention while you are trying to focus on something else. In conversation, we must learn to shut up the monkeys: to temporarily set aside our own ideas to focus on what others are saying.

Joining Art and Practice: The Challenge of Facilitation

A facilitator is the quintessential party host who draws people in, smoothes rough spots—and occasionally calls in the bouncer. The role requires sensitivity and subtlety, willingness to move in and out of the limelight, and ability to set aside personal interests and self-expression to encourage the free flow of ideas. More than anything, the job requires detachment. The facilitator stands one step removed from the conversation. The job is all about managing the exchange of ideas, and it's impossible to manage the process from the inside. The facilitator can't be invested in the discussion or its outcome. For teens, this approaches the impossible.

But the facilitator doesn't bear sole responsibility for creating good discussions. Book club works best when facilitation and participation operate seamlessly—that is, facilitators and participants share responsibility for moving the discussion along, asking thoughtful questions, including everyone, enforcing boundaries, keeping the discussion on track, and preventing disagreements from escalating into arguments. To help teens understand the give-and-take, spend a few minutes during one of the club's first meetings to explore facilitator's and participants' roles. The "Book Club Do's" reproducible handout for teens summarizes key responsibilities for both roles. The "Two Simple Things" reproducible handout reminds teens that they can "lead from within," fulfilling many of the facilitator's responsibilities even as they participate in the discussion and also reminds them that they can contribute even when they're not in the mood to talk.

BOOK CLUB DO'S

While the facilitator does this . . .

- Starts the ball rolling with a question or statement that is provocative, perplexing, or surprising.
- Asks questions that take the discussion in new directions.
- Draws everyone in without putting anyone on the spot.
- Keeps everyone focused on the book.
- Reminds people that book club is about exploring ideas.
- Challenges contradictory or inaccurate statements, assumptions or bias, and simplistic thinking.
- Prevents one or two voices from dominating.
- Helps people disagree without arguing.
- Enforces ground rules.
- Brings the conversation to a close.

Participants do this...

- Read the book. Even if you've already read it before.
- Bring some ideas to talk about.
- Take a break from the junk in your life. Leave it at the door.
- Follow the ground rules.
- Get outside your head. Try out new ways of seeing things and thinking about them.
- Listen attentively.
- Speak your mind.
- Stand up for yourself when someone crosses your boundaries or challenges your idea.
- Keep it civil!
- Know your strengths and weaknesses. Ask for help when you want it.*

*Great at looking up passages in the book, not so great at reading aloud? Find the passage and ask a friend to read it. Great at coming up with new ideas, not so great at standing up to a challenge? Get some allies. Say, "Am I the only one who thinks this?"

From *The Teen-Centered Book Club: Readers into Leaders* by Bonnie Kunzel and Constance Hardesty. Westport, CT: Libraries Unlimited. Copyright © 2006..

TWO SIMPLE THINGS YOU CAN DO TO MAKE BOOK CLUB BETTER . . . EVERY TIME

Be a Leader—Even if You're Not in Charge

In book club, everyone helps move the conversation along. You don't have to be the facilitator to ask a question, challenge someone's thinking, encourage people to stand up for themselves, enforce the ground rules, or anything else you can think of that will make the conversation more interesting and fruitful. In leadership-speak, it's called "leading from within," and it means that even if you're not in charge, you can help things run smoothly.

When You Don't Feel Like Talking—Be a Silent Partner

Let's say book club day comes around and you don't feel like talking. Should you just stay home? *No!!!* There are plenty of other ways you can contribute. Besides listening attentively or enforcing ground rules, you can ask questions or volunteer to be Keeper of the Time or Keeper of the List.

From *The Teen-Centered Book Club: Readers into Leaders* by Bonnie Kunzel and Constance Hardesty. Westport, CT: Libraries Unlimited. Copyright © 2006.

The age and maturity of club members will determine how active a role you'll play. For younger teens, you may start by serving as facilitator, preparing teens to grow into the role by reminding them to "lead from within." With more experienced or mature groups, you may coach teen facilitators as they take turns learning from experience. Simply let teens start where they are and grow into facilitation, shifting more responsibility to them as they become adept.

Managing the Flow of Ideas

A key facilitation skill is managing the flow of ideas. This involves encouraging the conversation to develop, neither skimming over ideas nor becoming bogged down. You do this by taking the conversation in new directions or by delving into ideas that excite the group, summarizing portions of the discussion, smoothing transitions and recapping what's been previously said. While deliberately *not* aiming to tie up all loose ends, you can encourage teens to look for connections among several ideas developed during the conversation—or during previous book club discussions. Here are some tips for managing the flow:

- **Listen more than you speak.** Observe more than you act.
- **Make notes** as people speak so you can summarize and revisit ideas.
- **Watch where the energy flows.** Encourage teens to pursue high-energy paths, but when the conversation falters or becomes repetitive or circular, drop in provocative statements or questions that lead in new directions.
- **Let teens blaze their own trails** to meaning and connection, whether the conversation becomes freewheeling, impassioned, silly, gross, or herky-jerky. That said, there's a fine line between freewheeling and chaotic, impassioned debate and vulgar discourse, taking a stand and speechifying. Teens usually will police one another. When they don't, call attention to the excesses and let them redirect themselves.
- **Balance your own participation.** Your job is to manage, not to contribute. But when you see missed connections and underdeveloped ideas, it's OK to mention them or to ask leading questions to develop them.

Obviously, teens will need to grow into the facilitator's role. No one is a natural. Each teen will bring unique strengths and weaknesses, such as generating excitement or enforcing ground rules. As each teen takes a turn at facilitating, your role is to let them fly in the areas where they excel, support them in areas where they are weak—and do it all unobtrusively. That makes your job approximately 100 times harder than theirs.

Wise Words

What is hard is to allow some silence. At first, I kept wanting to fill in with a question about the book. It took me a while to be able to allow a little silence, which gives people a chance to think an idea through and then express themselves. You get some of the more thoughtful observations that way.

Jan Klucevsek (Saal and LeClerc 1995, p. 34)

> **Tip!**
>
> At the New York Public Library, a book leader's success is measured by how much the group talks and how little the leader talks.
>
> (Saal and LeClerc 1995, p. 42)

Including Everyone in the Conversation

Inclusion becomes a challenge as book club conversation progresses. Early on, it's a matter of making sure that everyone who wants a turn gets a turn. As the conversation develops, it also becomes a matter of maintaining balance. Use verbal and nonverbal cues to invite reticent teens to talk and discourage garrulous teens from dominating. Here are some things to look for:

- **Notice which voices dominate and which ones are squeezed out.** Until you become adept at this, jot down names as people speak. If you have a visual memory, imagine a ball of yarn tossed from person to person as they speak; where is the web dense and where is it thin? Check your notes occasionally to see who hasn't spoken in a while.

- **Watch the gender balance.** Many teen girls, including strong, confident ones, tend to defer to boys in mixed groups. Adults do, too. Educators learn to recognize and compensate for such tendencies; we should, too. Awareness is half the battle; the other half is making sure that we consistently send messages to girls that their comments are as welcome and valid as boys' comments. John Gray points out an interesting phenomenon that has long been observed: When men and women participate equally in a conversation, people of both sexes perceive that the women "talked too much" or talked more than the men. Gray supports the established theory that such perception stems from a persistent belief that women should defer to men (Gray 2001).

- **Define participation broadly.** See the "Two Simple Things You Can Do . . ." handout. Teens don't have to speak to be active. And be sure to read the box "The Silent One" in this chapter.

- **Watch for anomalies.** It's a rare teen who doesn't leap at the chance to air thoughts and opinions. As you get to know the teens in your club, try to recognize patterns of behavior: who does and doesn't contribute, why and when. Later, when you spot anomalies, check them out.

- **Check in with quiet ones.** If a teen regularly sits silent, initiate a private, friendly check-in; then turn the conversation to book club. You may be surprised at what you learn.

- Invite everyone to join the conversation, but don't require it and don't call attention to reticent teens. If their body language tells you they'd like to speak, establish casual eye contact and ask a general, open-ended question.

- **Make space for teens** who are reticent, slow thinkers or slow speakers. Introduce a lull in the conversation with "Let's just think about this for a minute." "If you've had a chance to speak in the last five minutes, take a time out."
- **Accept** that not everyone will contribute to every conversation.

The Silent One

In *Good Books Lately,* Ellen Moore and Kira Stevens (2004) tell a story about a book group in which one member, Marion, never contributed to the conversation except to ask an occasional question. At one meeting, she opened up and joined the conversation, but that was it. *Years* went by until one club member recommended a Nancy Drew book. The club, bemused, agreed. At the next meeting, Marion confessed to the group that it was the first book she had ever read. During the previous months, the club member who had suggested the Nancy Drew book had been teaching Marion to read.

"She had wanted so badly to take part in the fellowship and discussion—based on something that she could not do—that she had shown up for every book group meeting for the better part of a decade just to be in the same room with a conversation she could not share," Moore and Stevens observed (2004).

Discussion Styles: It's More Than What You Say, It's How You Say It

It's a no-brainer to say that each of us adjusts how we speak to match the situation and audience as well as to express how we think or feel; and to reflect less tangible factors like our stress level, whether we feel defensive or safe, and so on. What we choose to talk about, how we talk about it, the angle or perspective we take, word choice, tone of voice—these are the building blocks of discussion styles.

Discussion styles are a big, cool amusement park for teens. Teens constantly try out styles for effect on others and on themselves. Often for teens, style *is* substance. Ironically, even as they are caught up in their own experiments, teens fall prey to others'. Book club helps them recognize discussion styles when they hear them (and use them). With a little self-awareness, they learn to strip away the style so that the content of the message shines through. When teens learn to do that, they can easily overcome the tendency to take discussion styles personally. As teens come to recognize how discussion styles work, they refine their own styles for maximum effect (to communicate more clearly or, frankly, to better manipulate others). Most important, teens discover that no matter what discussion style someone throws at them, they can handle it. This stands them in good stead whether they are facilitating or participating in the discussion.

Some discussion styles arise naturally from nature or nurture, and most are power plays. They're usually used early in the game, when teens are preoccupied with presenting their personas and jockeying for position. As the club evolves, discussion styles may become less important—or so ingrained that teens disregard them. This section describes several discussion styles, including strategies and scripts for handling them. Teens can easily learn to do this. You can help by distributing copies of this section, talking about discussion styles outside the heat of the moment (perhaps as a point of discussion when you open the meeting), and resisting the urge to rescue teens unless (especially in the case of younger teens) they really need it.

Introvert and the Extrovert

Some people like to talk through several ideas, getting to know their thoughts as they speak them aloud. Extroverts tend to be this way. It can drive introverts crazy. That's because introverts like to get their thoughts in order and even perhaps mentally rehearse what they'll say before they open their mouths. This can drive extroverts crazy. These discussion styles are the most authentic, growing as they do out of natural tendencies or preferences. The best we can do is encourage tolerance and make sure that both types get ample time to speak their minds.

Emotional Carrier Pigeon

People use emotional overtones to express feelings and thoughts simultaneously. The emotional message comes across as attitude, conveyed by word choice or tone of voice. Some emotional messages are: "This topic is really important to me," "This happened to me but I can't tell you about that," "I'm feeling hurt," or "I'm afraid you'll think what I say is stupid so I'm saying it in a way that cuts you off at the knees." Emotional overtones often sound combative or whiny. It may be necessary to help teens clarify what they are really saying by asking neutrally worded follow-up questions that help them separate the emotional overtones from the content of the message. Helping the teen to have his or her say while separating the emotional message from the content message is important because it gets at the fundamental message: "I need to be heard."

Rhetorical Gamer

A classic tactic in one-upmanship, nothing kills conversation like a rhetorical question does. Address them forthrightly. "Are you asking us a question or telling us what you think?" "Can you ask that in a way we can answer?" A light touch and a smile will take the sting out of the question. If you have a teen who frequently asks rhetorical questions, you may want to play an impromptu game: Explain what a rhetorical question is and how it's used to bully others, lead teens in creating a few examples, then ask teens to make up some rhetorical questions about the book—the sillier, the better—and pose the questions to the group. The point is for them to experience just how useless these kinds of questions are. If you have a habitual Rhetorical Gamer, create a signal for teens to use when they detect someone asking a rhetorical question or create a silly penalty to impose on someone who habitually does it.

Cross-Examiner

The Cross-Examiner has many strategies at his or her disposal: there's the rapid volley of questions thrown, picking at details, trick questions, misdirection, twisting words . . . if you've seen any lawyer-and-jury show, you get the idea. Clearly, it's a weapon rather than a tool of discovery. Call each strategy for what it is: "That's a trick question. Can you say it differently?" "Let's take your questions one by one." "Why are you asking that question?"

Note: Among like-minded teens who can give as good as they get, cross-examination can create value: They learn to withstand the onslaught and how to win by giving careful answers grounded in the book. At a higher level, by answering questions civilly and by posing thoughtful questions of their own, teens learn how to transform a cross-examination into an exploration. By surviving a cross-examination, teens learn the most important lesson of all: that they can do it.

Competitor

Many teens take a sporting approach to discussion, treating it as they would an athletic contest. As sports go, book club is more like fishing than football. Remind them—frequently—that in book club, the purpose of discussion is to discover and develop new ideas. You might say, "This is not a boxing match!" or "Let's not close our minds on that until we let all the facts in." Use humor and a light touch, keeping in mind that even teens who are very competitive can also be sensitive to slights. It's important to remember that not every spirited debate is competition; when teens are charged on the ideas, their energies will flow. The nature of competition is not in the speed or intensity of the discussion, but the spirit. In the midst of a high-energy discussion, ask yourself, Is this about winning and one-upmanship or is it about explaining and sharing ideas? As long as the book and ideas take front and center, you're probably OK.

Chronic Interrupter

Some people believe that immediately answering a question or responding to a comment—even if it means interrupting or cutting off their conversational partner's last sentence—shows that they are listening and actively engaged with the person speaking. Although this style of discussion drives some people crazy, others actually thrive on the energy. Listening to this type of conversation is like watching a basketball game, with the ball whizzing back and forth among many players. (Thanks to John Gray for the example.) As long as all the players are included and the discussion is developing, all is well. If some clubbers are sidelined, the discussion needs to slow down.

Caveat: There's a difference between vigorous give-and-take and the kind of interruption that says, "What I have to say is more interesting than what you're saying." This kind of interruption needs to be called every time it happens. Fortunately, you don't need to be the one to do it. Teach teens how to establish boundaries and insist that others respect them. It's easy enough. The first time it happens, the person being interrupted says in a neutral tone of voice, "I'd like to finish my thought." The second time, the person being interrupted uses stronger words but keeps the neutral tone, like this: "I'm not finished talking yet." The third time around, the person being interrupted can use even stronger words—still keeping the tone neutral: "I've asked you not to interrupt me. Please stop talking until I'm done." This kind of step-by-step escalation in language can go on and on: "I've told you three times to stop interrupting me. I'll tell you when I'm done." At some point, if the club has a chronic interrupter, you may have to call a time-out or do a game or role-play to get it under control. There's a fine line between allowing teens time to solve their problems and supporting them when they're struggling. Giving teens scripts, role-playing the scripts, and giving them permission to stand up for themselves will go a long way in helping them set their own boundaries.

Devil's Advocate

Whatever you say, I say the opposite. Whatever opinion you express, I challenge it. That's the devil's advocate. This isn't necessarily a bad thing; it can jump-start bland conversations in which everyone agrees and there's not much to say. But if it's overused, the group cannot work together to develop a single train of thought. Coming up against a devil's advocate at every turn is like stubbing your toe with every step; it makes reaching your destination much more difficult. When the devil's advocate is confounding the conversation rather than advancing it, enlist his or her support or ask her to table her objections for the sake of conversation. Tread gently; often, devil's advocates feel they are promoting multiple points of view and bringing to light perspectives that would otherwise go unnoticed—and often, they are. Value that even as you ask for momentary relief. "Pat, I love the way you're able to see things from many different perspectives without getting married to any one of them. For the next few minutes, would you put yourself inside Jan's point of view and help us see how it might play out?" "Pat, you're great at bringing up new angles. I wonder if you could hold off on giving us new angles for the next few minutes and join us in following this train of thought."

Belligerent Bully

There's no more obvious discussion style. Think political talk shows. Hip-hop. Truck commercials. It's all about style, not at all about content. Intimidation. Ridicule. Domination. Obfuscation. Provocation for its own sake. One-upmanship. If you strip the flash and dazzle, what you're left with is "Me cool. You dweeb" or "Because I said so" or "I like to see you squirm." Take strong, direct action that calls attention to the style, not the person. It's important to remember that even bullies can be fragile. The best way to defuse belligerence is to decode it, to separate the message from the style, exposing it for what it is. If the unspoken message is "I want to be sure I'm heard even though I think my message is unpopular," help the teen be heard. If the message is "Don't disagree with me," take the counterintuitive path and help the bully handle the challenge. (The assumption being that once a person is confident in handling challenges, they won't be so eager to head them off.) Always, always keep your comments grounded in the book: "J.J., I'm hearing you say [here restate the message stripping it of the belligerent overtones]. Is that right?" "Let's look at that passage in the book and see what the author says to create that impression." "Pat, I hear you, but I'm not sure I understand what you're getting at. Are you saying

'Because I said so?'" "Matt, I'm interested in what you're saying. But all the attitude is getting in the way. Can you say it more gently, so I can hear you better?" With bullying dominating all forms of media, it's easy for teens to take it as normal. Your role as "keeper of the safety zone" demands direct and sometimes drastic action. If a chronic bully just doesn't get it, he or she may need to leave the group.

Peacemaker

The peacemaker strives to smooth over every disagreement. This does not promote multiple points of view or encourage people to challenge one another's thinking. Help peacemakers understand that civil disagreements can lead to new insights, deeper understanding, and more meaningful connection than unexamined agreement. Some peacemakers see disagreements and energetic discourse as verbal violence. Book club discussions, by showing civil discourse in action, can help them see the difference.

Establishing and Enforcing Boundaries

No matter what their discussion style, to be healthy, safe, and socialized, teens need to learn to stand up for themselves appropriately. This isn't merely a leadership skill; it's a key life skill. In terms of leadership, establishing boundaries requires self-awareness, and enforcing boundaries requires discipline and diplomacy. In terms of life skills, establishing and enforcing boundaries defines and protects oneself. Boundaries make it possible to function and even to survive in the real world.

Teens are notoriously inept at this. Many don't know what their boundaries are, don't respect their own boundaries, have never considered whether their boundaries work for or against them, and have never consciously tried to enforce their boundaries. Trapped in unmindful emotional responses, a teen may become aggressively defensive over minor trespasses while submitting to gross violations. Book club helps teens learn to stand up for themselves in ways that work. Along the way, they learn to respect others' boundaries as well.

Boundaries don't just protect us; they express our values. (Think about how you interact with teens: Chances are the degree of familiarity you allow teens—where you draw the line—stems from your beliefs about what is appropriate intergenerational behavior.) With that in mind, it's critical that any boundary work you do with teens have nothing to do with influencing their values. Help teens learn to draw the line, but let them decide where to draw it. The "Establishing Your Boundaries" handout offers suggestions to help teens think about how they establish their boundaries. Boundaries can be fluid. As teens discover what works for them, it's worthwhile to periodically revisit the "Establishing Your Boundaries" handout and activity.

Finally, for all their vaunted rebelliousness, many teens find it difficult to do what it takes to enforce their boundaries. We often teach kids that their boundaries are unimportant, wrong, or downright bad. Almost everyone learns that it's rude to say no to adults in positions of authority; that it's selfish to insist other people do what we want; and (usually for girls) that it's unattractive to disagree or be strident. The "Stand Up!" handout for teens offers tips to turn some of that around in reasonable, effective ways.

ESTABLISHING YOUR BOUNDARIES

What's a Boundary?

It's a limit. You create boundaries when you set limits on what *other people* can do to you and how much influence they have over you. You also create boundaries when you decide what *you* will or won't do. The first kind of boundary protects you; the second reveals something about who you are and what you'll stand up for. Here are some examples of book club boundaries:

Don't mimic the way I talk.
Don't look at my scar.
I have a right to speak my mind.
I refuse to let people ridicule Jen.
I have a right to walk in here without being hassled.
People can challenge me, but they can't shut me up.
I decide.

Discover Your Boundaries!

Do this fast. Don't think. Just answer.

1. Name three things you don't let people do to you.

   Now name three things you don't let anyone do to you or your friends.

2. Name three things that you refuse to do.

   Now name three things you refuse to let other people do.

3. Name three things you have a right to demand for yourself.

   Now name three things you have a right to demand for others or the club.

You have a right to establish your own boundaries. And you have a right to stand up for them. Book club is a great place to do both.

Name three boundaries you want to have for yourself in book club.

Now, get ready to *stand up* for them!

From *The Teen-Centered Book Club: Readers into Leaders* by Bonnie Kunzel and Constance Hardesty. Westport, CT: Libraries Unlimited. Copyright © 2006.

STAND UP!

When you know what your boundaries are, you owe it to yourself to stand up for them—because standing up for them is standing up for yourself. So, how do you do it?

1. **Pick an easy boundary to enforce.** "I don't let people interrupt me" is a good one. It's easy to spot when it happens. It's easy to correct. And, because most people feel the same way you do (i.e., they can't stand being interrupted, either), they'll cheer for you when you stand up for yourself.
2. *Exude* confidence. Be direct. Look the person in the eye. Keep your voice strong, even if it's shaky. Don't whisper or shout. You're just talking.
3. **Keep it simple.** Don't explain, defend, or argue. You have the right to insist that other people respect your boundaries whether they like or understand them or think they are totally stupid. They're your boundaries and you're standing up for them. That's all your fellow clubbers need to know.

Keep on Standing Up

Have you ever noticed how many people don't like to take no for an answer? No matter what you say, they keep pushing the boundaries. You have to keep on standing up for yourself. How?

Each time someone crosses your boundary, use a little stronger language to tell them to stop it. Always, *always* keep your voice calm and confident; it works better than shouting. Here's how you can keep standing up to someone who won't stop interrupting you:

- The first time the Interrupter breaks in on you, say something simple like, "I'd like to finish my thought." Keep your voice calm and firm.
- The second time the Interrupter breaks in, use stronger words but keep your calm voice: "I'm not finished talking yet."
- The third time around, you can use even stronger words—still keeping your tone calm: "Please stop talking until I'm done."

This kind of step-by-step escalation in your language can go on and on. The fourth time someone interrupts you, say in your calm voice, "I've told you three times already to stop interrupting me. I'll tell you when I'm finished talking."

If someone in your book club is a Chronic Interrupter, the club might need to talk about it. Give the Chronic Interrupter a chance to explain what's going on and what it will take to make him or her stop.

STAND UP! (CONT'D)

Write Your Own Stand-Up Script!

It's good to be prepared. Write a little script for yourself, and next time someone tries to cross your boundaries, you'll be ready! Here's how:

- Choose a boundary that's important to you. Or choose an easy one for starters.

- Think about what you will say the first time, and the second time, and the third time someone crosses your boundary.

  - Pick a partner to play the part of Boundary Buster. Try out your script—and edit it to make it better.

Putting It into Action

So, how do you make your book club a place where teens can safely do all this?

- **Direct instruction.** During the first meeting and occasionally thereafter, provide a few minutes of structured "fun" time for teens to write scripts and to role-play boundary-enforcement strategies. Feel free to break into book club discussions when teaching moments present themselves. When a teen does something well, a quick compliment will call attention to it without interrupting the flow too much. If a teen fails to enforce a boundary (or violates others' boundaries at will), disrupt the conversation, focusing on the process, not the people.

- **Discuss.** Book discussion provides plenty of practice in standing up for oneself. On the best days, teens will be questioned and challenged. On worse days, they may be ganged-up-on, interrupted, or teased. As they respond to each situation (with your support as needed), they become both more aware of their boundaries and more expert and confident in enforcing them. Miss no opportunity to call teens (in public or private) on their failure to stand up for themselves and praise them (in public or private) profusely when they do—whether or not they succeed. Likewise, miss no opportunity to publicly call teens on their failure to respect another's boundaries.

- **Read.** Role models are always useful. Use plenty of nonfiction, and don't worry about salting the book list with issue books or strong female protagonists; it gets to be obvious. Regardless of what book the club reads, ask questions or make provocative statements that spur teens to investigate how characters establish and enforce boundaries—or how they don't—and the outcomes.

- **Take it in stride.** There may be tense moments when teens stand up for themselves against you. Whenever you can, welcome, honor, and (yes!) celebrate them: "Nancy, I really admire you for challenging us on that. You're right; we *should* think about why we're not reading any books by teen authors. I'm glad you brought it up. Good for you!" And when you can't respond to their challenge, when it's unsafe or violates your boundaries, you can reward them and model resistance at the same time: "Nancy, I can't change the book list for the group, but I'm impressed that you care enough to ask. Your idea is definitely worth talking about. Do you want to bring it up at the next meeting?" And when they stand up for their boundaries in a way that stings or annoys or angers or embarrasses you? Defuse the tension: Focus on the idea, not its expression. Be a model of magnanimity. Everyone's clumsy (and gratuitously nasty) sometimes. These are teens. It comes with the territory. Breathe. Count to 1 million. Let it be. You are doing great work here.

Grrrl Power(less)

Girls' unwillingness or inability to establish and enforce personal boundaries has implications that extend far beyond book club. In summer 2004, one of the hottest topics on the yalsa-bk Listserv was a *New York Times Sunday Magazine* article exposing yet again the well-documented fact that in many suburban, well-to-do middle schools, girls sexually service the boys in their social circles. Librarians on the Listserv asked one another again and again, "What can we do?"

Here's one idea: Make book club a safe place where girls develop the skill and the habit of standing up for themselves—and for respecting others who do. Note that we didn't say " . . . a safe place where girls *can* develop the skill and habit . . . " In book club, standing up for yourself is not an option; it's required and richly rewarded.

How do you do that? Body language comes first. Make eye contact with girls who look as if they'd like to speak. Nod your head slightly to encourage them. Raise your eyebrows very slightly. Gesture subtly with your hand. If it looks like the conversation is moving along, ask, "Has everyone had their say?"

Every time a girl speaks her mind, beam in approval and nod your head. If there's at least one girl in the club who is vocal and assertive, be sure to praise her when she expresses herself staunchly or responds well to argument. As teens see the signs of your approval, they will begin to mimic them . . . thus encouraging one another to speak up . . . thus creating an atmosphere in which it is actually safer to speak up than to sit in silence!

Be subtle! Don't embarrass anyone or single them out. Be indirect. For example, to encourage girls to stand firm in the face of arrogance or vociferousness, explain discussion styles and talk about ways to stand firm in the face of them. Several typical discussion styles are described in this chapter.

In private conversations, be more open. Prompt girls again and again to speak their minds and to keep on speaking their minds when someone disagrees with them. Praise them to the sky when they hold firm. Say things like this: "Nicole, how do you want to respond to that?" "Jessica, you had strong opinions on this topic last week. What do you think?" When they speak their minds, praise them on the spot (if it won't embarrass them) or privately during your good-bye: "Way to speak up Tay, I love to hear it." "Good job. Heather, I really admire the way you think on your feet." "Maggie, you did a great job of holding your own against Darrel. How did it feel? Are you OK?" And, the best praise of all (even if they don't show it): "I'm proud of you!"

The hope, of course, is that the habit of standing up for themselves leads to a new, stand-firm way of being that will serve them well in other, scarier places. Teens say to the world in dozens of ways, "I'm the boss of me." Make your book club a place where girls insist upon that. If girls can't say it to you and their club friends with confidence, how will they say it with conviction—for the umpteenth time—when they're being pressured to "hook up"?

KEEPING THE DISCUSSION ON TRACK

You've just read *Shattering Glass.* The discussion quickly turns to bullying. Someone tells about someone they know at school who is being bullied. Now the discussion is all about the kids and cliques at school. Your resident Goth, with that weird combination of self-effacement and pride, tells about how she's being bullied. Columbine High School and other school shootings come up. Simon Glass is long forgotten. Is this a real book discussion?

Every book club struggles with this question. What's the proper balance of personal and book talk? Which topics (gossip? advice? family secrets?) are off limits? When the group is discussing personal issues, should the facilitator steer it back to the book? How long should personal discussion go on before the facilitator steers it back? What happens when the talk veers from personal stories to last week's *Oprah* or *Jerry Springer Show*?

It's OK for the club to follow a long and winding road through everyone's personal experiences—but in the end and along the way, the purpose is not merely to throw stories at one another, but to build a shared experience that deepens each one's understanding or appreciation of his or her individual experience. And, because this is book club and the book is the shared experience, it's important that teens keep the discussion on track. The following reproducible handout for teens offers tips to help them do just that.

STAYING ON TOPIC

Book club discussions never follow a single track. But sometimes, they wander too far afield and stay there too long. If you're the leader, you need to bring them back home. How do you do that?

- **Ask people to read passages that illuminate their ideas and opinions.** ("For the next question, you have to answer by reading from the book.")
- **Ask people to tell their stories later.** ("Nat. I want to know what happened in the parking lot. Tell me later.")
- **Go back to the book again.** When someone tells a personal story, drop a question or observation that honors their story *and* brings the group back to the book. ("That's one way to get the bullies off your back. Too bad Simon never thought of that.")
- **Just say it.** When you need to be direct, be direct. ("So, how 'bout those Wee Free Men?")

From *The Teen-Centered Book Club: Readers into Leaders* by Bonnie Kunzel and Constance Hardesty. Westport, CT: Libraries Unlimited. Copyright © 2006.

Book Club Is Not Therapy!

Teens saturate book discussion with talk about the things that matter most—their normality (or perceived lack of), their future, their friends, their looks, their place in the world, their families, their hopes, their school experiences, the loneliness of absolute uniqueness, their cool (or perceived lack of), and the mundane, everyday reality of their lives. This can make for some dicey moments. If you read *The Watsons Go to Birmingham—1963* or *The Invisible Man* with African American teens, be prepared to hear about personal experiences with racial hatred. If you read *Jacob Have I Loved*, you'll hear about sibling relationships and family favorites. OK so far? What about substance abuse . . . or running away from home . . . or sexual exploration . . . or date rape . . . or self-mutilation?

Clearly, book clubs need some boundaries. And just as clearly, those boundaries will vary with every group, every book, every discussion. So the question is not what specific guidelines or rules you create, but what general principles you want to uphold. Stating your principles in a general way at the start of discussion that promises to raise painful issues will help to prevent trouble. Here's an example:

> Today, I'm going to do something I don't normally do. This is a tough book and it raises tough issues. So I'm asking you to think very carefully before you speak today. Some of us may have friends or know people who are struggling with the very same problem Joe faces in this book. That's none of the book club's business, so let's stay focused on the book and not talk about people's personal lives. Second, be gentle in what you say, so you don't accidentally hurt someone's feelings. And third, if you know someone who is having this problem, lots of adults know where to find help. You can email me or talk to me in private and I'll set you up with resources here in the library or help you find another adult who can do more. Or you can talk to another adult you trust.

When just-in-time interventions are called for, low-key, straightforward directives prevent embarrassment. Interrupt the speaker. Disrupt the conversation and redirect. Isn't that rude? Doesn't it violate teen autonomy? Absolutely. And normally, we'd help teens learn by resolving their own difficulties. But when a teen threatens to hurt him- or herself or others, it's the adult's responsibility to guarantee everyone's safety. Discussion often takes on a life of its own; caught up in it, teens may unwittingly say things that can lead to consequences they regret. So, while teens certainly deserve autonomy, it's unfair to shift all of the responsibility—and consequences—to them in the name of teen-centeredness.

By modeling tactful ways of redirecting conversation, you teach teens how to handle such situations, empowering them for future encounters. Celebrate the day a teen interrupts a peer to say, "Justin? Stick to the book." In the meantime, you are building trust by proving yourself an ally of each individual and the group a whole; they can rely on you to keep them safe and to handle situations when they are out of their depth.

Book Club Shouldn't Hurt!

Constance uses a single guiding principle for all of her work with teens: "This shouldn't hurt (you or other people)!" In practical terms, that spins out into a set of ground rules that she may or may not explicitly state:

- Book club is not therapy. It is not a place to bare your soul or share your intimate secrets. Please don't disclose your neuroses.
- Do not ask for or offer advice.
- Grandstanding (bragging about hurts, dysfunctions, or rule-breaking) and gossip are off-limits.
- When it comes to your safety, the adult has responsibilities that are not negated by club rules about confidentiality. Expect her to fulfill those responsibilities. Physical abuse from family members, boyfriends, self, or others; rape; severe bullying; substance abuse; suicidal tendencies: in each of these cases, the librarian has a legal and/or ethical obligation to report problems to legal authorities, parents, teachers, or principals.

KEEP DISAGREEMENTS FROM ESCALATING INTO ARGUMENTS

It would be nice to think that framing book discussion in terms of mutual discovery would create an atmosphere in which diversity in thought and opinion is honored. This requires a degree of detachment that only cats have mastered. Teens are emotionally embedded in their thoughts: What they think matters on an existential plane. In many ways, despite their penchant for experimentation, teens are even more entrenched than adults in notions of what defines "normal" and "right." For many teens, what they think and feel defines who they are. It's hard to maintain an air of detachment when your identity is at stake.

So turn the focus elsewhere. Frame book discussions in terms of their highest purpose: the search for truth (small *t*) and meaning. Back that up with some sound operational guidelines, two for participants and one for the facilitator:

- **For the participants:** (1) Be civil; and (2) Stick to specifics, backed by evidence. (See the "Handling Disagreements" reproducible handout for tips.)
- **For the facilitator:** Resist helping teens who are enmeshed in disagreement. Don't insult them by putting words in their mouths or by allowing other teens to leap into the breach. Encourage teens to police one another.

If someone is clearly at a loss to answer and looks to you for help, ask the challenger to rephrase the question or suggest another way into it. ("Jeremy, can you rephrase your question in terms of the tiger?" (*Life of Pi*) or "J.J., your challenge focuses on what's happening right here in this scene. What would happen if we looked at everything that happened in the weeks leading up to that minute?" (*Burning Up*). When a beleaguered teen gives up or clearly indicates he or she needs help, open it up to the group by saying something like "Any ideas?"

HANDLING DISAGREEMENTS

It's hard to be the first one to say, "I disagree." It takes courage. But if you do it, you'll be glad you did. It will make the book club stronger, and you will be one step further on your way to standing up for yourself.

And that's not all. It's amazing how often people start out disagreeing and end up discovering something completely new—something that has nothing to do with the original disagreement. Sometimes, disagreeing is the only way to get there. Of course, that can only happen the disagreement stays friendly.

Two ways to disagree:

When you want to speak your mind:

Be direct. Say, "I disagree." Then speak your mind.

When you want to hear what the other person has to say:
Keep your opinion to yourself—for now. For example, ask, "What did you like least about the character Aiden?" Later, you can mention that you loved the book (and Aiden) (*Blood and Chocolate*).

> *Everyone has the right to their own opinion, and everyone has a right to disagree with it. No one has the right to attack another person, or what that person thinks or feels.*

HANDLING DISAGREEMENTS (CONT'D)

10 Top Tips for Disagreeing in a Friendly Way

1. Stick to the book.
2. Use your manners.
3. Hold your own. When you're challenged, speak your mind.
4. Listen to *what* people say, not how they say it. Answer the *what.*
5. Choose your words carefully. Practice keeping your voice calm and even.
6. Listen. If you can't repeat what someone says, you haven't listened carefully enough. By the end of the discussion, you should be able to make other people's points as persuasively as they can. That doesn't mean you agree with them. It means you understand their views—and you still disagree with them.
7. Some discussions get intense. Deal with it. Breathe. Count to 10. Take a time out if you need to. Get a drink of water. Stop participating in the discussion and just listen for a while.
8. If someone doesn't understand what you're saying, make it clearer. But if they do understand and they simply disagree, don't keep trying to change their mind. Likewise, if someone keeps on repeating the same point, you can say, "I understand what you're saying. I just don't agree."
9. Sometimes, when things get hot, you can leave book club feeling badly and might even feel separated from your friends. It's natural; all the energy from the discussion is still there, and it needs time to dissipate. Go do something fun and noncompetitive. Have an ice cream. See a movie. Go swimming. Walk around the library and pick out books. Talk about something else for a while. Things will settle. You'll be fine.
10. Be honest. Be kind. Play fair.

From *The Teen-Centered Book Club: Readers into Leaders* by Bonnie Kunzel and Constance Hardesty. Westport, CT: Libraries Unlimited. Copyright © 2006.

Defusing Disagreements with Focus on Book Club Values

There is no right or wrong way to feel about a book. Most teens will mention this right away when generating the club's ground rules. Remind teens of this frequently—and reward them when they remind one another. If your teens tend to slip up, create friendly reminders and penalties. For example, you can set an "It's OK to think!" mascot (an oddly decorated stuffed animal or other artifact) in the center of the circle at the beginning of each meeting. Every time their eye alights on it, teens will remember to keep their minds open. Or, create light-hearted penalties offenders must perform when other teens catch their slips. For example, an offender must shake hands with the person they have offended, saying, "It's OK to think!" or "I lost my head, have you seen it?" On the other hand, if didacticism and intolerance are real problems for your group, intervene as directly and as often as necessary. It is your job to remind participants of book club values and basic courtesy when discussion veers into rough waters.

There's no absolute magic you can do here. But if you have established "It's OK to think!," helped teens facilitate the conversation to avoid personal attacks, and stepped in when things get rough, then (barring underlying animosities) any discomfort should work itself out.

What to Do When Teens Hate the Book

Some of the best discussions arise when teens disagree about the merits of a book. "I loved it!" "I hated it!" won't get you far, but if you can help teens air the reasons they feel the way they do, you have the beginnings of a fruitful discussion. The reproducible handout, "How to Talk about a Book You Can't Stand," helps teens think of ways to talk about books they dislike.

HOW TO TALK ABOUT A BOOK YOU CAN'T STAND

Almost everyone who's ever been in a book club says that great things happen when everyone *doesn't* like the same book. It gives everyone something to talk about. But . . . how do you speak politely about a truly horrible book?

- If you don't like a book, say so.

- If you didn't finish the book, say why.
- Don't get mad. It's the *book* you don't like.
- Criticize the book, not the person who chose it.
- Get past a simple "I didn't like it." Know what you don't like and why you don't like it.
- Read a passage from the book to show what you don't like. Then tell why you don't like it.
- Tell how the author might have changed the book or the writing to make it better.
- Enjoy your friends, even when you disagree.
- Be prepared for people to disagree with you. And be prepared to learn a lot about the book, the world, your friends—and maybe even yourself.

Here's a Way to Start

First say thank you to the person who suggested the book. Don't be sarcastic! Then say one good thing about the book (e.g., if you learned something new, it made you laugh, you like the jacket art). Doing those things sets a friendly tone, making it easier for people to hear your objections.

From *The Teen-Centered Book Club: Readers into Leaders* by Bonnie Kunzel and Constance Hardesty. Westport, CT: Libraries Unlimited. Copyright © 2006.

Brawlers and Softies

Every club has 'em—those who love the thrill of the fight and those who shrink from it. For book discussion to work, you'll need to stop the brawlers in their tracks and help softies feel safe enough to stand by their opinions.

Brawlers

Encourage brawlers to avoid rhetoric, vehemence, virulence, ridicule, and other forms of intimidation. If they're having a hard time separating civil from uncivil discourse, stop telling them and show them the difference with this game:

While the brawler speaks, take dictation.
Stop the conversation. Write what the brawler said on a whiteboard/display.
Ask teens to cross out all the words that are vulgar or incendiary.
What's left? What did the brawler actually say?

Softies

Whether motivated by lack of self-confidence, beliefs about acceptable behavior, or willingness to sacrifice their views to keep the peace, softies tend to keep silent, soft-pedal their beliefs, and back down in the face of challenges.

Subtly, through words and body language, make it clear that it's more acceptable for them to take a stand than to back down. Be *very* subtle; if you embarrass or hurt them, you'll lose their trust. Indirectly, perhaps in a general discussion of discussion styles, lead the club into a discussion of how apologies, self-deprecation, and soft-pedaling obscure the message just as much as smug, vulgar, and incendiary comments do.

The suggestions in the sidebar "Grrrl Power(less)" work as well for softies as for girls.

---

vulgar:

4 a: lacking in cultivation, perception, or taste: coarse b: morally crude, undeveloped, or unregenerate: gross c: ostentatious or excessive in expenditure or display: pretentious (*Webster's Ninth New Collegiate Dictionary*)

It is quite common for two men to argue with a lot of feeling in the tone of their voices, and neither feels personally attacked or gets personally defensive. A woman listening to the conflict may become alarmed, but men listening recognize that no one is being personally attacked and so all is OK. (Gray 2001, p. 106).

CLOSING THE DISCUSSION

Following a meaty discussion you might want to take a few minutes to assemble closing thoughts. Note that's *closing thoughts,* not *conclusions.* If the book is a good one, even the best consensus-building skills won't yield a single conclusion, unless it's shared wonder at the multiplicity of interpretations that can emanate from one source.

A good way to close book club discussion is with some kind of ritual or standard practice. This gives a sense of completion and signals the shift to other business or social time. A few ideas:

- Invite teens to take turns giving their final word on the book. This doesn't need to be a rating, just a thought.
- Read a poem aloud.
- Have teens fill out a comment card about the books read. Discourage them from rating the book. Instead ask them to write an intriguing thought, what they liked best about the book, or the main idea they came away with after discussion. Display and publish the cards every way you can: in a "Teen Book Club Picks" display in the YA section, posted on the Web site, published in the library (or city) newsletter or in the library column in the local newspaper.
- A very simple closing ritual is to say, "Thank you for a great discussion. I enjoyed it."
- If your teens have a bent toward the New Age, you could close with a chant, visualization, or silent meditation by candlelight.

Calming the Waters

For many girls and for some boys, all disagreement feels personal and antagonistic. One of the most helpful things you can do is help them recover from the spike of emotions that disagreement creates. Some light general conversation that brings teens together on a neutral subject, either one-on-one or as a whole group, can defuse the tension.

In the aftermath of a very heated discussion, direct intervention might be useful. Let teens know that everyone feels hyper or bruised after that kind of exchange and that it's a sign of how powerful both this book and ideas in general can be, when a room full of people become so personally involved in the discussion. This kind of talk reassures teens their feelings are normal, assures them they'll get over it, and helps them shift their focus from one another to the source of all that emotion—the book

---

CONCLUSION

Discussion is a huge topic, and clearly, it's beyond the scope of this book to cover it all. Authors like John Gray and Deborah Tannen have made a career out of the topic, with several books to their individual credit. We recommend them. But for the most part, discussions will go along with predictable highs and lows. Common sense, consideration of each teen's feelings, a steady focus on the book, and some attention to the common issues covered in this chapter will go a long way toward ensuring that your book club discussions leave everyone feeling satisfied, tired, and happy.

References

Gray, John. 2001. *Mars and Venus in the Workplace.* New York: HarperCollins.

Moore, Ellen, and Kira Stevens. 2004. *Good Books Lately.* New York: St. Martin's Press.

Saal, Rollene, and Paul LeClerc. 1995. *The New York Public Library Guide to Reading Groups.* New York: Crown Publishing Group.

Tannen, Deborah. 1987. *That's Not What I Meant!* New York: Ballantine.

YA Books Mentioned in This Chapter

Blood and Chocolate. Annette Curtis Klause New York: Laurel Leaf, 1999.

The Invisible Man. Ralph Ellison. New York: Vintage, 1995.

Jacob Have I Loved. Katherine Paterson. New York: HarperTrophy, 1990.

Shattering Glass. Gail Giles. New York: Simon Pulse, 2003.

The Watsons Go to Birmingham—1963. Christopher Paul Curtis. New York: Yearling, 1997.

The Wee Free Men. Terry Pratchett. New York: HarpherTrophy, 2004.

11

⬥■⬥　⬥■⬥　⬥■⬥

ONLY CONNECT: ACTIVITIES THAT BRING TEENS TOGETHER AROUND BOOKS

We've said it before, and we'll say it again: Adults join book clubs because of the books. Teens join book clubs because they are clubs.

The club's biggest draw is the rich opportunities it presents to help teens connect with book people, real and imagined. They read to connect with the characters, and they come to book club to connect with one another. Keep them coming back with activities that involve them body, mind, and heart with all the book people, real and imagined.

From start to finish, this chapter suggests activities for every type of club.

ICEBREAKERS

Have you ever in a gathering of teens who don't know one another well? They'll sit in their carefully spaced chairs, avoiding eye contact and guarding their tongues as if they were CIA agents, waiting for the program to begin.

And these kids are here to connect?

Yes! But they're at a loss to do it. After all, they don't want to do it "wrong" and wind up the club geek.

Icebreakers take are of all of that. Icebreakers give teens a focus other than their self-conscious selves, allowing them to relax and become familiar with one another. Use them early, use them often, whenever teens begin to form cliques or the club seems to be drifting apart. Build icebreakers around team-building and/or books, and you'll create an atmosphere of engagement and trust—the foundation of a great club!

These icebreakers prompt teens to reveal something about themselves and give them a chance to rub shoulders before the "serious work" of book club begins.

Paper Cup Pyramid

This team-building icebreaker appeals to active teens. It gives them something to do, it's easy to get right, and it helps teens become familiar and comfortable with one another as they focus on the task at hand.

Teens build a pyramid from paper cups using a simple tool. For each group of three teens you'll need the following:

10 small paper cups
1 sturdy rubber band
3 lengths of string, each about 1 foot long
several blindfolds (optional)

Tie the lengths of string to the rubber band. That's the tool. Teens use the tool to stack the cups in a pyramid.

In one book club, it took a group all of 60 seconds to finish the game. While others struggled, that group took it to the next level: Two team members were blindfolded, and the third team member gave them directions as the three built a new pyramid.

Two True, One Lie

Get teens talking about themselves without risking too much. Novel focus on creating a fun lie takes the pressure off self-revelation.

Everyone thinks up two facts or stories about themselves—plus one lie that could be taken for truth. Teens take turns telling their stories/facts to the group, and the group guesses which one is the lie. Ask follow-up questions to show your interest and encourage clubbers to do the same.

Let Me Ask You . . .

Provocative questions requiring creative answers incite teens to respond.

Ask a provocative question tied to the book under discussion, and open the floor to teens. Some examples (with the title of a book in parentheses):

* You're stranded on a deserted island with a character from any book. Who is it? (Any book)
* Who would you rather love? Someone who is sweet but selfish or someone who is embarrassing to be with but would do anything for you? (*Prom*)
* If you could start any kind of fad, what would it be? (*Bellwether*)

At amazon.com, enter the keyword "questions" to find many books of provocative questions you can easily use as springboards to create your own questions related to books. Among your many choices are several useful, fun, and well-illustrated books by James Saywell (1995) and/or Evelyn Macfarlane (1999).

CONNECTING AROUND THE BOOK

Discussion almost always enters into book club activities, because sharing thoughts and responses is what connecting is all about. That said, putting all hands to a common task builds a level of camaraderie in the moment and beyond, as teens create shared experiences and memories. Although some club activities have solitary, reflective moments, at some point, all of these activities bring teens together around books.

These activities are divided into writing, art, and service learning.

Writing

Many teens who love to read also love to write. It's the age of self-exploration and expression, and writing is just one of the powerful ways teens do that. The problem with writing, as many teens discover, is that it begs to be shared, but there are few opportunities or venues for doing so. Book club provides the venue!

Freewriting

A common approach to impromptu writing is called *freewriting*. Popularized by writing instructor and author Natalie Goldberg, it is a timed writing interval in which teens write every word that enters their heads, without stopping, no matter what. If the only words that come immediately to mind are "this is stupid," teens write that again and again, nonstop, until something else comes to mind.

A freewrite might easily read: "Chandra sitting next to me smells great. I want to ask her to go to the mall for ice cream. That time at the beach my brother spilled ice cream down his shirt and mom tore his shirt off and he ended up with a second-degree sunburn. If I could get past that *!"* Rowgerman, I'd hit level 5, I'm sick of level 4. Chandra smells great. She has a scar… stitches?"

The idea is that the writer can mine such freewriting for nuggets of gold, or that freewriting can empty the mind of chaotic "monkey thoughts" so the writer can focus on a specific idea. The ultimate hope is that some surprising thoughts will surface when the writing hand is forced and hurried—and uncensored.

To start a freewrite, simply explain what a freewrite is; then introduce the specific topic (examples follow) and set a timer for 5 or 10 minutes. Watch the timer; about 1 minute before time is up, say, "You have one minute left. Please finish up your thought." When time is up, immediately move on to discussion or activity—allow no extra time for stragglers.

The following writing activities all center around freewrites.

Writing Your Hopes

For all its desperation, adolescence is a time when teens begin to sketch their hopes for the future. Any book in which characters dream or think about or plan their futures makes a great springboard for asking teens to write about their hopes for their own futures.

For example, chapter 3 of *Olive's Ocean* begins with a diary passage recounting Olive's hopes for her life. (Olive has recently died.) To open a book club meeting, read the passage aloud; then give teens several moments to list their hopes. If teens are comfortable with one another, they can read their lists aloud.

If they are less prone to self-revelation, they can write one or two of their hopes on slips of paper. Drop the slips of paper into a bowl; then pull them out one by one to read aloud.

Some people like to put their lists away and pull them out much later (for adults, that might mean five years; for teens, five weeks) to see whether they progressed in the way of their dreams. Offer teens envelopes they can decorate and use to store their hope lists.

You Are What You Carry

Help teens explore unintentional self-revelation by asking, "What's in your knapsack?" Stuff a couple of knapsacks full of things that teens typically take to school—plus a few unusual items. (For example, for an exercise at *Writer's Digest*'s "The World's Largest Writing Workshop," Constance brought a purse containing a whisk and juniper berries, in addition to the usual accoutrements.)

Ask teens to work in groups to speculate about the person who carries those things. Then go to the book and look at the physical objects a certain character gathers about herself. Separately and together, what do those objects tell you about what's important to that character?

Take it to the next level by exploring the concept of the "baggage" we all carry with us. Read the opening paragraph of *The Things They Carried*; then ask teens what things they carry—seen and unseen.

Delve into the psyches of characters to discover what baggage they are carrying.

To keep it immediate to teens, explore questions of identity: "Does your baggage define you?" "Where does baggage come from?" "Are you doomed to carry it forever?"

What's Eating You?

Most books have at least one scene with characters eating, and those scenes (usually emotionally charged) almost always reveal relationships in action. Introduce this idea to teens and give them several moments to talk about an eating scene in the book they are reading (or, in the case of bookchatters, in any book they have read). Press them to back up what they say with telling details—that is, details that reveal something about the people and relationships involved (e.g., the way someone eats their food, the places they sit at the table, what is left unsaid, the tone of adjectives used to describe the food). Then introduce this writing activity:

Ask teens to remember a time they ate with family or friends. It could be a family meal or ice cream at the mall with a friend. Suggest they focus on sensory details, like smells and tastes, but let their thoughts go where they will. Ask teens to freewrite for 5 or 10 minutes, being sure to include telling details. Then ask them to begin a poem, short story, or essay using those telling details. If they're up for a challenge, suggest they write the scene using those details—but from a point of view not their own (e.g., the point of view of their little sister at the dinner table or a security guard at the mall. Sci-fi fans might even write the story from the point of view of a newscaster who can see into their home as they eat dinner in front of the television.)

Now revisit the eating scene in the book teens are reading—what additional clues or meaning do they find? Encourage them to covertly observe people eating, alone or together, to figure out what might be going on in their heads or in their relationships. They can share their "spy reports" to the group at the next meeting.

Critics' Circle

Encourage teens to write bookchats or reviews of their favorite books, for The List or for themselves. Review the basics of bookchats (summarize the book in a fun, engaging way that will entice others to read it) and reviews (summarize the plot and the book's strengths and shortcomings), some general advice (tell why you did or didn't like the book), and the Golden Rule of talking about books: Never Give Away the Ending!

Teens can publish the reviews to the Web site or in the library newsletter. They can create a display to feature the reviews with the books, or create a Readers Advisory notebook for the YA area of the library. They can submit the reviews for publication in the school or local newspaper, and offer to read them on-air for the local radio station. Though teens take the lead, you reap rewards, too: The more mileage you get out of teen creations, the more support you build for teen book club!

Visual Art

For many teens, there's no more natural expressive medium than visual art. Whether it's drawing, painting, sculpting, or crafting, artistically confident teens churn out creations by the truckload. And all of those creations, even the simplest beaded bracelet, reveal the person. Take advantage of teens' proclivity for "breaking all the rules" to encourage "nonartistic" teens (those who are convinced they can't do art) to try it anyway. Comfort them with parameters; while experimentation may be the name of the game, teens who lack self-confidence in this area will welcome some point of focus to shape their thinking.

The List

We can't think of a single type of book club that wouldn't have great fun (and find great use in) looking over titles read and recommended. The List, a comprehensive collection of those titles, offers a blank canvas for teens.

Start with the book itself, inviting teens to make a creative cover (clay or wood or fabric covers work as well as cardboard and binders), creative rings to hold the pages together (chains, bracelets, twine with a knot on one end and a loop on the other . . . anything that will clasp in some fashion), and creative pages (fabric, handmade paper, brown paper bags . . . you get the idea). Or, scale back the effort, asking teens to decorate the cover of a three-ring binder and create the booklist using fancy fonts on the computer.

If you have scrapbooking fans, turn their talents loose to transform The List into a scrapbook, each page featuring a different book. Encourage them to go past the book itself to document club meetings (discussion and activities) as well. After all, book club isn't just about books—it's about clubbers, too!

Encourage teens to start their own Lists at home. Several dedicated clubbers keep detailed lists of the books they've read, complete with reviews and ranking systems. Creating The List gives teens satisfaction today; in their adult years, The List offers a fascinating glimpse into who they once were.

This can easily lead into an identity-exploration activity similar to the writing activity, "You Are What You Carry." Assemble a display of books that "Bob" (a figment of your imagination) has read. Ask teens to speculate on what the collection reveals about Bob. To take it to the next level: Ask teens to think about the book the club is currently reading, then write a three-sentence review of it from Bob's point of view.

All in the Packaging: Book Jackets and Slipcases

One of the things that happen to popular books is that the covers become torn, dirty, or missing in action. Ask teens to comb the library shelves, searching out books with lost or damaged covers. Or have them choose books with great covers they'd like to protect with a slipcase.

This is a great time to introduce teens to the little-known world of fine-art, limited-edition publishers. Inspire them with a visit to Charnel House (www. charnelhouse.com), which packaged Dean Koontz's *Velocity* "bound and slipcased in white brocade Japanese silk with black stamping," or Hill House (www.hillhousepublishers.com), which packaged Neil Gaiman's *American Gods* in a wooden box that is "a beautiful example of the art of veneer, using an exotic rosewood from South America."

Offer a variety of craft materials (e.g., paints, pens, unusual papers, fabrics); then turn teens loose to create new dust jackets and slipcases. (You can purchase instruction booklets and kits for slipcases from Hollander's at www.hollanders. com.) Laminate the paper covers before adding three-dimensional décor like ribbons, buttons, beads, or charms. Display the books on the "What's New and Hot" in the YA area before shelving them.

Be sure to tell teens to use their own imaginations to create their art—no plagiarizing from the original cover!

Quilt It

With stamps and pens, patterns to trace, and freedom to wing it, anyone can make a quilt square.

Propose the idea of a hanging quilt to teens. The club may choose a theme for the quilt (e.g., a particular book, author, genre) and a design (e.g., quilt squares, one large piece of fabric). Or, each teen can follow his or her own creativity to produce one square of the quilt. Again, provide a wide variety of craft materials, and invite teens to bring some from home. Be creative with your craft materials. This isn't your granny's quilt: Matchbox® cars, artificial flowers, baby shoes, and other thrift-store treasures aren't out of line.

Find someone to sew the squares together (an experienced quilter will add nice touches, like strips of fabric between the squares) and quilt it. Then hang it somewhere very public—behind the circulation desk, in the lobby or meeting room, in city hall or a local bank—and let the world enjoy!

Dioramas and Murals

There was a time when every school kid made a shoebox diorama and groaned over it. The problem wasn't the art project—it was the subject matter. Make it relevant for teens by letting them choose the book and the scene, and the way they'd most like to present it. A diorama needn't be in a shoebox after all—it can be inside an old shoe, a Mason jar, a sugar-egg shell (available at craft stores around Easter). It can even be an edible scene on top of a cake!

Murals—temporary and permanent, on sidewalks and walls—are another tried-and-true art project for teens. Don't shy away because they've been done. From chalk drawings on concrete (à la *Mary Poppins*) to tiled mosaics (Ben Shahn's *The Passion of Sacco and Vanzetti* in marble and enamel on Syracuse University's Huntington Beard Crouse Hall), public art is a time-honored tradition. Expressing oneself means taking it public. Though we think of murals as visual art, they needn't be limited to images: Quotes and poetry selected and/or written by young adults (and others) are beautifully carved into the cement sidewalk skirting a parking lot adjacent to the Denver Public Library.

Displays

Reserve some space in library display areas for book club. Display book jackets and slipcases in a "Teen Book Club Favorites" display. Create bulletin boards featuring their book reviews.

Performing Arts

Singing, dancing, acting, reading aloud . . . for every teen with stage fright, it seems, there are a dozen hams. In Constance's experience inside every teen there lives a performing artist: The one who shies away from acting may embrace dancing . . . the one who wouldn't be caught dead dancing will sing till the cows come home . . . and the one who would rather die than go public conveys deep, nuanced feeling when reading on tape. Whatever your teens favor, individually or as a group, book club can provide outlets for that creative energy.

Book Club Follies

After as few as three meetings, clubbers have amassed enough reading and club experience to begin to create a Book Club Revue. Working individually, in pairs, or as a group, clubbers create a song, joke, skit, musical interlude, or vaudeville act around each book the club has read. The subject might be the book itself, or it might be what happened in book club when they tried to discuss it. (This is a great opportunity for teens to showcase what they've learned about civil discourse!) Clubbers can begin creating their acts as soon as they are comfortable with one another (generally, after the third meeting). Then they can add new acts for each book they read. By the time book club is over, you have a revue! Let teens practice it as often as they like before they take it public. They may be able to meet on their own or they may ask you to join them for rehearsals.

Dance It!

Many books feature cultures that may be unfamiliar to teens. If dance plays a role in the book or in the cultural setting, teens might enjoy a performance and even a lesson. Check local listings or Google to locate dance teachers or schools; then invite the teacher and/or students to perform for your club. Many teachers who present informational programs incorporate participation into their presentations.

Social dancing can be dicey with teens. Some love it; others are so self-conscious they can hardly bring themselves to shuffle their feet—or they simply won't show up for a club meeting that includes it. These teens may not be movement-phobic; they just aren't confident of their moves. A cultural dance program makes it easy for these teens to participate because everyone is on unfamiliar ground, and the movements are clearly defined.

Depending on interest, the dance performance/lesson may make a good program for library patrons in general. In that case, be sure to highlight the fact that the idea arose from a book club book, and mention the book prominently in advertisements for the event!

Reader's Theatre, with a Twist

Teens who want to stage plays join drama clubs. Book clubbers can enjoy a pared-down version of dramatic performance with reader's theatre. Teens select a dramatic scene (lots of tension, lots of dialogue), assign roles, do a few practice readings, and then convene to read the passage together. Releasing the words into the air, complete with individual interpretation and real-time interaction, creates a whole new experience for readers and listeners alike. Subtle meanings become apparent, and the dynamics of relationships leap to the fore. Teens will discover new insights into the text and the characters as they hear the passage come together. Be sure to take some time after reading to ask how the experience influenced their understanding of the action, character, or author's intent.

Taking reader's theatre public can be problematic because of copyright concerns. You may need to request permission to perform the piece (or, if necessary, to adapt a passage for use as a script), and your book club could be long disbanded before the permission is granted. On the other hand, if you can obtain permission, teens will have great fun performing—generating terrific public relations for the club!

If you do decide to perform a piece and you've gone to the trouble to obtain permission, do give some thought to the staging. Strictly speaking, reader's theatre is performed by people sitting in chairs against a plain background—as in chairs arranged in a half-circle in front of an audience. Rethink that if you can. How much more memorable might a reader's theatre of Whale Talk be if it were staged in the high school pool area, with the audience in the bleachers, the readers on a bench in front of the pool, and the swim team doing laps behind? That's a reader's theatre well worth taping—and showing to library directors, Friends, and city hall!

Books on Video or Audio Tape

This is another copyright quagmire. There are three ways to get around this.

First, use only original writing. Teens can record anything they've written in response to a book club book, including their reviews. As a matter of fact, book reviews on tape might be just the thing to complement all those books on tape out there!

If clubbers are dedicated to creating a quality work, they might be able to coordinate with an authorized organization that records books for the blind and disabled. Many of these organizations gain blanket permission to record a publisher's works. In effect, clubbers are acting as volunteers associated with the organization. This isn't a casual undertaking; such organizations expect quality work and often train volunteers in how to read.

If you can find a self-publisher or small publisher with popular titles (the Michigan chillers series is one), you might gain permission to record directly from the publisher.

You can avoid the whole issue by reading works in the public domain. *Frankenstein, The Tell-Tale Heart,* and anything Shakespeare are favorites. Let teens choose what they'd like to read for book club discussion; then embark on the recording. (For a high-quality recording, teens will want to explore the story to better understand the characters, and they'll need to practice extensively at home, before they record.)

Live Readings and Poetry Slams

Recording isn't for every read-aloud fan. Teens may enjoy a coffee-house atmosphere, where they read favorite pieces aloud to a live audience. Many teens *love* poetry slam competitions, in which they compete to perform poetry and/or create it on the fly.

These programs are easy to stage. You can create a coffee-house atmosphere during book club with comfortable chairs, lots to eat and drink, lowered lights and a makeshift stage complete with microphone. Or you can create a free-standing program in which all teens can participate, with clubbers as the core group.

CONTRIBUTING TO THE COMMON GOOD

Whether you use the term *service project, service learning,* or *community service,* the idea is simple: Teens contribute to the common good through social service volunteerism or service to the community at large.

Book club is an ideal springboard for service. The perennial favorite theme, Teens in Trouble, strikes the most direct hit for service learning; teens simply find creative, positive ways to address whatever issue lies at the heart of the book (e.g., abuse, alcoholism, homelessness, rape). Outside that genre, many books can spark good ideas. Because most novels' dramatic arc involvesconflict or dire straits of some kind, most books provide a hook for service learning.

Every service opportunity consists of three parts: to learn about the issue at hand, to put a human face on the problem, and to take humane action. The ultimate goal is less to solve the problem than to engage with fellow human beings who would otherwise remain objectified behind the label of "victim" or "loser." Without that goal, service becomes a mere transaction.

Learning about the issue at hand involves inviting speakers to book club, simulating difficult conditions (e.g., using constraints to simulate physical disabilities), watching movies or documentaries, reading fiction or nonfiction, and seeking out people who have lived, or are living, through the experience under study. All of these things can help teens learn about and put a human face on otherwise clichéd conditions. From there, it is a simple matter to brainstorm ideas for action, and then to plan and carry through. Some tried-and-true examples include reading to hospice or hospital patients, collecting toys for abused children, raising money for various causes, and so on. Teens will brainstorm ideas that will suit their interests, abilities, and availability.

Service need not always address social injustice and dire straits. Sometimes, serving the community means improving solutions already in place. Opportunities might include telling stories to children in Head Start, reading to elders in day care, helping to organize the library's annual book sale, walking dogs for an animal shelter, collecting books and supplies for underfunded schools, tutoring, and on and on. The "Be the Change" book club, described in chapter 4, gives an overview of service learning book clubs, including tips, cautions, and measures of success.

Show Off!

Many of these projects are PR opportunities waiting to happen. Take pictures and send them to the local newspaper. Invite television stations to visit the library to see teens in action or to see their art. Display art every safe place you can, from the library to a local bank lobby (preferably in glass cases). Perform for everyone—and be sure to stage at least one performance at the library (outside, when possible, so passersby can see).

Get on the agenda of city council, board of directors, Friends of the Library, civic clubs, and school board. Ask for booth space at a local book festival, county fair or farmer's market—anywhere people gather to browse. Display the artwork, perform the act—and stand back as teens act as ambassadors for book club.

Closings

It's always a good idea to formally close the book club meeting. Otherwise, there's a tentative, unfinished feeling as teens drift away. Book clubs use many different rituals to close their meetings, from a simple "Thank you for coming" to candles and meditation. Chapter 7, "The First Meeting," discusses closing rituals. Some rituals you might try include the following:

- **Close with Thanks.** Thank each teen for coming to the club and for specific insights, comments, questions, or actions that contributed to the club's discussion or activity.
- **Close with Round Robin or Talking Stick.** As the time nears for closing, ask teens to go around the circle and give a closing thought about the book. A variation on this is to use a talking stick; teens hold the stick as they speak. When they are finished speaking, they lay the stick down in the middle of the circle, where it remains until another teens picks it up and begins speaking. The purpose of the talking stick is to eliminate interruptions and to entice teens to speak.
- **Close with a Reading.** The discussion facilitator (librarian or teen) comes prepared with a passage to read at the close of the meeting. After reading the passage, the facilitator quietly says "Thank you for coming" to signal the end of the meeting.
- **Close with a Slogan.** In place of, or in addition to, "Thank you for coming," the book club may create a slogan or chant or cheer to close the meeting. This will arise spontaneously; if you try to deliberately create it, it will come across as lame. Definitely follow teens' lead on this one.

References

Macfarlane, Evelyn. 1999. *How Far Will You Go? Questions to Test Your Limits.* New York: Villard.

Saywell, James. 1995. *If: (Questions for the Game of Life), Vols. 1–3.* New York: Villard.

12

◇■◇　◇■◇　◇■◇

TAKING THE MEASURE OF YOUR SUCCESS: PAINLESS ASSESSMENT THAT PAYS OFF

Documentation. Feedback. Evaluation. Accountability. Advocacy. They all come together in the question: Is book club worth it? And all serve you well in everything from building a book club that serves real teens, to building support for the club, to putting your best foot forward in personnel reviews, to the sense of personal satisfaction you feel as you close the door on book club each month. To see how each builds on the other, let's start with a few definitions:

- **Documentation:** Gathering statistics and stories (with images) and comparing them to measures of success (benchmarks).
- **Feedback:** Soliciting insights, suggestions, and *complaints* from everyone involved in book club: teens, supporters, administrators, and you.
- **Evaluation:** Analyzing and reflecting upon the information you've gathered.
- **Accountability:** Using the evaluation to justify the program and the resources it requires.
- **Advocacy:** Building goodwill and support for book club and by extension the library.

Taken together, documentation, feedback, and evaluation sets assessment apart from assumption. It creates credibility by answering this question: "How do you know what you know?" It's one thing to have a gut-level feeling that attendance is growing; it's another to have the figures to prove it. Likewise, it's easy to assume that generous support means funders are wholly satisfied with book club; it's quite another to have them attest to it in writing. Finally, it's great to present your results in a nicely written report—but having teens report your results to stakeholders in person takes reporting to a whole new level!

Even as assessment clarifies your accomplishments to date, it also helps you move forward. And that's the reason to do it. Assessment is the means to this end: to serve teens better and better.

Collect What Matters; Let the Rest Go

We've all heard of those mad accumulators whose houses, cars, and pockets are so packed with must-haves they can barely move. And it may seem as if the plethora of tips in this chapter are leading you in that direction.

But no. Be a choosy collector. Stay focused on measures of success and gather only what you need. You'll find it much easier to collect and carry and much easier to organize, report and use.

Assessment Is Not ...

... discovering what you do well. It's about results. It's an important distinction. You could excel at everything you do and still not succeed—if you're doing the wrong things. Remember the proverb: Management is doing things right; leadership is doing the right things. Evaluation is a key leadership tool for you. By focusing on results rather than tasks, you discover how well you are doing the right things. Then you can make plans to do them better.

... quantitative only. There's a push right now for "data-driven decision making." For all its worth, quantitative data is rigidly compartmentalized and lacks context. Qualitative information puts statistics in context, revealing shades of gray, motivation, perception, and feelings. Of all the forms of qualitative information, stories are most compelling. That's why we urge you to collect statistics and stories—our shorthand for quantitative and qualitative information.

MAKING THE MOST OF ASSESSMENT: THE PAYOFF

If you use assessment to improve your book club, you're putting it to good use. But why stop there? The statistics and stories you gather, and the sense you make of them, are gold. Spend them in a dozen ways, from creating spin-off programs to elevating the status of the library itself. Here are just a few ways you can leverage what you learn from assessment:

- Help supporters say yes to book club by showing how book club serves teens and the community.
- Use statistics and stories in efforts to increase awareness and goodwill for book club (and by extension teen programming and the library).
- Gain greater latitude to innovate activities and spin-off programs based on what works well.

- Solve or avoid problems by knowing what doesn't work and why and then using what you know about what *does* work to fix (or avoid) problems.
- Identify exactly how book club helps the library achieve its goals. (If book club doesn't do that, it shouldn't be a library program.)
- Justify your time and other resources spent on the program: Specify where the time/budget goes and the return on each resource.
- Ask and answer "Is book club worthwhile?" in ways that address the interests and concerns of your various audiences (see chapter 3).
- Document your own performance to support job applications, promotions, salary requests, or periodic performance reviews.

Much has been written about evaluating teen programs. Instead of rehashing those resources here, we're going to look at specific ways you can use assessment to advance book club.

GETTING STARTED

Begin with the End in Mind

For all the uses you can put it to, assessment itself is straightforward: It's finding out whether you did the job you set out to do. Whenever assessment starts growing outside its bounds, check back against that foundation. If it's not about getting the job done, it's not assessment.

Since assessment is all about finding out whether you did the job you set out to do, go back to the very beginning: Refer back to your goal-to-action plan (chapter 3). What exactly *did* you set out to do? What are your purposes? What actions did you take? And what are your measures of success? Everything follows from them.

Fast Forward to the End

What will you do with the statistics and stories you collect? How many different ways will you use them, and to what ends? Take just one example: building support. Think about your supporters: parents, directors, friends, community partners, funders. With book club purposes and benchmarks firmly in mind, plan to collect the statistics and stories that speak directly to the interests and concerns of each group.

Let's say one purpose of book club is to develop leadership in teens, and your measure of success is that teens can discuss books civilly, even when they disagree. Table 12.1 offers some supporters' likely concerns and ways to address them with stories and statistics. To address supporters' concerns you need to anticipate them (see "Ask Supporters for Their Two Cents") and collect the stories and statistics you need. That's where a little planning pays big dividends.

Sneaky Story Collecting

It's easy to collect the stories you need from teens by subtly incorporate feedback-gathering into book club activities. For example, to collect stories about how teens learned to check themselves in the heat of an argument, propose a reflective freewrite on that topic (see chapter 11). Or, create a collage mural project about it. Start with conversation. Ask teens, "Do you remember how in half our meetings we used to get into shouting matches? You guys don't do that any more. What happened?" Let teens discuss how they've learned to manage their emotions (or at least their tongues), then ask, "What would you think about making a collage mural to show our evolution? The mural could show what you're doing differently, or how you think and feel when someone pushes your hot buttons, or just how you manage to control yourself and keep your mouth shut. It's something everyone struggles with, regardless of age. As a matter of fact, I think we could hang the mural in the library—I think a lot of our patrons would find it helpful!"

TABLE 12.1
Addressing Supporters' Concerns with Stories and Statistics.

Parents	I want my teen to grow up! (that is, gain emotional self-control)	Teens tell stories that explain how they learned to check themselves in the heat of an argument.
Library directors	Where is the direct link between book club and the library's mission?	Anecdotes show teens seeking information from several sources to support their points of view (rather than simply out-shout one another). An accompanying list documents the range of resources teens used.
Community partners/funders	How is book club relevant to helping teens cope in the "real" world?	In quotes and journal entries, teens explain how they used what they learned in book club to help them resolve disagreements at home, at school, among friends. You can add the workplace teamwork connection, or let your audience make that connection.

COLLECTING STATISTICS AND STORIES: DOCUMENTING
In Book Club

Even though assessment always comes at the end of discussions about programming, it pays to start documenting at the very first meeting. Create routines to collect statistics and jot quick notes about what you observe during meetings. The notes remind you of incidents (stories) as you saw them unfold. First-meeting statistics and stories are the baseline against which you track clubbers' progress.

Depending on the club and your measures of success, some things you may want to track include the following:

- Attendance
- What teens have read since the last meeting
- Depth and substantiveness of discussions
- How teens handle decision making
- How many times the facilitator intervenes to keep conversations civil
- How well teens stand up for their opinions
- How often meetings run over because teens aren't ready to give up on an idea

Offload the statistical work. A sign-in sheet (disguised as an entry form to win cheap trinkets) takes care of attendance. Let an Etiquette Enforcer count interventions, making a hatch mark on a stick every time he or she blows the whistle. That leaves you to capture stories as they unfold with a few quick notes.

It won't take long to collect the statistics and stories you need. It's time well spent; you'll use those statistics and stories over and over again in recruiting and promotion (see chapter 6) and improving book club.

Get Quotes! Take Pics!

When you're collecting stories and feedback, be sure to write down exactly what people say. It adds liveliness and even more credibility to your reports.

Ask for a picture to go with that quote. Pair them up to double your impact in annual reports, press releases, posters, and other marketing materials.

Get permission to use the photo and quote. If you can't get permission to use it with a name, ask for permission to use first name only or a anonymous attribution (teen, community partner, Friend of the Library).

Use a permissions form; you get the consent in writing *and* the proper form and spelling of their name!

Tips for Collecting Statistics and Stories

The best way to collect statistics and stories are covered in chapter 2. The "13+ Book Club Survey" is a reproducible you can use to collect feedback from teens. The techniques that work for teens also work for supporters, directors, and friends of the library: If you need to know what people think or how they behave, simply ask. If you want to know what they *do*, observe.

- To gauge awareness and goodwill, track mentions in all media (including online), thank you notes and other correspondence regarding book club. To give it additional weight, collect it all in a scrapbook, which teens can make and maintain (see chapter 11).
- Don't forget to save kudos you receive by email! Put them in your scrapbook as well.

- To organize your raw data, use the reproducible "Sample Form for Collecting Statistics and Stories," that follows. This form is for your own use, not for reporting purposes. Before you can report the results you'll need to analyze and reflect upon them; then you can report them in a context that explains their meaning. Later in this chapter we discuss how to do all that.

- To track external support, keep a list of past and present community partners or funders and each one's level of support.

- To track internal support, document the time, money, and other resources involved in planning and implementing book club, from year to year. Has budget/planning time increased? As they grow does the program get better? Do you stay within budget/schedule? What is the cost per teen? You absolutely need these kinds of statistics if you are going to ask for funding from outside agencies or for additional planning/prep time from your boss.

- For your professional purposes, track measures of success that relate to your professional responsibilities: Did you stay within the time/budget? Did you align book club purposes with the library's mission? Where did you fall down? What changes did you see in thoughtful reading, information literacy, leadership? Gather statistics and stories to lend credibility to your answers.

Sample Form for Collecting Statistics and Stories
to Assess the Goal-to-Action Plan in Figure 3.1.

Quantitative—General

1a Attendance total for all meetings:

1b. Attendance by meeting:
> Meeting 1
> Meeting 2
> Meeting 3
> Meeting 4
> Meeting 5
> Meeting 6

1c. Notes on anomalies or unusual situations relating to attendance:

Quantitative—Empathy*

Number of flags teens used to mark passages that stirred their emotions:
> Meeting 1
> Meeting 2
> Meeting 3
> Meeting 4
> Meeting 5
> Meeting 6

Range of responses:
> Happy
> Sad
> Mad
> Nostalgic

Other

1a. Number of teens who were able to flag the exact words or phrases that set of an emotional reaction as they read:

1b. Number of emotional triggers teens identified, total and by teen. (Get this figure by asking teens to count their flags.):

2. Number of teens who are able to identify important emotional moments for a character they dislike or don't understand:

3a. Number of teens who could name the core emotion at work in a particular passage they had flagged:

3b. Number and range of emotions teens identified:

4a. Number of teens who were able to find common ground with the character by linking the character's emotional experience to one of their own:

4b. Type and range of emotions that enabled teens to find common ground with a character they dislike or don't understand:

5. Number of words or phrases (identified by teens) that indicate teens are judging characters based on teens' own feelings or beliefs:

6a. Number of times teens were able to justify the character's motivations, emotions, thoughts, and actions even while explaining how all of these differ from the teens' own:

6b. Type and range of motivations, emotions, thoughts, and actions teens were able to understand in character, despite their difference from the teens' own motivations, emotions, thoughts, and actions:

7a. Number of teens who completed at least one book featuring a character they disliked or didn't understand:

7b. Total number of books teens finished, despite the fact that the books featured characters teens disliked or didn't understand (indicating growing empathy and tolerance of difference):

Quantitative—Thinking

1. Teens identified how many words indicating assumptions, generalizations and stereotypes:

2. Teens identified how many thinking flaws that occur most often in book club discussions:

2b. My count of thinking flaws that occur most often in book club discussion:

3. Number of teens able to name the thinking flaw they most often fall prey to:

4a. Number of teens who can identify how they catch themselves in the act of thinking or voicing a thinking flaw:

4b. Number, type, and range of thinking flaws teens identified in themselves:

5. Number of thinking flaws identified in book club discussions:
   Meeting 1
   Meeting 2
   Meeting 3
   Meeting 4
   Meeting 5
   Meeting 6

Qualitative—Empathy**

1. Teens' stories/observations about teens' ability to suspend personal judgment or emotional response to a book character:

2. Teens' stories/observations about teens' ability to find common ground with difficult characters—that is, characters they dislike or don't understand:

3. Teens' stories/observations about teens' ability to stick with books featuring characters they dislike or don't understand:

4. My stories/observations about teens' ability to suspend personal judgment or emotional response to a book character:

5. My stories/observations about teens' ability to find common ground with difficult characters—that is, characters they dislike or don't understand:

6. My stories/observations about teens' ability to stick with books featuring characters they dislike or don't understand:

Qualitative—Thinking

1. Teens' stories/observations about teens' ability to catch thinking flaws that other people make during book club discussions:

2. Teens' stories/observations about teens' ability to catch themselves in the act of making thinking flaws in book club discussions:

3. Teens' stories/observations about teens' ability to catch themselves in the act of making thinking flaws as they read or reflect on their reading:

4. My stories/observations about teens' ability to catch thinking flaws that other people make during book club discussions:

5. My stories/observations about teens' ability to catch themselves in the act of making thinking flaws in book club discussions:

6. My stories/observations about teens' ability to catch themselves in the act of making thinking flaws as they read or reflect on their reading:

---

*Note that numbers correspond to numbers the Measures of Success column in figure 3.1.

**Qualitative questions relate to the Priorities listed in figure 3.1.

From *The Teen-Centered Book Club: Readers into Leaders* by Bonnie Kunzel and Constance Hardesty. Westport, CT: Libraries Unlimited. Copyright © 2006.

Documentation can make or break assessment. People trust numbers and stories. As Walter and Meyers explain,

> librarians who are able to produce evaluation data that is *credible* and convincing . . . have an incredible advantage when it comes to telling their story to decision-makers. They can prove that what they do makes a positive difference in the lives of young adults they serve and in the community (Walter and Meyers 2003, p. 89).

Tell Your Own Story

In your book club notebook or in a separate journal, write your personal thoughts about book club. This journal is not about teens or the library or any audience but you. What was inspiring? What have you learned about teens, about literature, about yourself? What was your bleakest moment? How did you solve problems? What have you learned about leadership, about life? What will you carry into the future?

LISTENING FOR INSIGHTS AND OPINIONS: FEEDBACK

Feedback tells you what's working and what's not. Until you ask open-ended questions, you can only assume the stories behind the statistics. Feedback breaks down your assumptions and opens up a universe of insights, motivations and perceptions.

Too often feedback is a two-way street when it should be a 360-degree circle. If you want to know how book club is doing, ask a sampling of everyone involved. Begin with teens; then turn to colleagues, supervisors, library directors, boards of directors, friends of the library, parents, teachers, community partners, and funders.

Whether you conduct a sit-down Q&A session, chat with your colleagues en route to other things, broadcast an email, or make a few quick phone calls; there's no end to the benefits. Besides gaining insights, you create goodwill for book club every time you ask.

- For teens, ask questions like these: "Are meetings too long or too short?" "Are the date and time convenient?" "Do you feel included and listened to?" "Are the books good?" "How are you (the librarian) doing?" "What's good?" "What's missing?" "What would make book club perfect?"
- For others, ask open-ended questions about book club process (e.g., "Does the way you're handling book club cause any problems?") as well as measures of success. Listen for complaints and for ways to turn problems into praise.

Make it easy for people to give you feedback. The easier you make it for someone to tell you their complaints, the easier it is to fix them. And the easier you make it for someone to tell you their expectations, the easier it is for you to fulfill them. Whether you're fixing or fulfilling, be sure to document your success!

Tip!

One great way to gather feedback from teens is to put stacks of preprinted note cards and a Suggestion Box on the snacks table. One set of note cards might say "This was great!" on one side and "I hope *that* never happens again" on the other. Another set might say "Book club would be *perfect* if . . . " on one side and "Today in book club I learned. . ." on the other.

Ask Supporters for Their Two Cents

Asking and *listening* create goodwill among community partners, funders, and other supporters.

There is nothing more rude or less effective than approaching supporters only when you want something. Inviting supporters to voice their expectations and observations as you plan and deliver book club proves you understand what they hope to achieve and you are serious about making it happen. (If you aren't serious about achieving their goals, don't accept their support.)

A typical phone call might open with the pleasantries, then get to a series of specific questions:

What top three things would you particularly like to see book club do?
What three things would you most like to see changed? (For existing book club sponsors.)
Is there anything you particularly do not want to see book club do?
Is there any way book club can serve your organization?
How would you like to receive an assessment of book club—report, meeting, teen presentation, other?

That's it. You don't need to spend much time on this. Grantors likely will be surprised and perhaps mystified by your initiative in asking the questions. They will understand your reasoning when you and/or the teens deliver the assessment.

Of course, asking for feedback creates the expectation that you will follow up on it. Guide the conversation carefully and be frank about what is suitable and realistic—or not.

ANALYZING AND REFLECTING: EVALUATING

Statistics and stories are piling up. If you've been disciplined about what you collect, you have a manageable amount of information that practically sorts itself by purpose, audience, and measures of success. That makes it easy to look past the particular statistics and stories to see what they *mean*.

Evaluation steps back to look at the big picture and then zooms in to analyze the pieces and parts and how they fit together. Librarians and educators devote a great deal of energy to fostering teens' critical thinking skills; think of evaluation as a real-life test of *your* skills.

There's no one best way to evaluate data. If you tend to be analytical, you'll start with the small bits to amass a whole, or you'll deconstruct the whole into its bits. If you process information perceptively, you'll begin with the whole mess and let it speak to you. Wherever you begin, you'll need to cross over to the other side; evaluation is where analysis and perception (reflection) come together.

Before you begin to examine and reflect on the statistics and stories you've gathered, put on a filter. Your filter, once again, is your purposes, audiences, and measures of success. If you don't stay focused on these, even a small bit of information can become overwhelming.

Look for patterns, trends, causes, connections, anomalies, surprises, no-brainers, and gaps. Choose the outstanding positives and negatives; then probe for causes. For your professional purposes, some causes might include people, library policy, meeting space, processes, attitudes, your skills (or lack of), and resources. Think about implications for teens in terms of their *whole* lives: academic achievement *and* personal pleasure, information literacy *and* trivial pursuits, lifelong learning *and* lifetime fulfillment.

We're conditioned to look for what causes bad things to happen, but it pays to look for the good as well: Did book club excel because certain resources were available? because you were able to draw on other staffers' skills? because library policy defends teens' right to read? Connecting positive outcomes to their causes tells you what resources you need to build future book clubs. Linking resources to positive results makes it easy for supporters to say yes to book club.

Resist the Bright Baubles!

It's inevitable: As you explore the information you've gathered, bright gems will snag your attention; for example, you might note that there was a stretch of weeks when only the younger clubbers showed up, or that more teens showed up in even-numbered months than in odd-numbered ones, or that discussion was especially lively for books with female authors. Make a note if you'd like to return to them later—but for now stay on task. You're here to answer one question: Is book club worthwhile?

Making Sense of What You See

How do stories and statistics turn into implications and patterns? And how do you relate what you learn to your audience's interests and concerns? To follow the previous example through this step, see Table 12.2.

TABLE 12.2
Finding Patterns and Discerning Meaning from Statistics and Stories.

Teens	Self-awareness	Teens need fewer interventions now than when they began (8 in the first meeting, 1 in the last). Except in one area: sex. When that subject comes up, teens revert to boy-versus-girl rivalry, gossip or rants with no holds barred.
Parents	Emotional self-control	Teens say they have learned to check themselves, but I observe they still rely on external prompts to pull them up short when their emotions get carried away. It's true that the Etiquette Enforcer intervenes less often; instead, teens take their cues from one another. They have always been sensitive to body language; now they are more savvy about reading the signals and changing their behavior. That's the easy half of the battle. I notice that during discussions about sex no one gives the "stop it" cues.
Library directors	Library mission	In the last 6 meetings, teens used 19 different information resources to back up their opinions or to give depth to their booktalks—sometimes running out of the room mid-discussion to retrieve a bit of needed information. Most still go first to Google, but they are becoming selective about which Google references they use. Since a "war of the words" fiasco (in the second meeting) in which clubbers threw all kinds of unreliable information at each another, every clubber has made a point of challenging the reliability of information teens bring to book club. Despite the negative tone, it drives home that veracity matters. Teens have really come to "own" this; it's part of the club's culture now.
Community partners/ funders	Preparation for the real world	Teens say that book club has no relevance to their real lives, but their stories say something different. Teens talk about their lives as if they were one long battle against teachers, parents, even friends. It's a minefield out there, and every disagreement has the potential to escalate into a life-or-death threat. But in book club, teens have started to relax; at each meeting, they tolerated disagreement for longer periods of time before discussions disintegrated. At the second-to-last meeting, teens talked through a controversial issue (felony murder) to reach a resolution. They didn't try to reach a consensus, but they did sincerely acknowledge that there are valid arguments on both sides of the issue. They were able to do that because they had instant access to a portable laptop with wireless Internet access. Teens could step out of the conversation to check their facts (or try to debunk another teen's facts); they reentered the conversation with reliable information, and the time out for research settled their emotions a bit. Teens learned two things: reliable information trumps bad information, and taking time out to focus on facts is one way to manage their emotions. Having the donated laptop made it happen!
You	Professional purposes	When we started, teens were all too willing to go to the mat with nothing more than assumptions and vague generalizations. Two things put a stop to that: We took a "time out" for a quickie lesson in how to evaluate information sources, and I obtained a laptop (with wireless Internet access) for clubbers to use so they could retrieve information just-in-time without leaving the room. Since missing the action is a huge de-motivator for these teens, having the computer in the meeting space made all the difference.

> **Tip!**
>
> What people say is subjective. What you observe is subjective. You make subjective choices about what statistics to track. When you evaluate all three in light of one another (and with an awareness of your own biases), you can come to some reasonably "objective" conclusions.

REPORTING: HELPING OTHERS MAKE SENSE OF IT, TOO

Just as you suspected, book club has had great results—and you have the statistics and stories to prove it. Now to let others know, too.

There's only one hard-and-fast rule for reporting results: Speak to your audience. You've sorted their interests and concerns and matched them to your measures of success. Keep that momentum as you decide *how* to tell your story. Different audiences respond to different ways of presenting information. Will you use charts or paragraphs? Annual report or PowerPoint presentation? Personal appearance or Web presence? Press release or phone call? Will you open your report with statistics or stories or with a history of book club? How do you decide where to begin?

Use Teens to Demonstrate Results

There's nothing like a real, live teen to make book club come alive. Make teens part of your presentation whenever you deliver results about book club. Take them to your next Friends or Board meeting to booktalk their favorite books. Have them create a PowerPoint presentation featuring highlights and accomplishments. Invite them to write a regular column for the library newsletter or Web site. Help them put together a book club follies or revue to perform at a special, year-end book club event to which you invite all sponsors, Friends, directors, management, parents, and other stakeholders.

Put It in Writing ...

Let's start with the easy question: Format. For internal purposes (a report to the director or your personnel file), you might write a formal evaluation report. But most of the time, you'll simply incorporate what you've learned from your evaluation into the kind of marketing and promotional materials discussed in-depth in chapter 6.

Writing is thinking; the better you organize your material, the easier the words will come. Some people get through this on natural knack. For everyone else, here's a system that nearly always works. The format is only a shell; as you fill it in be sure to tailor the message and tone to your audience(s):

- For each audience, make a little card that lists interests and concerns along with relevant measures of success. Keep that list handy!

- Choose an audience. Make an idea web or mind map to connect interests and concerns to measures of success to the statistics and stories that back them up.
- For that audience, choose the interest or concern they feel most strongly about *or* where you had stunning success.
- Tell a story about that success. It doesn't need to be the great American novel. If you're lifting the story from a feedback form or from your notes, you may be able to repeat it verbatim. Work in a little context if you need to, as in "Tanya didn't speak until the third book club meeting, but when she did, she amazed us!"
- Next to the story, create a chart or graph that backs up the story with statistics.
- After the story, say, "That's just one of the great results we've seen in Teen Book Club." Then list other successes that address your audience's interests and concerns.
- *Optional:* After the list, elaborate. For each success, give a little context plus a story and chart (if available). Run through the whole list of successes that way.
- Conclude by putting it all together, then taking it to a higher level. When you look at all of your successes as a whole, what do they add up to? And what does that mean to teens, the audience, the community?
- Report the gaps. Assessment isn't only about success. Be honest about challenges, setbacks, and outright failures, and how you addressed them.
- Repeat for every different audience. Feel free to reuse stories and statistics, tailoring what you say to address the interests and concerns of each audience.

The conclusion is the most difficult part of the report, and it's the one that gets skipped most often. It's also the most compelling. Let's see how it might come together. Using the existing example, we see that clubbers do the following:

- Don't check their own emotions but respond to external cues
- Can calm their emotions or at least their behaviors when someone prompts them to
- Avidly challenge the veracity of one another's information
- Value the power of reliable information to back up what they say—and can find reliable information to do it
- Tolerate the discomfort of disagreement when they're in an environment that encourages lively, not hurtful, discussions
- Can talk through their differences to reach a resolution, even if it's an open-ended one

Putting it all together, you can see that book clubbers are becoming better at standing up for themselves, saying what they believe, holding their own, and questioning the facts they are given. Those are all natural teen tendencies; in book club teens learn to convert their tendencies into tools they can deliberately use whenever they like. Equally important, they're acquiring the practice and confidence they need to call on those skills in "real" life.

Now, what does all that relate to adults' concerns about emotional self-control, developmental assets, and so on? Take the number-one adult concern about teens: Peer pressure. Book club gives teens the tools and practice they need to resist peer pressure. And resisting peer pressure has implications for teens now in their social lives and in the future as they participate on teams in the workplace. Focus on peer pressure, and you can speak to the concerns of every supporter.

The picture is not completely rosy: Teens don't check their own emotions but rely on external prompts. But other skills compensate. Imagine this: A girl and a boy in the backroom at a party. Emotions run high. He makes a certain advance. She resists, but weakly. She's not managing her emotions well and the external prompts certainly aren't helping. Then he draws close and whispers, "Everyone does it." The girl's head tilts; her lips curl sweetly. "Oh, *really?*" she says. "Can you verify that?"

A FINAL THOUGHT

When you're mulling over "Is book club worthwhile?" take a few moments to answer that question for yourself. After all, this is your book club too. You've put in the hours of effort. You've rounded up the snacks and the chairs. You've had a rare, close-up view of teens becoming their own persons. You've witnessed the heartwarming moments and the hair-raising frustrations. You've seen teens become more competent, more thoughtful, more compassionate. And you've seen their spectacular failures, when everything disintegrates into condescension and tears. You've listened to stories about they've learned, and how they've carried that into the world.

Now as you reflect on it, the good, bad, and mundane—with no expectations, no measure of success, no audience but you—answer for yourself: Is book club worth it?

Reference

Walter, Virgina A., and Elaine Meyers. 2003. *Teens and Libraries: Getting It Right.* Chicago: American Library Association.

APPENDIX A

◇◼◇　◇◼◇　◇◼◇

BOOK CLUB VALUES

Book clubs operate on certain values: Respect. Openness. Intellectual rigor. Often, the values go unsaid, and that's a mistake. Teens literally talk their values into being. Naming and talking about book club values give them shape and substance; they're no longer amorphous concepts drifting about the periphery of conscious thought. Talking about values honors teens' skepticism of received wisdom and challenges them answer their perennial "Why!?" It helps teens define what book club values mean to them and how they will act upon them. The result? Teens own the values; they are right-here, right-now and they have muscle.

Teens participating in book club must ascribe to certain values in order for the discussion to work. Ascribing to the values means understanding explicitly what those values mean. You can't insist on *civility* and teens can't agree to it no one knows what exactly it means. That sounds elementary, and that's exactly the level we find teens who are new to book club. They may be proficient at parroting standard ground rules, but can they explain why the rules matter? Book club values fill that gap.

The following paragraphs outline a few major book club values. This is a starting point, not a definitive overview. Talk it through with your teens to flesh out the core values in a way that best serves your group.

RESPECT IS MORE IMPORTANT THAN AGREEMENT

Ultimately, the purpose of book club is to think empathically and critically together—which can only happen in an atmosphere made safe by a mutual respect that embraces ideas and process as well as people.

Respect means approaching every aspect of book group—people, books, ideas, the discussion process—with a willingness to engage as equals. People often say that teens consider themselves the center of the universe. Respect allows them to share that space with others. A treatise on "what respect looks like" could (and does) fill volumes. But for book clubs, it mostly looks like courtesy, authentic participation, empathy, forthrightness, responsibility, a generosity of mind, willingness to temporarily suspend the primacy of one's own opinions, and inclusion.

Respect implies the imperative to do no harm. But that does *not* mean tolerating faulty thinking, overlooking flaws or taking a laissez-faire attitude that anything goes. Rather, it means addressing concerns—forthrightly and considerately.

EXPLORATION IS MORE MEANINGFUL THAN CONQUEST

We measure book club success in *eureka!* moments, not in unanimity. Though persuasion is a key leadership skill, we don't advocate it for book club. A preoccupation with lining everyone up behind one idea short-circuits learning by focusing on what is already known (or assumed) rather than with revelation and discovery.

During open-ended discussions you'll often wonder, "Did we all read the same book?" The answer is yes and no. We all bring our own perceptions to create a personal interpretation of the book. In sharing our interpretations, we not only enrich one another's understanding, but the friction or fusion among diverse perspectives may generate entirely new interpretations and understandings. Those are our *eureka!* moments.

In the end, book club is about how well we seek out and respond to diverse ideas, opinions, beliefs, information, modes of thought, feelings, and behavior—the defining aspects of people we encounter every day. The more book club promotes teens' flexibility, the better they will adapt to the diversity they will encounter throughout their lives and the more broad-reaching leaders they will be.

NO ONE HAS THE RIGHT TO AN UNFOUNDED OPINION

American folk wisdom says the First Amendment guarantees the right to an opinion, unfounded or not. As if. There is no such thing as an unfounded opinion. Thoughts and feelings don't materialize out of nowhere. They rise from the conglomeration of our prior knowledge, which includes ideas, information, assumptions, biases, emotions, and the unspoken impressions we gather from Madison Avenue, Hollywood, important people in our lives—and yes, books!

Substantiating an opinion with solid evidence demands intellectual rigor. With friendly, neutrally phrased questions ("How do you know that?" "How do you know that you know it?" "What clues lead you in that direction?" "Are you sure?") you can help teens detach from their opinions and dig deep to discover exactly what leads them to certain conclusions.

As they learn to use evidence and reason to substantiate their ideas and opinions, teens gain a powerful leadership tool. When a person can't justify his ideas or perceptions, what tools can he use to respond to challenges or build support? Too often we see the dearth in inflammatory language, belligerence, and debate focused more on cutting the legs out from one another than explaining one's own views. These are the tools of helplessness. Book club empowers teens to do better.

Perhaps most important, as teens learn to ferret out faulty (and good) thinking and false (and true) conclusions, they discover that they can choose what they think and feel and believe—and *do*.

A Caveat

Book club values are not universally endorsed. Some parents and teens may require predefined boundaries, either-or thinking, and prescribed conclusions. The bottom line: If teens (or parents acting for teens) reject fundamental book club values, then this library program may not be for them. Book clubs thrive, founder, or die based on how steadfastly book club members adhere to the values. Insist that in book club, book club values stand.

APPENDIX B

◇■◇　◇■◇　◇■◇

AN ARRAY OF BOOK CLUB BACKUP QUESTIONS

If the suggestions in chapter 9 weren't enough for you, here are additional ideas for backup questions to use when book club conversations lag. Don't stop here—brainstorm your own backup questions now and as you read each of the club's books.

- Is the author trying to beat you over the head with a theme or message? Do you get the idea the author cares passionately about the issue?
- With some books, you know exactly where it's going from the first page. Do you like being surprised, or do you like knowing where you're going? Do you ever read the end of the book before you've finished it? Did this book unfold the way you expected it to?
- Did you like the book? Did you enjoy reading it? Have you ever liked a book that you didn't enjoy reading?
- Who has read something else by this author? Some critics say that every book an author writes is really just the same book in different disguises. Would you say that's true of this author?
- In most books everything makes sense (in one way or another) in the end. This is called the "pretense of orderliness." Is your world like that? Is it fair for authors to present the world as an orderly place?
- Some people say our lives are all about the "life choices" we make. Others say our choices are bound by our "life chances," that is, the accident of our birth (e.g., age, sex, race, economic class, cultural background, geographic location). If one of the characters in this book had had different life chances, how would that have changed his/her life choices?
- One great thing about YA books is that they don't always stick to the easy truths, like "good wins over evil" or "friendship lasts forever." What's the truth of this book? Is the truth of this book also true in your world?

- Do you like one type of book better than another?
- What ethical choice did the character make? What did you think of that choice? Is there more than one good choice here? Who decides what the good choice is? Who decides that for the character? Who decides that for you?
- Do you think the author disagrees with what some of the characters do? How does the author let you know what he or she thinks of what's going on in the book?
- Is the author using this story to get a message across? Is it subtle or do you feel like he or she is shoving it down your throat? Did it work—that is, do you get the message and do you agree with it?
- Authors choose their words carefully. Think of the difference between describing someone as "willowy," "thin as a bicycle," or "anorexic." Find a passage in the book that shows some attitude. What is the real message here?
- Overall, what is the attitude you feel from this book? optimistic? depressed? goofy? sarcastic? good-naturedly obnoxious? cautionary? patronizing? What kind of attitude do you like in books? What do you not like? If you were going to pick out a new book to read, would you look for one with a certain kind of attitude?
- Is there something in the book that didn't make sense to you?
- Did your opinions about any of the characters change as the book went on? Did the change surprise you? Did it seem natural and realistic? If you had the kind of experiences the character had, would you change in the same way? People say you can't change what happens to you, but you can choose how you react. Is that really true?
- Was this book entertaining? Would you recommend it to a friend? to your parents? What kind of person would you recommend it to? Who would you *not* recommend it to? Why?
- Tell teens something about the author that is relevant to the book. Then ask, "If you knew that about the author, would it have helped you to understand the book? Do you think you should have to know about the author to enjoy the book?"
- Did the book live up to its opening line? Authors work hard on the first page of their books, because most readers decide whether to read the whole book based on the first few lines. Did this author keep up the good work throughout the book?
- Did you finish this book? Do you feel like you have to finish every book you start, even if you don't like it?
- Do you ever read ahead? Does that affect whether you finish a book?
- What's the difference between realistic and believable? Do characters have to be realistic to be believable?
- There's a style of writing called realism, in which everything occurs exactly as it would in the real world. (One famous American author, Theodore Dreiser, was so carried away with realism he even checked the Chicago train schedules to make sure his fictional trains left on time!)

There's another style called magical realism, in which fantastic things happen. Have you read any magical realism? Would you like to try it?

- Pick something a character does that is totally wrong—stupid, illegal, self-destructive, and so on. What in the world was she thinking when she did that? What did she hope to achieve? Did it get her what she wanted? How far would you go to get what you wanted?

- When a person does something he or she would not normally do, we call that acting "out of character." Is that possible? If you do something, doesn't that mean it's part of your character? In contrast, if we can never act out of character, how can we change and grow? Do any of the people in this book act out of character? What makes them do it? What happens as a result?

- If you see something in a book and you can't figure out why the author made a point of putting it there, it may be a symbol. Symbols are like secret codes (e.g., birds often relate to death or the spirit world). The frustrating thing is that symbols are like hieroglyphics: If you don't know the secret code, you can't figure them out. Let's see if we can figure out what the mysterious things in this book might mean. (This is a good time to introduce a few dictionaries of symbolism.)

- Is there a Great Theme in Literature in this book? Would the book still be worth reading even if you ignored the Great Theme?

- Does everyone have a right to their own opinion, really? Are there any limits on that? What if the opinion is based on ignorance? lies? gossip? racial hatred? assumptions or stereotypes? If everyone has a right to their own opinion, do they have a right to express it? People like to say every right comes with responsibilities. What responsibilities go with the right to having your own opinion?

- Do you think an author's writing style reveals something about the author? For example, do you think authors who write about gritty urban life must have lived that life?

INDEX

ABOUT THE AUTHORS

BONNIE KUNZEL, Teen Specialist in the Youth Services Department of Princeton Public Library in Mercer County, New Jersey, is former president of the Young Adult Library Services Association (YALSA). She is the coauthor with Diana Herald of *Strictly Science Fiction* (LU, 2001), and has published extensively in professional journals.

CONSTANCE HARDESTY is a YA programming and book club specialist with more than 20 years' experience working with teens and adults in educational and recreational settings. From writing workshops for middle schoolers to continuing education courses for educators, she focuses on connecting people with ideas through the written word. Her writing has received several awards from the American Booksellers Association, National Parenting Publications Awards, Associated Press, and others.